# Ballet Basics

## FIFTH EDITION

Sandra Noll Hammond

Boston   Burr Ridge, IL   Dubuque, IA   Madison, WI   New York
San Francisco   St. Louis   Bangkok   Bogotá   Caracas   Kuala Lumpur
Lisbon   London   Madrid   Mexico City   Milan   Montreal   New Delhi
Santiago   Seoul   Singapore   Sydney   Taipei   Toronto

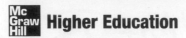

**Higher Education**

BALLET BASICS
Published by McGraw-Hill, an imprint of The McGraw-Hill Companies, Inc. 1221 Avenue of the Americas, New York, NY 10020. Copyright © 2004 by the McGraw-Hill Companies, Inc. All rights reserved. Previous editions © 2000, 1993, 1984, 1974 by Mayfield Publishing Company. No part of this publication may be reproduced or distributed in any form or by any means, or stored in a database or retrieval system, without the prior written permission of The McGraw-Hill Companies, Inc., including but not limited to, in any network or other electronic storage or transmission, or broadcast for distance learning. Some ancillaries, including electronic and print components, may not be available to customers outside the United States.

This book is printed on acid-free paper.

2 3 4 5 6 7 8 9 0  FGR/FGR  0 9 8 7 6 5 4

ISBN: 0-07-255714-1

Publisher: Jane Karpacz
Sponsoring editor: Vicki Malinee
Development editor: Carlotta Seely
Marketing manager: Pam Cooper
Production editor: Jennifer Chambliss
Production supervisor: Tandra Jorgensen
Design manager: Jean Mailander
Interior and cover design: Jean Mailander
Art editor: Cristin Yancey
Compositor: Thompson Type
Text and paper: Printed in 10/12.5 Minister Light on 45# New Era Matte
Printer: Quebecor World in Fairfield, PA

**Library of Congress Cataloging In-Publication Data**

Hammond, Sandra Noll.
    Ballet Basics / Sandra Noll Hammond.—5th ed.
        p.cm.
    ISBN 0-07-255714-1
        1. Ballet—Handbooks, manuals, etc.  I. Title

GV1788.H35 2003
792.8—dc21

200352721

www.mhhe.com

# Contents

# Foreword

by Maria T. Vegh
Director, Maria Vegh Ballet Center

Someone once wrote that "Dancing is the loftiest, the most moving, the most beautiful of the arts, because it is no mere translation or abstraction from life . . . dance is the only art wherein we ourselves are the stuff of which it is made." Yes.

Dance is universal; virtually all cultures have devised a bewildering variety of forms within which to express the joy of movement. And perhaps nowhere has this joy been more carefully crafted and defined than in the Western tradition of classical ballet, where the difficult, the sometimes seemingly impossible, is made to look effortless.

We have often assumed that the professional aspirations of young women and men require commitment and hard work at an early age. Such assumptions are normally well-founded. But as Ms. Hammond states almost immediately in her preface, there are are compelling reasons for late adolescents and adults (women and men) to study ballet. "Ballet . . . challenges the entire body." Again, yes. A student will "soon be immersed in an art rich in more than five centuries of history." That, too. To these crucial points I would only emphasize a third: The older student can come to experience the body as expressed through a vocabulary in which precision and nuance are paramount.

Precision and nuance lie behind this book. I have known Ms. Hammond for many years; I have watched this wonderful, unusual book as it has grown through four editions, and now in this new century in a fifth edition. I have used the book in my work with older individuals who aspire to experientially understand what ballet is about. Ms. Hammond takes what can seem daunting to the student (vocabulary, basic positions, etc.) and makes it accessible. As she rightly stresses, a person who essentially masters the information in her book will come to a new appreciation and understanding, not only of ballet but also of herself or himself as a person.

I am indeed pleased to write this introductory word and recommendation.

*Ms. Maria Vegh, formerly codirector (with David Howard) of the Harkness Research and Training Center in New York, is now director of the Maria Vegh Ballet Centre, dedicated to the training of advanced dancers who aspire to professional careers. A well-known master teacher, Ms. Vegh regularly conducts ballet workshops throughout the country and abroad, most recently in Japan and Peru.*

# Preface

The popular image of the beginning ballet student is that of a knobby-kneed eight- or ten-year-old girl, eyes sparkling with dreams of becoming a ballerina. This book, however, is written for the beginning ballet student who is at least eight years older than that dreamy-eyed child. For a variety of reasons, this person, male or female, has enrolled in an adult beginning ballet class—in a department of physical education or performing arts at a college or university, in a community or arts center, in a private studio or professional dancing school. No matter where the ballet class meets, certain fundamental activities and protocol will be observed.

This book introduces and explains the basic fundamentals of the ballet class—ballet technique at the barre and in the center, the dress and comportment of the student, the function of the classroom, and the role of the teacher. In addition, the text offers suggestions on the care and strengthening of the dancer's instrument—the body—and information about the ballet profession. The final chapter gives an overview of ballet history, tracing the development of ballet technique and the contributions of some of the important artists in the ballet tradition.

The study of ballet as a means to a career as a professional ballet dancer is not very realistic for the adult beginner. There are a few, very rare, exceptions of talented latecomers who began the study of ballet in their late teens and eventually joined one company or another as professional dancers. But even those rare cases are almost always men who came to ballet after several years of training in other forms of dance (tap, jazz, or folk) or in a related activity such as gymnastics.

It is assumed, therefore, that the reader probably does not dream of becoming a professional ballet dancer. Is there a valid reason for an adult to study ballet? I believe the answer is yes and, moreover, a plural yes.

Ballet technique involves and challenges the entire body. Its intricacies and harmonies stimulate the mind as well as the muscles. For total body exercise, it has few equals. The determined student may even discover performing, teaching, and choreographing opportunities in the ever-multiplying amateur groups, civic or regional. Ballet training is widely recognized as a valuable foundation for other dance forms in which there indeed may be professional performing careers for those beginning relatively late in life. Certainly, new and expanded opportunities exist in ballet-related fields, for which an understanding of ballet technique is a benefit and often a requirement.

The execution of ballet technique can do more than exercise muscles and strengthen ligaments or provide an outlet for the performing urge. When done carefully and correctly, it can improve body posture and carriage and, eventually, the actual shape of the body. It can stimulate the appreciation of dance as a medium of expression, thus developing a more informed audience. Admittedly, progress in these directions may be slow in an adult after years of habitual careless posture, accumulated tensions, and desultory attendance at dance concerts. For the person who would attempt to correct such habits, the ballet classroom is one place to begin, the modern-dance classroom being, of course, another.

A student who has chosen the ballet classroom will soon be immersed in an art rich in more than five centuries of history, an art form worthy of serious study by an adult. The evolution of ballet is detailed in many fascinating books, but reading about ballet cannot begin to impart the excitement and understanding that study from a good classroom teacher can—a teacher whose expertise is part of that historical legacy. Books such as this one are offered as an aid to, not a substitute for, that study.

## NEW TO THIS EDITION

### Updated Content

This new edition contains updated content throughout, including the latest teaching practices. In addition, new illustrations have been added to highlight alternative positions and demonstrate correct technique.

### Study Questions and Topics

Chapters 1 through 4 begin with a list of questions that prompt the reader to think about the key points, such as what clothing should be worn to ballet class, why barre work is important, and what the eleven body positions for ballet are. Chapters 5 through 7 are introduced by a list of study topics, including foot disorders, dance therapy, and the development of ballet in the United States.

## Making Progress

These new concluding sections for the technique chapters (Chapters 2 through 4) explain how different individuals advance and how to improve one's technique. Topics include how the unique nature of an individual's body affects his or her progress, the use of visualization in ballet, and making each dance movement visually appealing.

## New or Expanded Topics

### Chapter 1 The Ballet Class

- New section on how to choose the right teacher and class
- Revised discussion of correct breathing
- Expanded explanation of turnout

### Chapter 2 Ballet Technique: Barre Work

- New illustrations showing direction of *en dehors* and *en dedans* for *ronds de jambes*
- How to use the barre and correct preparation of the arm at barre
- Proper use of individual range of turnout
- Revised descriptions of selected exercises and suggestions for practice
- Expanded discussion of stretching
- Use of body imagery in practice of barre exercises

### Chapter 3 Ballet Technique: Center Work

- New example of *adagio* sequence
- New illustrations for alternate preparation for *pirouette en dedans*
- Descriptions for *pirouettes* and preparatory exercises
- Expanded discussion of *port de bras*
- How barre exercises are performed in center floor
- Use of body imagery
- Kinesiological implications of the exercises

### Chapter 4 Ballet Technique: *Allegro*

- Reorganization of material for greater clarity
- New example of *grand allegro* combination
- New illustrations for *chassé en l'air à la seconde* and *pas de basque sauté en avant*
- Expanded discussion of *chassés*

### Chapter 5 The Ballet Body

- New discussion of somatic approaches to achieving one's potential
- New section on yoga
- New discussion of cardiorespiratory exercise
- New section on strength training
- Increased emphasis on individual variations of body structure
- Expanded discussion of flexibility exercise
- Revised section on injuries and ailments
- Expanded discussion of foot care
- Revised section on proper nutrition, including health hazards of smoking

### Chapter 6 The Ballet Profession

- Sharpened focus on the adult beginner and the profession
- New section on computer technology
- Updated material in all sections on other ballet-related careers

### Chapter 7 Ballet History

- Condensation of information for better presentation
- Updated references

### Successful Features

**Illustrations**   One of the features that sets this book apart from other ballet books is the way it is illustrated. Simple and clear, the illustrations keep the reader's eye focused on the position or step being demonstrated. When appropriate, the illustrations show a view of the dancer from the back, offering an excellent learning advantage. Illustrations and their corresponding text are placed as closely together as possible for ideal presentation.

**Format**   The various ballet steps and movements are presented in a standard format. The pronunciation of each ballet term is given immediately following its heading. This is followed by sections on the definition, purpose, and description of the step or movement. Next, reminders, suggestions, and related exercises are presented. This simple pattern makes the content easy to understand and remember.

**Selected Reading and Viewing**   The Selected Resources list at the end of the book has been completely updated. It includes sections on General Reference, Ballet Technique, Ballet Health, Ballet Profession, Ballet History, American Periodicals, and Internet Sources for Ballet Video/DVD Selections, Ballet Companies, and Dance Libraries and Organizations.

**Technical Terms Index**   In addition to a general index, this book features an index of technical terms. This helpful guide shows at a glance where to find the main discussion of a particular term, including its definition and related illustrations.

## SUPPLEMENTS

**PageOut: The Course Website Development Center (*www.pageout.net*)**
PageOut, free to instructors who use a McGraw-Hill textbook, is an online program you can use to create your own course website. PageOut offers the following features:

- A course home page
- An instructor home page
- A syllabus (interactive and customizable, including quizzing, instructor notes, and links to the text's Online Learning Center)
- Web links
- Discussions (multiple discussion areas per class)
- An online gradebook
- Links to student web pages

Contact your McGraw-Hill sales representative to obtain a password.

**Primis Online (*www.mhhe.com/primis/online*)**   Primis Online is a database-driven publishing system that allows instructors to create content-rich textbooks, lab manuals, or readers for their courses directly from the Primis website. The customized text can be delivered in print or electronic (eBook) form. A Primis eBook is a digital version of the customized text (sold directly to students as a file downloadable to their computer or accessed online by a password).

Although this fifth edition contains expanded, updated material in each chapter, the intention of the book remains the same: to provide an auxiliary source for the beginning-level ballet class by supplying information about basic ballet technique and an introduction to the world of ballet.

## ACKNOWLEDGMENTS

I wish to thank my ballet instructors who, through the years, have indirectly helped me write this book, especially Margaret Craske and Antony Tudor, The Juilliard School and the Metropolitan Opera School of Ballet; Alan Howard, Pacific Ballet, San Francisco; Thalia Mara and Arthur Mahoney, School of Ballet Repertory, New York City; Dolores Mitrovich, Tucson, Arizona; and my very first teachers, Toby Jorgensen and Sue Keller, Fayetteville, Arkansas.

I also want to thank the many ballet instructors and students who, during the past three decades, have used *Ballet Basics*. Their comments always have been helpful and their enthusiasm much appreciated. I am grateful that *Ballet Basics* is continuing into the twenty-first century with the publishing expertise of the McGraw-Hill Health and Human Performance Team: Jane Karpacz, publisher; Vicki Malinee, sponsoring editor; Carlotta Seely, development editor; Pam Cooper, marketing manager; Jennifer Chambliss, production editor; Tandra Jorgensen, production supervisor; Jean Mailander, designer; Cristin Yancey, art editor, Joe Webb, copyeditor; Tara Joffe, proofreader; and Melanie Belkin, indexer.

Finally, I am especially thankful for the many suggestions from the reviewers of the fourth edition of *Ballet Basics*. The contributions of the following reviewers have helped to improve this new edition in many ways:

Anjali Austin
    Florida State University

Lenna DeMarco
    Glendale Community College

Philippa Frame
    Arizona State University

Patty Graham
    Columbia College

Susan R. Koff
    Louisiana State University

Catherine A. Schaeffer
    Valdosta State University

Sandra Noll Hammond

# The Ballet Class

This chapter will help you answer these questions about your first ballet class:

- What should you wear to ballet class?
- Why is class attendance and behavior important?
- What is meant by correct alignment of the body, and why is it important?
- What is turnout, and why must it be done correctly?
- What are the five positions of the feet?
- What are some of the rules for positions of the arms?

The necessary elements of any ballet class—the teacher, the studio, the student, the music, the language—and the fundamental principles of ballet technique are the subjects of this chapter.

Beginning ballet classes usually meet two or three times a week, with each class typically lasting an hour or an hour and a half. Dancers often refer to "taking class" rather than "going to class" because much is offered in the ballet studio that can be taken by the serious and willing student. Taking class can become a regular part of a dancer's life. It is the special time, in a special place, for continual artistic enrichment and personal discovery, as well as for improvement and day-to-day maintenance of the dance instrument itself—the body.

## THE TEACHER

A well-qualified teacher is most important to a ballet class. Before enrolling in a beginning ballet class, a student might ask permission to watch a class and thereby have a chance to observe the teacher in action. A student new to ballet probably does not have specific knowledge about ballet technique and style, but by watching a class it is possible to answer some general questions about the teacher and about the way the students are responding to the work they are given. For example, some general questions are: Does the teacher seem interested in the students' progress? Is the teacher enthusiastic, encouraging, and positive in attitude? Does the teacher explain and demonstrate the exercises clearly so that the students seem to understand what they are to do (and what they are not to do)? Does the teacher give corrections and suggestions clearly? Are those corrections and suggestions about improving postural alignment as well as about how the steps and exercises are to be performed? Does the teacher make you wish that you were taking the class?

The teacher of a beginning class for adults need not be a retired *prima ballerina* or *premier danseur* with firsthand acquaintance of famous ballet roles, but she or he should have a sound knowledge of ballet technique and an understanding of human anatomy. The instrument being trained is the human body; the teacher's job is, therefore, a complex and responsible one.

Although a teacher's knowledge and demonstration of ballet steps is, of course, essential for a beginning class, the teacher first must explain basic movements and exercises. These slow, elementary exercises may seem totally unrelated to the brilliant footwork of dancers seen on stage and screen. Those serene artists show no signs of effort, sweat, or fatigue, but a visit backstage at a performance or to a professional class will quickly dispel the vision of effortless motion. To dance is to work, and to work very hard. It is the teacher's job to guide that work soundly, and the good teacher can make it exciting and enjoyable.

Teaching methods and manners vary. One teacher may be "dressed out" in practice clothes like the rest of the class; another may wear street clothes. A teacher's voice may be loud, accompanied by hand clapping or finger snapping, or it may be soft, as though only two persons were in the studio. Many teachers employ a variety of styles and resort to a number of ways of reaching the students—serious, joking, angry, anecdotal.

Corrections and suggestions are basic ingredients to instruction, and a good teacher knows when and how to give them. Basically there are two kinds of correction—that given to the entire class and that given to an individual. Take heed of both! A soloist with a famous company has said that she always listened to a class correction as though it were said to her personally. When an individual correction is given, it should not be received as an embarrassing insult, and one hopes it would not be offered in such a manner. Most teachers have a genuine interest in the progress of their pupils and a dedication to ballet. A correction is an aid to progress, and the teacher is likely to lose interest in the student who ignores or systematically forgets corrections. If corrections apply to a serious structural problem and are still ignored, the student may be asked to withdraw from the class. Ballet technique is a powerful tool for building strong bodies, but when done incorrectly it is equally powerful in damaging them. The teacher of a beginning class for adults should not expect the technical perfection of a younger student enrolled in a professional ballet school. Neither should the adult who enrolls in a ballet class expect to float randomly around the room as music plays somewhere in the background.

A certain formalism in manners as well as style has continued from ballet's aristocratic heritage in royal courts. (See "Social and Theatrical Dances of the Renaissance and Early Baroque Periods" and "Birth of the Classical Ballet" in Chapter 7.) Thus, in class a certain politeness prevails, and the ballet teacher may expect to be addressed as Miss, Madame, or Mr. Such-and-Such even though some students in the class may be older than the teacher or on a first-name basis outside of class. Although this procedure may sound austere, it is a part of the ballet tradition of respectful demeanor. It does not detract from the teacher's availability to answer serious questions and listen to individual problems.

Adult classes offer both teacher and students the opportunity to discuss artistic and historical matters as well as technical concerns of ballet. The classroom should be a place to ask politely as well as to listen respectfully.

## THE STUDIO

The ballet classroom is an unpretentious place, for the needs of the class are simple, though specific. Typically, the room is fairly large, often approximating the rectangular shape and size of a stage. A wooden floor is essential. Dancers prefer it to be "raised" (the boards resting on padded joists, or supports) so as to allow a certain give under the weight of the body. This slight cushioning effect helps reduce fatigue and prevent injuries that can occur from dancing on a concrete floor. The raised floor usually is made of hardwood with its surface smooth but not slick. A once-familiar sight before ballet class was the teacher sprinkling the floor with a watering can to prevent a slippery surface. Today, the wood floors of most studios and stages have vinyl coverings, such as Marly or Rosco-floors, that provide a smooth, nonslippery dance surface.

Every ballet studio contains *barres,* which are long railings made of wood or metal pipes, either attached to the walls or supported from the floor. A studio may also contain portable barres. Whether permanent or portable, barres have to be steady, offering the student a secure place to begin the lesson. The average height of the barre from the floor is three feet, six inches, but obviously some adjustment can be made for the very short or very tall person. (See "Use of the Barre" in Chapter 2 for further discussion of the relationship between the barre and the student.)

Usually at least one wall of the studio contains a mirror. Often, one entire wall is covered by mirrors and designated the "front" of the room because the dancers usually face that wall when they leave the barre to do center work. The mirror allows the dancer to check instantly the correctness of a position or movement. Nevertheless, students can become so accustomed to dancing before their own images that facing a nonmirrored wall leaves them at a loss. (This loss is nothing, however, compared with that felt by the dancer, trained and rehearsed in a mirrored studio, who first sets foot on a stage and looks out, not to mirrors but the blackness of the auditorium.) Focusing on the mirror can often distort a position and actually make some movements more difficult (especially turns). A teacher is wise to change, at least occasionally, the "front" of the room to a nonmirrored wall.

A studio needs to be well ventilated, but not drafty, and sufficiently warm to allow the muscles of the body to work easily. Few ballet facilities are luxurious; many are barely adequate, and some are depressingly dingy. But the art of ballet transcends these surroundings as it passes from the careful teacher to the hard-working students, for ballet is not contained within the walls of the studio but within the body, mind, and spirit of the dancers.

## THE STUDENT

Enrollment in a beginning ballet class should—but often does not—depend on permission of the instructor after a personal interview. It is important for the teacher to know whether the student has any physical handicaps, particularly problems of the heart, spine, hips, knees, or feet. Certain physical problems may not preclude ballet study, but they may temper the way training is approached. (See "The Ballet Physique" and "Preventing Injury" in Chapter 5.) A student should inform the teacher of any medical condition and of any injury, especially if an injury occurs in class.

### Clothing

Students admitted into a beginning ballet class will need certain equipment: tights, leotard, and soft ballet shoes. Because of the great variety of dancewear now available, it is wise to check with the instructor for the preferred style and color of such items before purchasing them. In a college or university dance course, instructions about equipment often are given at the first class meeting.

Classroom dress for a woman means tights (usually pink), covering the body from feet to waist, and leotard (often black) worn over the tights from the hips to the shoulders. These practice clothes are made of a stretchable material that can be worn skintight while allowing full freedom of movement with the outline of the body seen clearly. This exposure is often an unnerving experience for the beginner, but it is vital for the teacher, who is concerned with correct placement and movement of the body. Actually, tights and leotard are much less revealing than a bathing suit. They soon begin to feel like a second skin and as appropriate for the study of ballet as a bathing suit is for swimming. It is unnecessary to wear underpants beneath the tights, but if worn, they should be of bikini style and must never show below the leotard. The long line of the leg must not be shortened by the outline of an undergarment or by a leotard pulled down to an unflattering straight angle on the thigh. To prevent possible tearing of breast tissue, a well-supporting dance or sports bra should be worn if bra size is 32B or more.

The male dancer wears heavier tights, often black, and a plain tank top or T-shirt tucked into the tights. Under the tights, he wears a dance belt of the same color as the tights, made of elastic and strong cloth, with the wide cloth part worn in front. The dance belt gives more support and protection to the genitals than does an ordinary athletic supporter. To prevent a baggy look, the tights must be pulled up so that they fit firmly at the crotch. They can be secured in this position by elastic suspenders attached to the top of the tights and carried over the shoulders; or a belt can be worn around the waist with the top of the tights rolled over it.

**Ballet Shoes** Ballet dancing usually is associated with "toe dancing," but beginning students never wear toe shoes—dancers refer to them as *pointe shoes*. Beginners, both male and female, wear soft ballet slippers, made of leather or canvas, that have been constructed to give protection while allowing flexibility to the feet. Other soft shoes, such as gymnastic or jazz shoes, do not allow the feet to work properly in ballet exercises, nor do they give the correct "line" to the feet.

The ballet shoe gives the ballet dancer the best possible base from which to work, but it may feel strange indeed when first tried on! The shoe should fit the foot as snugly as a glove fits the hand, but there should still be room for the toes to lie flat, although there needn't be extra space at the end of the toes as in a normal street shoe. (Long toenails can result in a misfitted shoe, painful bruising later on, or both. See "Minor Foot Ailments" in Chapter 5 for proper nail care.) An American-made ballet shoe is purchased usually at least one size, sometimes two sizes, smaller than a street shoe. Individual differences, such as a particularly long big toe, call for different considerations when buying or ordering ballet shoes.

It is best to have the teacher check the fit before the student wears the shoes. The teacher can also show where to sew on the elastic that will keep the heel of the shoe in place. Elastic strips usually come with ballet shoes, but they are seldom sewn on by the manufacturer. Many studios prefer women students to use satin ribbons instead (available at the same shoe store where the shoes were bought), which are tied around the ankle exactly as ribbons for pointe shoes are. To determine the proper position for the ribbon or elastic on the shoe, fold the heel inward until it lies flat on the sole of the shoe. The elastic or ribbon should be sewn directly in front of this fold.

Like any other shoes, ballet shoes need to be broken in before they are worn for any length of time, such as a period of an entire class. After the teacher has checked the correctness of the fit, the shoes can be softened by bending them back and forth in the hands. Then they should be worn for short periods around the house, but never outside; the soles must be kept free from dirt that might track onto the studio floor.

There is no right or left to ballet shoes when they are new. Because the shoes are soft, however, and tend to mold to the feet, most dancers prefer not to switch them once the molding process has begun. The softness of the shoes also causes them to stretch with continual wear, and the resulting looseness can be adjusted by tightening the strings at the front of the shoe. These strings must never hang out but should always be tucked into the shoe. Professional ballet-company members can be subject to fines if caught with dangling shoestrings or ribbons on stage.

## Care and Use of Equipment

Outfitting oneself for a ballet class involves initial expenses that often are hard on a student budget, but equipment bought for a first class should last for many years if it is properly used and cared for. The shoes, which will be the first item to wear out, should be removed immediately after class and allowed to air before being stored in a dance bag or locker. Because it is unwise and uncomfortable to keep wearing damp practice clothes after class, the student should shower immediately and change into dry clothes. After every class, the dance clothes should be washed in mild soap and warm water, with fabric softener added to prolong the stretchiness of the leotards and tights. The garments should be allowed to hang dry, as they will shrink in the hot temperatures of most dryers.

**Accessories**   Students who continue in dance may want to add to their basic dance wardrobe. Dancers are fond of wearing many layers of dance clothing to concentrate heat where it is most needed, removing one or more of these layers as muscles get warm. The most frequent additions to the basic wardrobe are leg and ankle warmers, made of wool, cotton, or acrylic knit and worn over the ordinary dance tights. A close-fitting sweater is some-times worn, especially in cold weather. The current popularity of dancewear with the general public creates a vast selection of new styles and fabrics from which to choose. For class use, however, any dance garment should neither hinder the dancer's movement nor obstruct the clear outline of the body. Loose or bulky garments, such as sweatpants or nylon "bloomers" and jack-ets, are fine for preclass warm-up but not for class, because they may hide technical faults or structural problems from the teacher and thus invite weakness or injury.

## Hair and Jewelry

Hair should be fastened securely to keep it off the face and neck. Hair falling into the eyes or whipping about the face in turns or jumps is distracting and can be dangerous. Practical aids such as headbands, hair clips or pins, or elastic bands should be used if the hair is long. This advice applies to men as well as women. When glasses are worn, it is advisable to secure them with a stretch band, available at sporting-goods stores. Try to keep jewelry to a minimum, not only for the important sake of a neat, uncluttered appearance but also for the sake of safety. Watches, large rings, dangling earrings, and bracelets can be hazardous and distracting to the wearer as well as to other dancers.

## Attendance

Proper equipment and grooming are necessary, but equally important is regular attendance in classes. Attendance should become a habit, for only by regular work will improvement be possible. If one day a student is "not feeling up to par" but is not really ill, perhaps arrangements can be made to observe class. A great deal is learned from watching others and from writing down the exercises they perform. The student should note her or his observations, not only of the classwork but also of the explanations and suggestions for improvement given by the teacher.

Taking a ballet class in the evening, after a day of hard work, may require great discipline, but more often than not the body will respond surprisingly well and be revived by the workout. Exercises and stretches frequently make a person feel better, as is often the case for women with menstrual cramps. Dancers must—and students would do well to—continue their regular activities during menstruation. If a woman has to miss one class a month, she should, if possible, try to make it up in another section at the same technical level. If many absences occur, the body (and mind) will not be able to catch up with the rest of the class.

## Behavior in Class

More is expected, however, than merely bringing a body to class regularly, for ballet includes the intellectual and emotional being as well as the physical. Studying ballet requires full attention during class; it requires eyes and ears that are open for all available dance clues, a mouth that is closed to chatter (and empty of chewing gum), and a mind and body that are quietly ready for the work ahead.

Alert observation is crucial for learning in a movement discipline such as ballet, where exercises and patterns are typically demonstrated by the instructor for the students to follow. The ability to quickly and correctly imitate a movement phrase is important in the highly competitive professional dance world. That world is virtually closed to those who do not have that ability. For professional and amateur alike, correct performance of a movement helps prevent injury.

Although the mind cannot control specific muscles, if it correctly understands the idea of a movement, then correct muscles will function when the movement is executed. Correct execution cannot always be achieved simply by unthinkingly copying another's movement pattern. Be open to suggestions; be willing to try new ways of learning; and don't be afraid to ask questions or to make mistakes.

Remember that the face is part of the dance image. Agnes de Mille, choreographer and wise and witty author, had these words of advice for the dance student: "Do not grimace while you practice. Learn to make all the necessary effort with a quiet, controlled face—a quiet face, mark you, not a dull face."[1]

Good manners are expected in the classroom. For instance, when a progression of movement is to begin from one side of the studio, a slow saunter to the designated area is no more appropriate than a fast sprint to the front of the line. In classes containing students of several levels of technique, common protocol is for the more advanced dancers to stand in the front line or to lead off in a combination. In a class of all beginners, it is both wise and courteous to be ready to move to the front but not to expect always to be there. Be aware that everyone in class needs space in which to move. Learning to move while keeping a certain distance from and a certain relationship to other dancers is one of the challenges and rewards of dance study.

If students stop work more than momentarily in a class, they should not start again during that class period. Injuries can occur when cooled muscles are suddenly asked to work vigorously. Similarly, latecomers should not expect to take class if the first exercises have been missed. Dance study is a cumulative experience, each lesson building on the one before, just as the exercises of each lesson build on one another.

Again to quote de Mille: "Remember always that the point of every exercise is to strengthen and soften, that the object is not how high, how fast, or how long, but how harmonious and how lovely. Do the exercises slowly and carefully at first. Forget speed. Speed will take care of itself later."[2]

## THE MUSIC

The integral relationship of ballet and music is nicely summed up by choreographer and teacher George Balanchine as he described his collaboration with composer Igor Stravinsky: "His music provides the dancer's floor. It's the reason for us to move. Without the music, we don't want to move."[3]

Prior to the twentieth century, most ballet teachers were men. They usually accompanied their own classes, playing a small violin while students performed their exercises. A violinist typically would be hired to accompany classes taught by a woman or taught in a professional academy. Today, the piano is the classroom instrument, and the piano accompanist is a vital component of every class. When a good accompanist is not available, a teacher may use recordings such as tapes or CDs—perhaps those made especially for ballet classes—with appropriate selections for different exercises.

Music can be selected from a variety of sources: piano pieces from nineteenth-century composers such as Franz Schubert and Frédéric Chopin, as well as piano adaptations from ballet scores of Léo Delibes,

Cesare Pugni, and Peter I. Tchaikovsky. Twentieth-century marches, rags, and show tunes can provide appropriate accompaniment for certain movements, as can compositions from later composers such as Francis Poulenc and Sergei Prokofiev.

Knowledge of music is useful for the study of ballet. Even students who have not studied music will soon learn to count it; that is, they will hear the musical *beat* or pulse and will recognize a few fundamental musical rhythms and be able to keep time with them.

During class, the instructor may demonstrate an exercise and then count it, for example, "1 and 2 and 3 and 4." The numbers are the beats, with number 1 having the strongest beat, or accent. This group of four beats makes a *measure* of 4/4 time (or *meter*). The first number tells how many beats are in the measure. The second number tells what kind of note—in this case a quarter note—gets one beat. A series of measures is called a *phrase*. Strong and weak accents within the measure create a certain *rhythm*.

The musical meters that are used most often in beginning ballet classes are listed as follows. They are divided into measures, as indicated by the / mark. The heavy accent of each rhythm is indicated by underlining the number; the lighter accent, by the symbol ´. Each example is four measures long. Count these rhythms out loud; then try clapping or walking to them, accenting the first count of each measure:

2/4:  1̲ 2 / 1̲ 2 / 1̲ 2 / 1̲ 2 /
4/4:  1̲ 2 3́ 4 / 1̲ 2 3́ 4 / 1̲ 2 3́ 4 / 1̲ 2 3́ 4 /
3/4:  1̲ 2 3 / 1̲ 2 3 / 1̲ 2 3 / 1̲ 2 3 /
6/8:  1̲ 2 3 4́ 5 6 / 1̲ 2 3 4́ 5 6 / 1̲ 2 3 4́ 5 6 / 1̲ 2 3 4́ 5 6 /

The speed (*tempo*) of these rhythms can vary from a fast beat (*allegro*) to a slow one (*adagio*). Dance movements use these same terms: fast steps are called *allegro;* slow, sustained movements are called *adagio* (or the French form, *adage*).

Ballet exercises are usually done an even number of times; that is, a step is repeated four or eight or sixteen times. (Sometimes, a step may be done three times with a hold or pause in place of the fourth step.) Similarly, combinations of steps usually are done four or eight times. This practice is in contrast to modern dance exercises, which often are done an odd number of times (three, five, seven). Moreover, modern dancers frequently use many different meters for one dance phrase (such as 1̲ 2 3 / 1̲ 2 3́ 4 / 1̲ 2 / 1̲ 2 3́ 4 . . .). Rarely does a ballet teacher experiment in these ways, although occasionally such experiments may be rewarding, especially when working with an accompanist who is adept at improvising.

A ballet exercise or combination of steps will sometimes be learned first in one meter, such as 2/4, then tried in another, such as 6/8. The steps will look and feel slightly different when such a change is made. A change in *tempo* will have an effect also; for example, a faster tempo requires smaller movements covering less space. Changes in meter and tempo can help improve rhythmic awareness, sharpen the articulation of dance movements, and bring forth the variety of expressions of a given step.

To help students know when to be ready to begin an exercise, the accompanist will play a few notes of introduction, which the teacher may count aloud. This is called the *preparation.* Tune in to these cues and be prepared to move at the designated time, not several beats later.

Rhythm, beat, measure, phrase, tempo—all may seem bewildering to the beginner. A teacher recognizes this confusion and will try to help. For instance, a particular exercise for the leg may be demonstrated and then described by the teacher as "point, lift, point, close." The teacher may then count the exercise as "one, two, three, four." The music will play the same rhythm. And in time, the student will become equally acquainted with other musical forms, such as the waltz (3/4, with the accent on the first beat), the polka (2/4), and the mazurka (also 3/4, but with the accent on the second beat).

Although responding to the musical beat is fundamental to dance, the classroom would be dull indeed if the musical accompaniment offered merely a flat, steady rhythm. Students' ears should be trained along with their muscles. Phrases of movement and music are the goal—not just steps or notes.

## THE LANGUAGE

Because ballet was first nurtured in the royal courts and academies of France, French became the language of the art. All ballet exercises, steps, body positions, and movement directions have French names. These names are in use in every ballet studio the world over, although such wide diffusion has led to certain differences, even corruption, in specific terminology.

It is advantageous to have studied French, but students who have not will soon have a number of French words in their vocabulary after a few classes in ballet. When understood, these words can greatly simplify directions that a teacher might otherwise have to use. In addition, the terminology simplifies the task of writing down class work or choreography, should that sometime be necessary or desirable.

## STYLE

As might be expected, such a global art includes some regional differences in training and in the manner in which steps and poses are executed—differences in style. Briefly described, the French have emphasized charm and elegance, whereas the Italian school has stressed technical virtuosity. The Russian school was founded by French ballet masters, but later it adopted and adapted the more brilliant technique of the Italians. The combination of these and other sources produced the strength and flair characteristic of Russian dancers. In contrast, the British style is less flamboyant, more serene. The Danish school has maintained the exuberant lightness and speed of its French-trained nineteenth-century mentor, August Bournonville. The methods of two outstanding teachers, Enrico Cecchetti (1850–1928) and Agrippina Vaganova (1879–1951), have created methods of technique now being handed down by their many pupils. And there is an American style, a blend of French, Italian, and Russian influences with a distinctive dose of American restless energy and youthful spirit as manifest in the popular ballets by George Balanchine (1904–1983). The style of a class will reflect one of these or other schools, depending on the training of the teacher.

This book is offered as a general ballet text rather than a presentation of one particular instructional method or performing style. It does, however, reflect much of the author's training with Margaret Craske and Dolores Mitrovich in the Cecchetti tradition and with Thalia Mara and Arthur Mahoney in the Russian style, which they had received from their teachers, such as Olga Preobrajenska (1870–1962) and Adolph Bolm (1884–1951).

## THE FUNDAMENTAL PRINCIPLES

A first lesson in ballet may seem more like a class in basic anatomy than a dancing class. But without an understanding of proper body alignment and placement, there can be no progress in work toward balance and form, toward freedom and economy of movement. The very exercises that lead to control, strength, and beauty of line in ballet can also lead to weaknesses and injuries when attempted by a poorly aligned body.

The correct application of turnout of the legs is fundamental to the proper use of ballet's five positions of the feet. These five positions, along with the basic positions of the arms and head, constitute the foundation of ballet technique.

### Alignment

*Alignment* in ballet essentially means good posture; that is, the various body parts—head, shoulders, arms, ribs, hips, legs, feet—are in correct relative position with one another. Bad posture can result in a slump, with rounded shoulders and droopy head, or a sway, with the pelvis tilted forward, causing a hollow look to the lower back. These distortions in alignment are detrimental enough to an ordinary body, but they can be positively hazardous for the ballet student. In his book *Dancing without Danger,* Donald F. Featherstone warns of the cumulative effect of poor alignment: "Any departure from the balanced posture will strain muscles and ligaments and cause undue friction in joints—if one segment of the body is out of line, all others will be affected."[4]

Ballet *placement* refers to a well-aligned body that is shifted slightly forward from the ankle over the ball of the foot. Thus, when standing with the

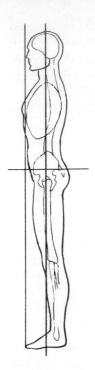
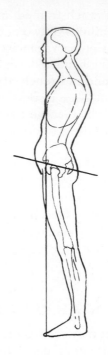
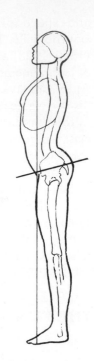

Good posture                                    Poor posture

legs parallel and the focus straight ahead, a direct vertical line could be drawn from between the eyes, down through the navel, to the tips of the toes. A dancer is said to be *placed* when the muscles of the body have become educated to assume such a position of correct alignment without effort. Once achieved, good posture requires less effort to maintain than poor posture. Each body is different, however, and correct placement is a slow process that requires many classes, often many years, of work. In ballet, the body is always active, not static, and thus requires a dynamic yet subtle realigning each time it assumes new and different poses.

Some dancers and ballet teachers use specific anatomical terminology, whereas others use more general language, imagery, or both to convey the fundamentals of correct alignment necessary for ballet. It is helpful to contemplate these fundamentals one at a time, keeping in mind that the goal is to find the most efficient posture for the work ahead.

**The Feet** To begin an understanding of proper alignment and placement for ballet, stand with the feet a few inches apart, pointing straight ahead. The feet should feel relaxed, the toes flat, with the weight of the body resting mainly on three points: the heel, the base of the big toe, and the little toe. In this position, as in the ballet positions discussed later, the arch of the foot is supported, the ankles are prevented from rolling inward or outward, and the body is given a strong base from which to work.

**The Legs**   Straighten the knees firmly, *but do not push them back;* they should be directly over the feet. Now bend the knees, keeping the heels on the floor, and check to see that the knees are pointing directly over the front of the feet. This knee-over-foot alignment is correct for any bend of the knees, whether in this parallel position or in the turned-out positions of ballet. Begin to straighten the knees and also begin to sense a lengthening of the thighs.

**The Torso**   The pelvis should be in a midway position, neither tucking under nor sticking out. To check this position, place the palm of one hand on the abdomen (which ought to feel flat and compressed) and the back of the other hand on the lower spine (the "small of the back"). The front hand should be perpendicular to the floor and the back hand nearly so. The natural curves of the spine, which allow it to be flexible and to absorb shock, must be neither exaggerated nor entirely flattened out. Maintaining a firm abdomen and an extended spine will help achieve correct alignment in a more efficient way than the inappropriate admonition to "tuck under your hips."

The rib cage should be directly in line with the hips. At no time should the rib cage feel rigid or forced forward; breathing should remain normal.

To feel the correct position of the shoulders, lift them up toward the ears, hold them there a few seconds, and then let them drop. Now feel the shoulder blades resting downward. The shoulders will be low but not pulled backward. Let the arms hang naturally from this position with the hands relaxed (shake them first to relieve any tension) and the fingers and thumbs separated naturally

**The Head**   The head must be in alignment with the ribs and hips. The back of the neck is kept long, for it is a continuation of the spine, on which the head lightly rests. The chin is parallel to the floor but never thrust forward. The eyes look forward, not down.

**Other Methods**   It is not unusual to find lessons in body alignment occurring with students not standing, as just described, but lying on the floor. New approaches to understanding movement—changing habitual muscle and neurological patterns, releasing tensions, conditioning and strengthening the body, as well as achieving more efficient posture—are some of the goals of today's many body-therapy and conditioning methods. Pioneers in the development of these methods include Dr. Lulu E. Sweigard, Frederick M. Alexander, Irmgard Bartenieff, Moshe Feldenkrais, Joseph Pilates, and Zena Rommett. (For further discussion, see "Mind/Body Approaches" and "Conditioning Methods" in Chapter 5.) Such methods are being integrated into the work of some dancers and instructors as they seek new and more appropriate ways of performing, teaching, and, not least, aligning the bones of the body.

## Correct Breathing

Correct use of the breath is fundamental to the dynamic condition of proper alignment and for enhancing ballet movements as well as for sustaining the vigor necessary for a strenuous class. Correct breathing technique can add different dynamics, such as flowing or sharpness, to movements. Consider what Ellen Jacob said in her book *Dancing: A Guide to the Dancer You Can Be:*

> The ultimate skill that every dancer strives for is to work with concentration and calm control of the body, but without tension. To achieve this, the breath is instrumental. . . . Ballet dancing, which seems to mask ordinary human function, achieves its characteristic lightness and elegance with the use of breath. The inhaled breath can literally lift you up in the air as you jump or are raised by a partner. . . . All movement must have breath and flow; otherwise it looks flat and lifeless.[5]

Correct breathing usually means lateral breathing, in which the ribs expand sideways as air fills the middle and lower parts of the lungs. The following exercise can help improve awareness of good breathing technique:

> Standing in proper alignment and with the legs parallel rather than turned out; place the hands on the sides of the ribs. Keeping the diaphragm fairly still, inhale and feel the lateral expansion of the ribs. With the exhale of the breath, feel the ribs return to their former position.

When the arms hang naturally from the shoulders, they can reflect this expansion by slightly opening and rising to the sides during inhalation, then returning gently as the breath is exhaled. This natural action is fundamental to the movement of the arms (called *port de bras* in ballet); when the body rises onto the toes or into the air during steps or springs, it will inhale naturally, and the arms will naturally want to lift also. As the body returns to the ground, the breath will be exhaled, and the arms will lower. Breathing during exercise will not be in a constant, even rhythm, however. The body will naturally want to inhale longer and deeper, or quicker and more shallow, depending on the difficulty and the speed of an exercise.

Deeper breathing can help reduce tensions in the body and thus can contribute to increased flexibility. The following exercise, from a dance therapist, can help develop deeper breathing:

> Stand, arms at the sides, and breathe in through the nose, filling the abdomen with one deep breath. Holding the breath, bend forward, allowing the spine to curve, sharply contract and exhale the air through the mouth. With the abdomen completely empty of air, return to the upright position. Repeat.[6]

The releasing of muscular tension by this exercise also contributes to a gentle stretch, sensed especially in the lower back and down the legs.

## Turnout

The student also must deal with another essential element related to alignment: the turnout of the legs at the hip joints. The legs are rotated outward from that joint *only as far as that position can be maintained by the rotator muscles around the hip joint, without disturbing body alignment.* A "complete" turnout of 180 degrees is very seldom realistic for most beginning students, and it is not a requirement for enrolling in a ballet class. Individual body differences—the shape of the pelvic structure and the tightness or restrictions of the inward and outward rotator muscles—determine the natural degree of turnout for each person. Whatever that degree, the arches of the feet must remain lifted and the ankles straight. Remember that the weight of the body rests on the base of the big and little toes and the heel. As discussed in a preceding section, correct ballet placement requires the weight to be shifted slightly forward from the ankle so that it rests more on the balls of the feet than back on the heels. In maintaining this posture, it is important that the pelvis not tilt forward nor the buttocks tuck under. The knees should always be in line with the feet, following the same rule of alignment as in the parallel position: when the knees are bent, they ought to be over the center of the feet.

Although this turned-out position may feel strange at first, it is important to understand that the turnout of the legs in ballet is merely an exaggeration of a perfectly normal action of the human body. The top of the thighbone (femur) can rotate either inward or outward in the hip socket. Ballet technique has simply capitalized on the outward-rotation possibility. Maintaining the turnout should cause no sense of strain or tension. The body must not be stiff and locked in position. It must be firm, yet at ease and free to move.

Realistic turnout
for many
beginners

Historically, the desire for extreme turnout developed slowly—by 1700 the angle of turnout was typically 90 degrees; by 1800 it was ideally 180 degrees. A similar progression is mirrored in a student's training; a beginner works from positions of lesser turnout, advancing gradually to more turned-out positions as the body gains in strength and learns to maintain correct alignment. This process must be done slowly and carefully. Forcing a turnout can cause serious injury and muscular imbalance. And remember, a 180-degree turnout is not a requirement for beginning ballet classes!

## THE FIVE POSITIONS OF THE FEET

The five positions of the feet, codified in the late seventeenth century, are the foundations of ballet technique. (See "Birth of the Classical Ballet" in Chapter 7 for the historical context.) Every ballet step, movement, and pose relates in some way to one or more of these positions. In all five positions, the weight must be equally distributed on both feet, the legs straight unless purposefully flexed. The hips remain squared to the front, the pelvis in its upright position, and the legs turned out from the hip joints. For clarity, positions with 180-degree turnout are described and illustrated here. A beginning student, however, will realistically work from positions of more modest

**15**

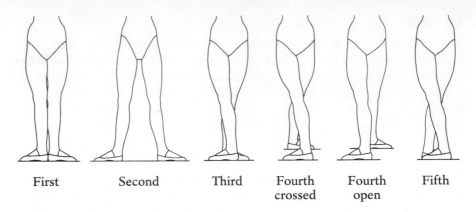

First    Second    Third    Fourth crossed    Fourth open    Fifth

turnout, as shown in the examples on the preceding page. The five positions are as follows:

First position: the legs turned out from the hips, the heels and knees touching, the feet forming a straight line

Second position: the legs turned out from the hips, as in first position, but the heels separated and directly under the shoulders

Third position: the legs turned out from the hips, one foot directly in front of the other, with the heel of each foot touching the middle of the other foot

Fourth position: the legs turned out from the hips, one foot directly forward of the other and one foot length apart (for crossed fourth position) or forward the same distance from first position (for open fourth position)

Fifth position: the legs turned out from the hips, one foot directly in front of the other, with the heel of the front foot at the joint or at the tip of the toe of the back foot

At the beginning of training, it is wise to begin and end exercises in first position; later exercises can be done from third, and finally from the more demanding fifth position.

## POSITIONS OF THE ARMS

The positions of the arms correspond to the positions of the feet. However, no rule says that if the feet are in fifth position, the arms must always be in a particular position. Some variation occurs in the numbering and naming of the basic arm positions in different teaching methods. It is pointless to argue over numbers or names; learn those used in your school and concentrate on the desired shape of the arms. Although there are slight variations in the style of the positions, the following general rules of form can be helpful for most basic positions: The arms curve gently from shoulder to fingertip, eliminating the pointed look of the elbows. The hands are held simply, the wrists neither stiff nor floppy, the fingers curved and only slightly separated, with the thumb and middle finger brought relatively close together but not in a forced manner. In midlevel positions, either to the front or to the side, the arms may have a gradual slope downward from the shoulders to the elbows, then to the wrists, and finally to the fingers. The arms should move freely from the shoulder sockets so as not to raise or pull the shoulders. When the hand is over the head, it should be just within the line of vision as the performer looks straight forward.

The following descriptions and illustrations represent only one of several possibilities for terminology, style, and numbering of arm positions; others are equally valid.

Basic positions in which the arms and hands are to the side of the body and, usually, just slightly forward:

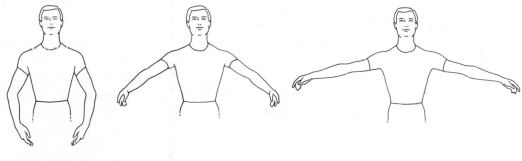

First (preparatory)          *Demi-seconde*                          Second

Basic positions in which the hands are centered on the body, only a few inches apart, the arms forming an oval shape:

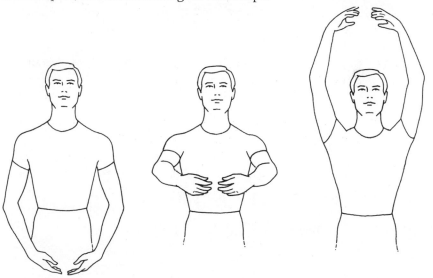

*Bras bas (fifth en bas)*      *Bras avant (fifth en avant)*      *Bras hauts (fifth en haut)*
(arms low)                     (arms forward)                     (arms high)

Possible variations of these basic positions, which have a variety of different names and numbers, include:

## POSITIONS OF THE HEAD

During barre work in beginning classes, the position of the head seldom varies. It is held regally on a long neck, with chin parallel to the floor and eyes looking (not staring) straight forward. This position sets the tone for the elegant style of ballet, but in center work the head must learn to move in harmony with the rest of the body. Five different positions of the head can be used:

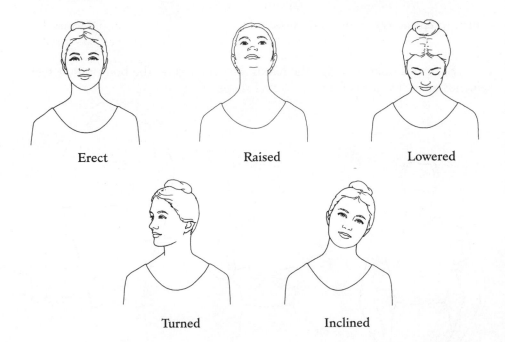

Erect        Raised        Lowered

Turned        Inclined

These positions can be combined, for instance:

Turned and inclined      Lowered and turned

## SPECIAL CONSIDERATIONS

### Balancing on One Leg

A dancer's body is expected to be centered, the weight of the body resting evenly on both feet while imaginary lines dissect the body vertically from head to toe and horizontally across the body at hip level. However, a shift of weight to one foot, with the other leg extended or raised, brings a challenge to this sense of center. The vertical center line moves from the supporting ankle up through the top of the body, until it is in line with the center of the supporting foot. Turnout on the supporting leg is maintained through control of the rotator muscles around the hip joint. A horizontal line must be maintained across the hips, avoiding any tendency to "sit" into the supporting leg or to raise the other hip.

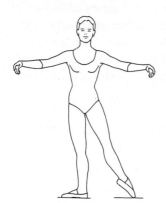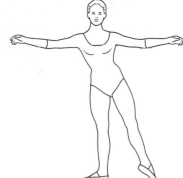

Properly balanced                       Improperly balanced

### Balancing on the Ball of the Foot

All five positions of the feet can be done with the heels raised and the weight on only the balls of the feet. The balance is centered between the metatarsal heads at the bases of the big toe and the second toe. If the foot leans

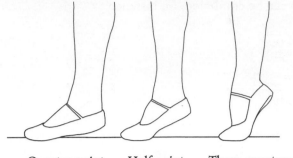

Quarter point    Half point    Three-quarter point

toward only the big toe or toward the little toe, it is said to be *sickled,* a potentially harmful position for the ankles and knees as well as for the feet.

In beginning work, balances ae taken on quarter point and on half point. After sufficient strength is acquired, balances can be done on three-quarter point. Before attempting balances, the following exercise, done one foot at a time, can help with awareness of proper alignment of the foot to leg:

*Practice*
Stand with the feet parallel. Lift one heel as high as possible (allowing the knee to bend) while keeping the ball of that foot firmly on the floor. The ankle and knee should be in line with the big toe and the second toe. Now try practicing this position with the legs turned out.

## Pointing the Foot

The pointed foot extends from the ankle joint through a series of arches of the foot (including the longitudinal or long arch along the inner side of the foot and the transverse arch across the forefoot) to the toes. The toes compress together in a stretched, rather than a curled or knuckled-under, position. The center of the foot and the toes form a direct line with the ankle.

*Practice*
Sit on the floor, or well back in a chair, legs together and straight, the feet flexed (bent) at the ankles. Slowly begin arching the feet, working

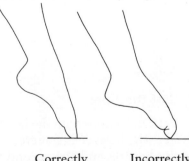

Correctly          Incorrectly
pointed foot      pointed foot

inch by inch from the ankle through the insteps of the feet to the balls of the feet and then to the toes. The knees should remain straight. The toes should appear as a continuation of the arch of the pointed foot, creating a smooth line with the leg. The toes are pressed together but are not "knuckled under."

## Warm-Up

Dancers frequently like to limber their bodies gently before the class begins. This warm-up can help awaken the muscles, as well as the mind, for the work ahead by raising the body temperature and increasing the supply of blood.

Some teachers may even begin the lesson with certain preparatory exercises, not leaving beginners to warm up on their own. Following are examples of simple movements that may be used as a warm-up. Note that these movements are done slowly and without jumps or extreme stretches; gradually, over time, increase the number of repetitions.

### Practice

To warm the neck area: Bend the head forward, then lift the face toward the ceiling. Tilt the head from side to side. Turn the head from side to side. Roll the head in a circle.

To warm the chest area: Lift the shoulders toward the ears and let them drop. Circle the shoulders forward, up, and back, then reverse the circle. Circle the arms forward, up, and back, then reverse the circle.

To stretch out the entire body: Reach upward, sideward, and forward.

To activate the reflexes: Bend slowly forward, starting with the head and "rolling" down through each vertebra of the spine. "Hang" in this forward position with the body relaxed, the knees slightly bent. Reverse the movements, returning to an upright position with the body in correct alignment. Do this in parallel position, then in first position.

To warm the ankles and feet: Circle the foot at the ankle. Flex and point the foot (as described earlier). Lift the heel of one foot while pressing the ball of that foot on the floor; complete the arching of the foot by pointing through the toes and allowing them to leave the floor slightly. Reverse the action by rolling down through the toes to the ball of the foot, then lowering the heel. Using this action, slowly prance in parallel position.

To warm up the hip joint: Lift the knee several times to the front; gently swing the leg forward and backward.

To warm the calf muscles: Face the barre with the legs parallel and the feet a few inches apart. Lean into the barre, keeping the legs straight and the heels firmly on the floor. Hold this position and then return to the original stance.

To strengthen the abdominal muscles while lying on the back, knees bent and the soles of the feet on the floor: Clasp the hands in front of the body and reach forward between the knees, raising first the head, then the shoulders and upper back off the floor. Keep the waist pressed to the floor and the stomach flat. Slowly return to the original position by reversing the action.

## MAKING PROGRESS

People learn at different speeds and in very individual ways. Each body is unique; no two dancers have exactly the same physique and therefore no two dancers' training will progress in the same way. A dancer with a long-limbed body may have great flexibility and a pleasing line in movement but may need extra work to gain strength for balances, turns, and quick jumps. A dancer with a more compactly built body may learn easily to balance, turn, and jump but may need extra work to maintain stretch and to develop a pleasing line. For every physical strength, there is usually a related weakness, and vice versa. Respect the uniqueness of your body. Learn to listen to your body as it begins to assimilate a new way of moving—ballet technique.

A beginning ballet class challenges "traditional" learning habits because it engages a multiplicity of sensory, kinesthetic, and mental channels. Eyes must catch the visual image demonstrated; ears must tune in to the rhythmic and harmonic patterns of the music; the mind must analyze complex movement details. Sometimes muscles respond and remember before the conscious mind does.

Technical progress usually occurs in a stair-step fashion rather than in a smooth, continuously ascending line. Thus, technical plateaus—periods seemingly without change (that is, improvement)—are inevitable. And then, a glorious breakthrough will occur, and another stair step will have been climbed. That is the time to congratulate yourself and enjoy the pleasures of accomplishment. Then, once more, have the discipline to continue, for the key to progress is regular class attendance and consistent work—mind, senses, and muscles fully involved.

To get the most benefits from your ballet training, make a habit of getting to class on time, being properly dressed, arriving and staying alert, having a positive attitude, and in all respects being ready to dance!

## NOTES

1. Agnes de Mille, *To a Young Dancer* (Boston: Little, Brown, 1960), 24.
2. Ibid.
3. Quoted in Selma Jeanne Cohen, ed., *Dance as a Theatre Art: Source Readings in Dance History from 1581 to the Present,* 2d ed. (Hightstown, N.J.: Princeton Book, 1991), 190.
4. Donald F. Featherstone, *Dancing without Danger* (South Brunswick, N.J., and New York: Barnes, 1970), 65.
5. Ellen Jacob, *Dancing: A Guide to the Dancer You Can Be* (Reading, Mass: Addison-Wesley, 1981), 210.
6. Raoul Gelabert, *Anatomy for the Dancer,* vol. 2 (New York: Dance Magazine, 1966), 55.

# Ballet Technique:
## Barre Work

After reading this chapter, you should be able to answer these questions about barre work:

- Why is barre work important?
- What is meant by the "preparation of the arm"?
- What are the three most fundamental exercises at the barre? Describe them.
- What are the similarities and the differences between *battement tendu, battement dégagé,* and *grand battement*?
- What are the similarities and the differences between a *rond de jambe à terre en dehors* and a *rond de jambe à terre en dedans*?
- What is the leg action of *développé* and the coordinated movement of the arm?
- What are some important things to remember when you stretch?

The first formal segment of classroom instruction begins with exercises done at the barre. Although each exercise has its own purpose, barre work as a whole is designed to strengthen the feet, legs, and back; to increase range of movement (especially at the hip); to attain balance and control; to stabilize turnout; and to gain speed in the feet and lightness in the legs—in other words, to instill the mechanics of and build the foundation for ballet technique. Because of these important factors, barre work may comprise most of the lesson during the first weeks of ballet training. Gradually, the time spent in barre exercises is reduced, but it seldom is less than half of the class period.

## USE OF THE BARRE

The barre is meant as a hand support only, steadying the body but not bearing its weight. In the early stages of training while doing many exercises, the student faces the barre with both hands resting lightly on it, close together, and the elbows relaxed and slightly bent. This position gives the beginner an extra aid in centering the body because the hips and shoulders can be kept parallel with the horizontal line of the barre (see figure on page 25). Later, most exercises are done with the body sideways to the barre, hence the earlier term *side practice* was used when referring to barre work. When standing sideways to the barre, the leg farther from the barre (the outside leg) typically is the gesture leg of the exercise. Because exercises traditionally begin with the right leg as the gesture leg, the dancer begins with the left hand (the inside hand) on the barre. The hand should rest on the barre somewhat forward of the line of the shoulder, the fingers on top of the barre with the thumb along the side of the barre rather than below it. The body should be far enough from the barre to allow the inside elbow to be relaxed and slightly bent. The outside arm is low and slightly curved (as shown in the preparatory position illustrated on page 44).

Before an exercise begins, the outside arm makes a *preparation,* such as the following example, done in four counts:

1. With breath, open the arm slightly to the side, the *demi-seconde* position.
2. Lower the arm to *bras bas* position.
3. Raise the arm forward to *bras avant* position.
4. Open the arm outward to second position.

These four movements can be accompanied by coordinated movements of the head. The instructor may count the preparation as "5, 6, 7, 8," and then the actual barre exercise will begin on count "1." When an exercise is completed, both arms are lowered, and the final position is held momentarily before turning to repeat the exercise with the other leg.

### Suggestions

To enhance the sense of being centered over the legs, it is helpful to make the preparation with both arms, raising them forward so that the hands are centered on the torso, opening them outward to the side, and then taking the barre with the inside hand. Review the arm positions illustrated in Chapter 1, pages 17 and 18, then practice the arm preparation with one arm and then with both arms. To help avoid "right-leggedness," it is wise to occasionally begin exercises with the left leg.

### SEQUENCE OF EXERCISES

No universally accepted order of sequence for barre exercises exists, but in most classes work at barre begins with the most basic movement of ballet, the *plié,* or bend of the legs, and finishes with the vigorous movements of grand battement, or large beating action of the leg. Although the sequence varies somewhat from teacher to teacher and from school to school, in general the smaller, slower movements are done first, legs are gradually warmed up from the feet to the knees to the hips, and combinations of movements grow from simple to more complex.

The barre exercises discussed in the following pages are arranged in broad general categories that do not reflect any preferred order of teaching. Because they lay the foundation for the entire technique of ballet, they will be described in some detail, the three most fundamental exercises deserving first attention.

The illustrations show the dancers using complete turnout of the legs, but students should remember always to work only within their own range of turnout. And, it must be remembered that the most specific instructions, cautions, or hints from a printed page cannot *teach* the mechanics and artistry of ballet even to the most willing student. Neither can the finest illustrations. Therefore, the following pages are not intended as do-it-yourself instructions but rather as resources for, and supplements to, classroom study.

## THREE FUNDAMENTAL EXERCISES: *PLIÉ, ÉLEVÉ/RELEVÉ, AND BATTEMENT TENDU*

The following three exercises represent ballet's most fundamental movements of the legs—bending and straightening the knees, raising and lowering the heels, and stretching the foot along the floor to a pointed position before returning it to a closed position.

### *Plié* (plee-AY)

**Definition**   A *plié* is a bending movement of the legs, beginning at the top of the thighs, through the knees, and into the ankles. A half-bend is called a *demi-plié* (d'mee-plee-AY); a deep bend, a *grand plié* (grahn plee-AY). (Technically, a bend on only one leg is not a *plié* but a *fondu*.)

■ *Demi-plié* in first position

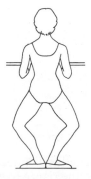

Balanced, smooth motion

**Purpose**  Almost every step in ballet—certainly every jumping movement—involves a bending movement of the legs. The correct execution of the *demi-plié* (and the *fondu*) gives a springy quality to steps of elevation and a lightness to all dance movements. The *grand plié* is important in stretching and strengthening the legs because the entire weight of the upper body is lowered and raised by the legs. Both *demi-plié* and *grand plié* require even distribution of the weight on both feet, thus making it easier to center the body and to master the turnout of the legs. Both types of *plié* increase the circulation of the blood in the legs, thus facilitating warm-up. Knowing how and when to bend and straighten the knees is the cornerstone of ballet technique.

**Description**  *Pliés* are done in all positions of the feet. During the *demi-plié,* the heels never leave the floor. The movement begins in the high, inner side of the thighs. The knees open outward in a direct line over the toes until the depth of the *demi-plié* is reached (determined by the length of the Achilles tendon connecting the calf muscle and the heel). Then the legs return to their original straight position.

The *grand plié* begins exactly as the *demi-plié,* but when the maximum stretch of the Achilles tendon is felt, the heels are allowed to release from the floor and the knees continue to bend over the feet until, ideally, the thighs are almost parallel with the floor. Immediately the action is reversed: The heels press into the floor, the knees straighten, and the thighs continue to lengthen upward until the original position is attained. The *grand plié* thus described is done in all positions except the second and the open fourth positions, where, because of the spread of the legs, the heels need not and should not be released from the floor.

■ *Grand plié* in first position

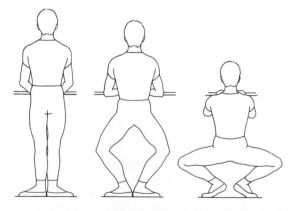

A two-way motion: the spine lengthens upward as the body descends, then reaches downward on the return to the original position

Thighs rotate sideward as well as lower downward

**Reminders**   In all *pliés,* the body must be centered over the feet. The spine must remain erect, with the pelvis in the midway position—that is, neither pushed forward nor released backward. Be sure that the turnout of the legs remains within the natural range and is not forced by any movement of the feet during the *plié.* The feet should be securely placed on the floor but not tense, with the arches supported so they do not roll. The correct alignment of the ankles should be maintained without tension at the depth of the *demi-plié.* The weight of the body must not settle into the knees at the depth of the *grand plié.* The movement of the *plié* should be smooth and slow but without pauses at any point in the exercise. The straightening of the legs must be done as carefully as the bending of them. When the legs are crossed, as in third, fourth, and fifth positions, it is important that the weight continue to be distributed evenly on both feet. (The temptation often is to lean toward the back foot.) These crossed positions also require great care in opening the knees equally, so that one knee lowers to the same level as the other. (The tendency often is to drop the back knee, especially in the fourth position.) The depth of the *grand plié* is determined by the strength of the muscles on the inner side of the thighs and by the length of the Achilles tendon. Therefore, the thighs ought not to be lowered all the way to the horizontal position unless correct body alignment can be maintained throughout the *plié.*

**Suggestions**   It is important to think of the *plié* as an outward motion rather than a descending one. Try to feel tall, lifting and lengthening the body—long spine, long legs—as the thighs and knees are reaching sideward during the *plié.* This sense of oppositional suspension—upward and outward—makes the difference between a simple bend of the knees and a ballet *plié.*

Learn to execute the *demi-plié* correctly before attempting the *grand plié.* Begin the study of *pliés* in the first and second positions; later add the third position and when sufficient strength has developed, the fourth and fifth

■ Incorrect *pliés*

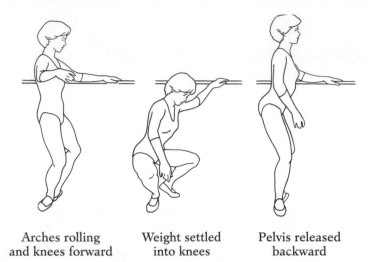

Arches rolling
and knees forward

Weight settled
into knees

Pelvis released
backward

positions. When changing to a new position, move only one foot and do not look at it. Learn the *pliés* facing the barre before trying them sideways or with movements of the arm.

Because *grand pliés* are an especially strenuous exercise for the knees, they should be limited in number and performed after the legs are warmed up. Thus, while *demi-pliés* are appropriate as a first exercise, *grand pliés* may be more safely and effectively performed later in the barre sequence.

### *Élevé* (el-e-VAY)/*Relevé* (ruhl-e-VAY)

**Definition**    An *élevé* is a rise from straight legs to the balls of the feet, the *demi-pointes* (d'mee-PWAHNT). When the rise is made from a preceding *demi-plié,* it is called *relevé,* meaning raised or relifted.

**Purpose**    Strength, suppleness, and control of the feet are developed by both the *élevé* and the *relevé.* As the thighs lengthen upward during the rise, the knees and the muscles of the legs are strengthened also, building a strong, secure position on *demi-pointes,* so important for balances, turns, and many steps of ballet, including those later done on full pointe by advanced students (traditionally, women only). Because it combines both a bend and a rise, the *relevé* serves also as a preparatory exercise for jumps. A *relevé* often is used for a balanced pose, even at the finish of an exercise at the barre.

**Description**    *Élevés* and *relevés* are done in all positions of the feet. In the simpler movement, the *élevé,* the heels and legs stretch upward from the floor as the body rises to the *demi-pointes.* As the heels press downward in the return to the floor, the legs continue to lengthen as the body returns to

■ *Relevé* to three-quarter point

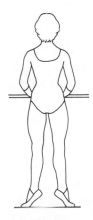

Verticality with strong upward thrust

its original position without a bend of the knees. Although *demi-pointe* literally means half-point, the term often is used for any of three levels—quarter, half, and three-quarter—that denote the relative distance of the heels from the floor. (See "Balancing on the Ball of the Foot" in Chapter 1)

The *relevé* is preceded and followed by a *demi-plié,* therefore requiring a high degree of coordination: the push of the heels from the floor must be properly timed with the straightening of the knees and lengthening upward of the thighs; the lowering of the heels to the floor and the bending of the legs must be carefully controlled but without tension.

The action can be smooth, with the heels raised and lowered in the same spot, or the action can be quick and springy, with a firm push against the

■ *Sous-sus*　　　　　　　　■ *Échappé relevé*

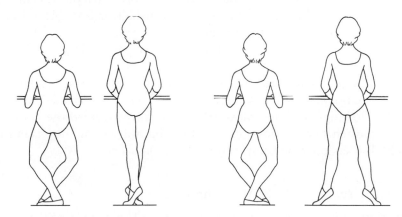

Connecting the preparatory *demi-plié* with the light spring to the *demi-pointes*

floor that pulls the toes underneath the ankles in the *demi-pointe* position. Two basic *relevés* of the latter type are the *sous-sus* and the *échappé*. The *sous-sus* (soo-siu) is a *relevé* made with a slight spring that allows the feet to slide together from fifth position *demi-plié* to a tight fifth position on *demi-pointes* while the feet move equally toward the center of the body. The *échappé* (ay-shah-PAY) is a *relevé* made with a slight spring that allows the feet to slide apart from fifth position *demi-plié* to an open position on *demi-pointes* (to second position; later to fourth) while the feet move equally from the center of the body. After both types of springing *relevés*, the feet return to their original position in *demi-plié*, also by means of a slight spring.

**Reminders**   In all *demi-pointes* positions on two feet, the body must be centered over both feet. The turnout of the legs must be maintained throughout the raising and lowering of the heels. The body should be lengthened as much as possible so that the weight rests lightly on the balls of the feet, toward the first three toes (beginners should never rise to the full pointe; this movement is done only by advanced students who wear shoes specially constructed for work on full pointe). The feet must never be allowed to roll either in or out because that weakens the ankles and the arches of the feet. The knees must be straight in *demi-pointes* positions.

**Suggestions**   Learn the *élevé* in first and second positions; later practice it in the other positions of the feet. When the principles of *élevé* have been mastered, add the *relevés*, beginning with those requiring slow, smooth action. Later try the springing *relevés*. The exercises first should be practiced facing the barre. When releasing the barre for a balance in *relevé*, think of the balance as an active pose—the body maintaining correct alignment, the abdominal muscles strong, and the spine and legs lengthened.

**Related Exercises**   *Relevés* also can be taken to only one foot following a *demi-plié* from any of the five positions of the feet or from a position in *fondu*. The raised foot, well pointed and turned out, usually is brought in front or in back of the supporting ankle or knee. From there it can return to a *demi-plié* position, or it can remain lifted while the supporting foot lowers into a *fondu* position.

   A *demi-détourné* (d'mee-day-toor-NAY) is useful in making a half-turn pivot to face the other direction at the barre, thus changing sides for an exercise. Following a *sous-sus*, make a half-turn pivot toward the back foot. The feet thus change relationship—the foot that was behind now is in front. Both heels then lower on completion of the *demi-détourné*.

### *Battement Tendu* (baht-MAH*n* tah*n*-DIU)

**Definition**   Literally, *battement* means "beating." There are more than twenty types of ballet *battements*, but the most fundamental is the *battement tendu*, often simply called *tendu* ("stretched"). In this exercise, the gesture foot, starting from a closed position, is extended along the floor until it is fully arched and the toes pointed (the stretching movement); then it is returned to a closed position at the supporting leg (the beating movement).

**Purpose** More than any exercise, the *battement tendu* strengthens the foot by alternating the tension of arching and pointing the foot with the relaxation of the toes and then the arch as the foot returns along the floor. The strong closing of the leg after the stretch strengthens the inner muscles of the thighs and engages the muscles of the buttocks. The *tendu* is basic to many other exercises and steps of ballet, and because it is typically the first exercise done with one leg at the barre it is basic to the centering of the body on the supporting leg.

**Description** In *battements tendus,* the toes never leave the floor. The movement is initiated at the top of the leg; turnout is controlled through use of the rotator and accessory muscles around the hip joint as the foot slides outward from a closed position (first, third, or fifth) until the heel has to be raised in order not to shift the center of the body away from the supporting leg. Immediately, the foot begins to arch, first through the instep and then through the ball of the foot and through the toes until the maximum stretch of the *tendu* is reached. To return to the closed position, first the ball of the foot relaxes and then the instep, until all tension is released and the heel is placed firmly on the floor, the thighs drawn together, and the weight again centered over both feet. Both legs remain straight throughout the exercise.

Tendus are done to the front (*à la quatrième devant*), to the side (*à la seconde*), and to the back (*à la quatrième derrière*). When an exercise is done consecutively to these directions, it is said to be done *en croix* (ahn krwah)—in the shape of a cross. When the gesture leg is extended, the tips of the toes touching the floor, foot fully arched, and knee straight, the position is termed *pointe tendue* (pwahn*t* tah*n*-DIU)—"point stretched."

**Reminders** Correct body alignment must be maintained, and special care must be taken not to "sit" into the supporting hip. Turnout of the supporting leg and foot is essential so that the hip does not release and the foot does not roll. Weight should never shift to the extended foot, thus putting pressure on the pointed toes. The knee of the gesture leg should remain straight as the leg opens and closes. Proper alignment of the heel and the toes is maintained by keeping the heel forward, which also helps ensure the turned-out shape of the leg.

In *battements tendus* to the side, the movement of the foot should travel along a path indicated by the degree of turnout. For example, when standing in first position, the *battement* will describe a line outward from the big toe. The direction of the path will therefore be one's personal *à la seconde* rather than directly "to the side."

■ *Battement tendu à la seconde*

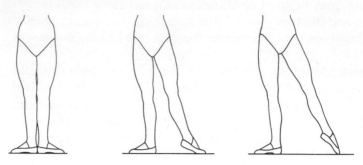

Stretching and elongating the leg and foot outward—
then reversing the direction to return with a strong close

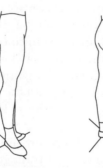

Correct alignment for
degree of turnout

**Incorrect**
**alignment**

In *battements tendus* to the front (*à la quatrième devant*), the heel leads
the way forward so that the bone at the inside of the ankle remains forward
as much as possible. As the foot returns, the toes lead the way to the closed
position, and the inside anklebone remains forward. In this way, correct
alignment is maintained, and the foot does not sickle.

The process is reversed for *battements tendus* to the back (*à la quatrième
derrière*): the toes lead the way backward, and the heel leads the way for the
return, with the bone at the outside of the ankle pointing backward as much
as possible throughout the exercise. A lengthening of the torso upward with
some shift of the body weight forward will help accommodate the slight forward tilt of the pelvis in *tendus* to the back. In *battements tendus* to the front
or side, the foot should point to the tip of the big toe (and often of the second toe as well). However, when performed to the back, the point is to the
tip of the *side* of the big toe.

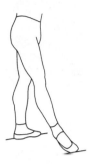

Inside of the ankle reaching forward        **Incorrect** or
                                            "sickled" position

**Suggestions**   Begin the study of this exercise by stretching the foot *à la seconde* from first position, later from third position (better to use a good third than a poor fifth position), closing in front each time for a series of *battements,* then closing in back each time. Later, the closings can alternate front and back of the supporting foot and to *demi-plié* as well as the straight position.

    *Battements tendus* forward or backward are best learned from third position (and later practiced from fifth position) rather than first position because the point of the foot in line with the crossed position gives a clearer concept of the basic front direction (*quatrième devant*) and back direction (*quatrième derrière*). Artistic preference and individual body construction will determine whether the toes of the extended foot are directly in line with the center of the body or more in line with the heel of the supporting foot.

    In a beginning class, *battements* should first be practiced slowly and evenly without frequent change of direction. Gradually speed can be increased and an accent given to the closing of each *battement.*

**Related Exercises**   A *battement soutenu* is performed with a *fondu* on the supporting leg: Keeping the gesture leg straight, slide the gesture foot along the floor to *pointe tendue* while bending the supporting leg. Return the foot to a closed position while straightening the supporting leg. An alternative exercise is a slow *battement tendu* closing to a *demi-plié* in first, third, or fifth position.

    A *battement tendu relevé* involves a lowering and relifting of the extended foot: Slide the gesture foot out to *pointe tendue à la seconde,* keeping the weight centered over the supporting foot. Release the arches of the foot and lower the heel to second position as the weight centers between both feet. Relift the gesture heel and reach the foot as the weight returns over the supporting foot. Slide the foot into a closed position.

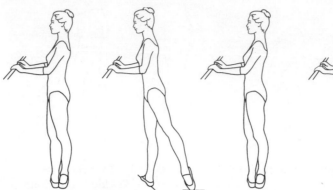

Energy flowing upward as foot extends backward

**Incorrect** *battement*
alignment

## OTHER BASIC *BATTEMENTS*

### *Battement Dégagé* (baht-MAHn day-gah-ZHAY)

**Definition**   A *battement dégagé* is a *battement* disengaged from the floor; it is sometimes called *battement tendu jeté* ("thrown"), *battement glissé* ("glided"), or simply *dégagé* ("disengaged").

**Purpose**   The chief function of the *dégagé* is to develop speed and lightness in pointing the feet. The *dégagé* helps the arches and ankles to become supple and prepares them for the quick movements in jumps. The rapid opening and closing of the leg is the foundation for *allegro* steps with beats (*batterie*). The *dégagé* is part of many ballet steps, such as the brushing action in a *glissade*.

**Description**   The movement begins in the same way as *battement tendu,* but the action continues so that the gesture foot leaves the floor a few inches, well pointed, before sliding back to the closed position. The action can be described as a brush of the foot outward and a slide inward.

**Reminders**   The advice for the correct execution of *battements tendus* is equally applicable for *battements dégagés,* except that the toes are allowed to leave the floor. Care must be taken, however, that the toes rise only a very few inches. If the leg is raised too high, the capacity for speed is lost. Faults in many *allegro* steps can be traced to errors made in *dégagés*, especially the failure to touch the pointed toes on the floor before sliding the foot to the closed position. The timing of the exercise should emphasize the closing of the *dégagé*.

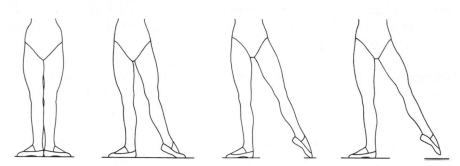

Lightly brush from the floor, then touch the toes to the floor
before reversing the action for the quick slide to close

**Suggestions**   As in *battement tendu,* the study of *battement dégagé* begins in
first position with the movement done *à la seconde.* It can be broken down
as follows: Brush away from the closed position (finishing with the foot
slightly off the floor). Touch the toes to the floor. Slide the foot back to the
closed position. Each part of the exercise can receive a separate count, with
another count for a hold in the closed position (to allow time for the foot to
relax): Brush (count 1), touch the toes (count 2), close (count 3), hold the
position (count 4). Later, it can be done in two counts: Brush (count 1),
touch the toes (and), close (count 2), hold (and). Eventually the *dégagé* is
done with the entire movement happening on the "and," with the closing to
position on the count. The breakdown of the exercise can, of course, also be
followed in learning *dégagé* to the front and to the back, from third or fifth
position, and with a closing to *demi-plié.*

**Related Exercises**   *Battements dégagés en cloche* (ahn KLOHSH) are performed forward and backward through first position and usually occur in a
series: Brush the gesture foot forward, slide it back to first position, immediately brush the foot backward, and continue as a swinging, pendulum-like
motion through first position.
   *Battements dégagés* may be performed with a *fondu* on the supporting leg
in an action similar to *battements soutenus* as previously described.

## Grand Battement (grahn baht-MAHn)

**Definition**   The *grand battement* is a large beating action of the leg, a continuation of the basic *battement dégagé.* It sometimes is called *grand battement jeté.*

**Purpose**   The forceful sweeping lift of the leg into the air limbers and
stretches the legs. It helps loosen the hip joint while it strengthens the

control of the hip muscles. Properly done, the *grand battement* creates a lightness in the legs necessary for steps of high elevation such as *grand jeté*. It also increases the height of the extension of the legs, valuable for *développés* and other exercises of *adagio*.

**Description**   The movement begins in the same way as the *dégagé* but is continued upward to hip height (higher or lower, depending on the stretch of the legs and control of the body); then the leg is lowered with control until the toes touch the floor and the foot closes as in previous exercises for *battements*. *Grands battements* are done to the front, to the side, and to the back.

**Reminders**   Follow all of the basic rules of the *battement tendu* and *dégagé*, being especially careful to keep the thighs rotated outward and the weight over the supporting foot. To achieve the desired lightness of the leg, its lift should be initiated by the brush of the foot along the floor, not by the pickup of the thigh. The knees must not bend, nor should the heel of the supporting foot leave the floor. Continue to maintain a well-lengthened torso with ribs facing forward, a relaxed neck and throat, stable but not stiff arms, and the hand held without tension on the barre. Note that the pelvis will tip slightly sideward when the leg is raised to hip level *à la seconde*. To permit the leg to rise to the back, the pelvis and torso will tilt slightly forward, and then the body returns to its vertical position as the foot closes.

**Suggestions**   Practice *grands battements* at 45 degrees until proper placement and turnout can be maintained at 90 degrees or higher. Break down

■ Height of the leg for *grand battement à la quatrième devant, à la seconde, à la quatrième derrière* at 90 degrees

Strong, smooth brushes with energy flowing from center of body
through hips, legs, and foot

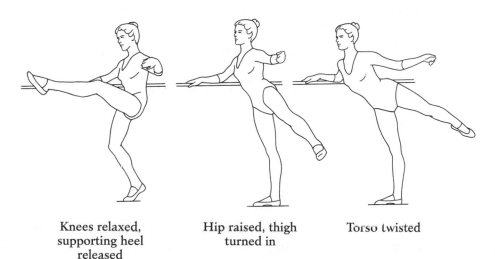

| Knees relaxed, supporting heel released | Hip raised, thigh turned in | Torso twisted |

the exercise as follows: From a closed position (first, third, or fifth), brush the leg into the air (count 1), lower it to *pointe tendue* (count 2), and return it to the closed position (count 3). Eventually, the exercise can be done with the entire movement happening on "and," with the closing of the foot on the count. This movement must be achieved with control; do not drop the leg as it lowers or slam the foot into the floor!

**Related Exercise**  *Grands battements* may be executed *en cloche* as in *battements dégagés* but with a higher brush of the leg forward and backward, passing smoothly through a turned-out first position each time.

## Battement Frappé (baht-MAHn frah-PAY)

**Definition**  A *battement frappé* is a strong brush outward from a raised position at the ankle of the supporting leg; it often is called simply *frappé,* which means "struck."

**Purpose**  The muscles in the foot are stimulated and strengthened by the brush outward along the floor. Articulation of movement through the ankle is improved by the constant alternating motions of extension and release in the foot. This builds speed and flexibility needed in jumping steps, particularly the *jetés.*

**Description**  The *battement frappé à la seconde* begins with the ankle of the gesture foot slightly flexed, the heel touching just above the front of the supporting ankle, and the toes near the floor. The ball of the gesture foot brushes strongly against the floor to *dégagé* position *à la seconde,* knee and

■ *Battement frappé à la seconde*

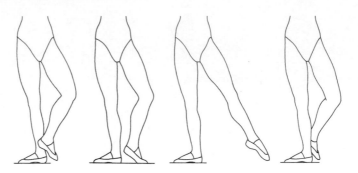

Energetic brush outward from clear placement at supporting ankle

foot fully extended. The foot returns quickly to the back of the supporting ankle without touching the floor, ready to begin again.

**Reminders** The supporting side of the body must remain lifted and lengthened so that the weight remains centered over the supporting foot, thus avoiding either sitting into the hip or pulling away from the supporting heel. The action of the *frappé* happens from the knee down, so the thigh does not raise and lower. The ball of the foot should brush briskly along the floor but never pound against the surface. The brush *à la seconde* should always be in the direction determined by one's turnout. Both the knee and the foot should be taut at the finish of the outward motion.

**Suggestions** In the early stages, the *frappé* can be done in four counts: Brush to the extended position just off the floor (count 1), hold this position (count 2), return to the position at the supporting leg (count 3), hold (count 4). Later, a ¾ rhythm can be tried: Brush and hold the position (counts 1, 2) and return to the supporting leg (count 3). Eventually, the *frappé* is done on one count, with the accent on the brush outward and the return on the "and." The exercise can later be done to the front and to the back as well as to the side.

**Related Exercise** *Battement frappé double* (DOO-bluh) is a doubling of the beating action at the ankle: From a *dégagé* or *pointe tendue* position *à la seconde,* bring the foot inward to beat in front of, and then immediately behind, the supporting ankle, then brush outward as described above. Reverse the action, beating back and then front before brushing outward.

### *Petit Battement sur le Cou-de-Pied*
(p'TEE baht-MAHn suir l'koo-duh-pee-AY)

**Definition** *Petit battement sur le cou-de-pied* means, literally, "small beat on the neck of the foot."

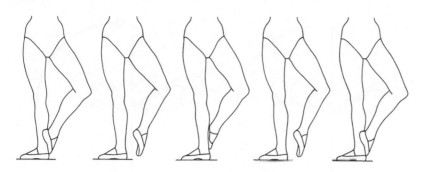

Small, rapid gestures with a bright playful quality

**Purpose**   The exercise is important in developing speed and precision in movement, particularly for *allegro* steps with beats or rapid accents.

**Description**   The exercise begins with the gesture foot placed *sur le cou-de-pied,* at the ankle of the supporting foot. (The exact position varies in different schools of technique—the foot may be "wrapped" around the ankle, heel in front and toes in back; extended downward along the side of the ankle; fully pointed in front or in back of the ankle; or relaxed, heel touching the ankle and all five toes on the floor in *demi-pointe* position.) The *battements* consist of small, rapid, out-and-in movements of the gesture foot as it rebounds slightly from each contact in front of and behind the supporting ankle; movement is from below the knee only.

**Reminders**   Keep the heel of the beating foot well forward and do not change the shape of the foot as it moves out and in around the supporting ankle. Keep the thigh of the gesture leg pressed well outward, hip remaining in place, and the knee relaxed so that the action of the beat is made with the lower leg only.

**Suggestions**   To sense the quality of moving the lower leg freely from the knee joint: Stand sideways to the barre with the legs in parallel position, flex the outside leg so that the ball of the foot rests lightly on the floor, and place the free hand on the raised thigh. Keep the thigh immobile and the knee relaxed as the lower leg swings evenly forward and back. Next, perform this exercise with a turnout, allowing the working foot to swing evenly across in front and in back of the supporting foot. Later, speed is increased and accents can be added (back, *front,* hold; back, *front,* hold; and so on).

## CIRCULAR MOVEMENTS

Circular movements of the leg, either along the ground or in the air, are important elements of barre work and are later incorporated into exercises in center floor as well.

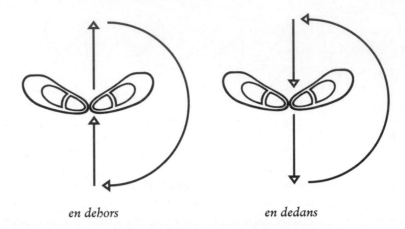

*en dehors*                    *en dedans*

### *Rond de Jambe à Terre* (rohn duh zhahnb ah TAIR)

**Definition**   More than a dozen exercises bear the general term *rond de jambe* (literally, "circle or round of the leg"). The most basic is *rond de jambe à terre* (or *par terre*), in which the gesture foot describes a semicircle on the ground. When the foot travels in an arc from the front to the back, it is called an "outward" (*en dehors*) *rond de jambe*. When it travels from the back to the front, it is called an "inward" (*en dedans*) *rond de jambe*.

**Purpose**   In *ronds de jambe,* the muscles and ligaments of the hip are exercised to allow the leg to move freely in a circular motion without disturbing the immobility of the torso. Characteristics of this movement are found in such steps as *pas de basque.*

**Description**   For *ronds de jambe en dehors,* extend the gesture foot forward from first position in the same way as for *battement tendu devant,* carry the toes in an arc along the ground through *pointe tendue à la seconde* to *pointe tendue derrière* behind first position. Then slide the foot forward to first position in the same way as the closing of a *battement tendu.* The direction of the entire exercise is reversed for *ronds de jambe en dedans.* The exercise usually is done to a $^3/_4$ rhythm, with an entire semicircle completed during one measure. A series of *ronds de jambe* may be executed continuously without pause or with accents given at *pointe tendue* positions (*devant* or *à la seconde* when taken *en dehors, derrière* or *à la seconde* when taken *en dedans*).

**Reminders**   The toes of the gesture foot remain in contact with the floor during the entire exercise. The gesture foot must remain fully arched as it traces the arc of the semicircle; take care not to shorten the arc near the *pointes tendues* positions to the front or to the back. As the foot passes through first position, it should relax but never roll. Both legs must remain thoroughly extended throughout the exercise with the body lengthened up-

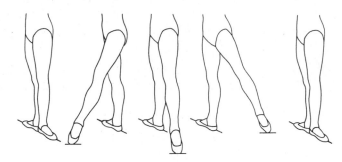

*Pointes tendues* positions joined by a smooth arcing motion,
passing through first position to continue

ward and centered over the supporting foot. The supporting leg must resist
any temptation to rotate inward, thus defeating one purpose of *rond de
jambe*—improvement of turnout.

**Suggestions**   The *rond de jambe* is best learned slowly, with a pause at each
position of the arc (front, side, back) and at the first position.

**Related Exercises**   A helpful exercise for emphasizing turnout is the *demi-
rond de jambe à terre:* To perform *en dehors* from first position, extend the foot
to *pointe tendue devant* and quickly carry it *à la seconde,* hold at the *pointe tendue* position, and then close to first position. Reverse the action for *demi-
rond de jambe en dedans.*

    A *demi-rond de jambe* lifted to 45 degrees in the air—that is, at half height
or *à la demi-hauteur* (ah la d'mee-oh-TUHR)—introduces the important
pelvic, torso, and weight adjustments necessary when the leg travels in the
air from one direction to another. To perform *en dehors,* brush the gesture
foot forward from first or fifth position as in a *battement dégagé* to 45 degrees
*à la quatrième devant.* Leading with the foot, carry the leg *à la seconde* at the
same height, maintaining turnout and keeping the weight centered over the
supporting foot. Lower to *pointe tendue,* and close to first or fifth position.
To continue *en dehors,* brush the gesture foot *à la seconde* to 45 degrees. As
the foot leads around at the same level to *quatrième derrière,* the pelvis will
tilt slightly forward so the torso must lengthen upward and also forward, allowing the center of weight to shift more forward. Lower to *pointe tendue,*
returning the body to its normal upright position as the foot closes to first or
fifth position. Reverse the actions to perform the exercise *en dedans.*

## ADDITIONAL BASIC EXERCISES

Out of the multitude of possible exercises to be included in barre work, only
four more are given here. Again, the reader is reminded that no "proper"
order of exercises has been implied in this chapter. Rather, exercises have

Coordination of opposites: strong verticality of support side of body
with horizontal circling of gesture leg

been grouped according to general characteristics, with the following exercises sharing a folding-and-unfolding design for the leg or torso.

### Battement Retiré (baht-MAHn ruh-tih-RAY)

**Definition**    The *battement retiré* is a "withdrawing" of the gesture foot from the floor until it touches the front, side, or back of the supporting knee. The term *passé* is sometimes used when the withdrawing foot passes from fifth position front to fifth position back and vice versa.

**Purpose**    This exercise is an integral part of many movements in ballet, such as *développés* and *pas de chats*. It has great value in warming up the

■ *Retiré*          ■ Incorrect *retiré*

Stable balance over support
and clear design of gesture leg

thighs and in strengthening the muscles in the waist and back. *Retirés* (or *passés*) also can improve balance and turnout.

**Description**   From fifth position, crisply draw up the front leg, keeping the toes in contact with the supporting leg, to a fully pointed position in front or to the hollow of the supporting knee; return the foot to the closed position as the weight centers again over both feet. When the back foot performs a *retiré,* the toes of the gesture foot draw up either behind or to the hollow of the supporting knee.

**Reminders**   The thighs of both legs must remain well turned out and the pelvis level throughout the exercise. The heel of the gesture foot does not touch the supporting leg in the *retiré* positions. Initiate the action of *retiré* by the push of the foot from the floor rather than by a pickup of the thigh; keep the elongation of the pointed foot as long as possible during the return, releasing first the toes, then the ball of the foot, and finally the heel into the closed position.

**Suggestions**   To ensure correct body alignment, learn the exercise facing the barre. Use third position if fifth is not yet secure and a lower *retiré* position if the pelvis cannot remain level when the thigh is raised. Practice slowly in sequential action: Sharply arch the foot just in front of and above the supporting ankle as the body centers over the supporting leg, draw the foot up to *retiré* position, hold, and return to the beginning position.

**Related Exercises**   When *retiré* is executed from a *demi-plié* to a *relevé,* it becomes an important practice for *pirouettes. Retiré* also can be used in an exercise to prepare for *rond de jambe en l'air: Dégagé à la seconde* to 45 degrees, bring the toes to *retiré* position without lowering the thigh, extend the leg again at the same height, continue in a series, and then lower to a closed position.

### *Développé* (day-vloh-PAY)

**Definition**   In the *développé,* the gesture leg is slowly "developed" by being drawn up to *retiré* position and then extended to an open position at 45 degrees or higher to the front, side, or back.

**Purpose**   This movement is one of the most fundamental exercises of *adagio* (the slow, sustained movements of ballet), for it is the method by which the leg can arrive at many ballet positions, such as *arabesque.* Done repeatedly as an exercise, *développés* have great strengthening value for the muscles of the abdomen, legs, and back, thus improving the ability to sustain an extension of the leg in the air.

**Description**   Arch the gesture foot at the ankle, draw it up along the supporting leg to a *retiré* position, smoothly unfold the leg to the appropriate height *à la quatrième devant, à la seconde,* or *à la quatrième derrière.* These movements usually are accompanied by a *port de bras*—a coordinated movement of the outside arm: Raise the arm from a position *en bas* to *en avant* as the foot goes to *retiré* and open the arm to second position or raise it *en haut* as the leg unfolds.

**Reminders**   Arch the gesture foot as soon as it leaves the closed position, and keep the pointed toes close to the supporting leg until they reach the *retiré* position. Establish the appropriate height of the thigh, and then unfold the lower leg at that level. Maintain a strong turnout of both legs, torso lengthened upward with the ribs facing forward and the body centered over the supporting foot. Note that the pelvis will tilt slightly sideward in a *développé* to 90 degrees *à la seconde,* and it will tilt slightly forward in *develop-*

■ *Développé à la seconde*

Extending a design into space

*pés* to the back. Briefly hold the extended position before lowering the leg smoothly to the closed position, the weight centering over both feet.

**Suggestions**    First master the control and balance necessary for the *retiré* before attempting the *développé*. Ideally, the *développé* should be done slowly and smoothly in one continuous flow from the closed position to the extended position. Nevertheless, it is helpful to practice the exercise with slight pauses of the foot, first at the ankle, then at the knee, then at the halfway position before full extension, and finally at the full height of the *développé*. It is best first to learn the leg movements alone before adding coordinated arm movements.

## Battement Fondu (baht-MAHn fohn-DIU)

**Definition**    *Battement fondu* ("melting") is a compound exercise consisting of a bending of the supporting leg and then a straightening of that leg as the gesture leg unfolds from a *cou-de-pied* position to *pointe tendue* (or higher).

**Purpose**    The basic action of *battement fondu*—the coordinated bending and straightening of the legs—is inherent to many *allegro* steps and movements of *adagio*. It is especially beneficial as an exercise for jumps, because it works the muscles of the legs needed in jumping. When taken to the *demi-pointe*, *battement fondu* exercises the foot also.

**Description**    From *pointe tendue à la seconde*, bring the fully arched foot to *cou-de-pied devant* as the supporting leg bends. (A bend on one leg is a *fondu*.) Then simultaneously straighten both legs as the gesture foot opens

■ *Battement fondu à la seconde*

Smooth harmony of legs unfolding simultaneously

to *pointe tendue devant*. Continue with the same action, unfolding the leg *à la seconde* and then *à la quatrième derrière*.

**Reminders** Emphasize equal turnout and harmonious bending and straightening of both legs. The gesture foot remains fully arched and the body well-lifted over the supporting leg throughout the exercise.

**Suggestions** A preliminary exercise can be helpful: Raise the front foot to *cou-de-pied devant* as the supporting leg bends, close to fifth position as both legs straighten; reverse the exercise, raising the foot to *cou-de-pied derrière*. Later, when *battements fondus* are performed from the *pointe tendue* position, the initial movement can be a slight lift of the foot—as though the leg takes a breath—before the knees bend. This can help counteract any tendency to sink or drop into the *fondu*.

**Related Exercises** *Battement fondu* may be done *en l'air*, unfolding the leg to *dégagé* height or higher, depending on development of the necessary strength and control of the legs, pelvis, and torso. Later a *relevé* may accompany the unfolding of the leg *en l'air*.

### *Port de Bras au Corps Cambré* (por duh BRAH oh kor kahn-BRAY)

**Definition** *Port de bras au corps cambré* means, literally, "carriage of the arms with an arched body." Often the shortened term *cambré* is used when referring to the bending of the body backward or sideward from the waist. The forward bend from the hip joints sometimes is termed *penché* or *port de corps* forward.

■ *Port de corps* forward

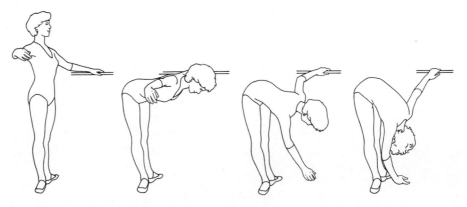

Lengthening upward and forward, then releasing inward

**Purpose**   This exercise is important because it involves movements of the head, arms, and torso, and not, as in all other barre exercises, movement of the legs. It also limbers and relaxes the upper body and coordinates arm and head movements—all necessary for fluidity of motion.

**Description**   For the forward bend, lengthen the torso upward as it begins to reach forward from the hip joints and keep the spine extended as long as possible; curve the spine downward, relaxing the neck, until the head is near the knees. Return to the upright position by retracing the path of the forward bend or by uncurling (rolling up) through the spine.

Begin the *cambré* backward by lifting the chest and face as the outside arm rises toward the ceiling; then arch the upper back while maintaining the upright position of the lower back and pelvis. The ribs should remain facing forward, and the hand should be centered slightly forward of the top of the head. Turn the head in the direction of the raised arm. Return to the upright position by retracing the path of the backward bend or by opening the arm outward to second position as the back straightens.

The *cambré* sideward occurs from the waist with the torso well lengthened. Raise the outside arm overhead, reach upward and sideward with the spine, stretching the outside ribs and allowing the inside ribs to fold in gently. Keep the hand centered slightly forward of the top of the head. Keep the head focused front or turn it in the direction of the *cambré*.

**Reminders**   Even though words such as *bend* and *arch* are used when describing these exercises, it is important to remember that the exercises begin with breath and with a lengthening of the entire body. The legs remain straight and vertical with the weight of the body evenly distributed on both feet when these exercises are done from any of the five positions of the feet. Avoid straining the neck, raising the shoulders, or shortening the lower spine, especially in the *cambré* backward. In any *cambré* position, the hand of the raised arm should never go back past the top of the head. All movements should be done smoothly, with the arm flowing into gently curved positions.

**Suggestions**   Feel as though each vertebra is lengthening during the *cambrés* and that it is the spine that takes the arm into the *cambré* positions, not the arm that pulls the spine. An intake of breath beginning just before and continuing during the exercises enhances the sense of lengthening into the *cambrés*. These *cambré* exercises should be learned in first position before they are attempted in other positions. Learn the forward bend as a half-bend; that is, stretch forward until the upper body is parallel to the floor (or as parallel as possible, given the flexibility of the legs), and then return to the upright position. The *cambré* backward at first can be learned facing the barre.

## STRETCHES

Today, most ballet instructors incorporate stretches in their class work. This often occurs at or toward the end of barre work (sometimes even at the end of class), because, to avoid possible injury and to maximize the benefits of stretches, the body must first be thoroughly warmed up. A teacher usually gives the class a specific sequence of stretches that are to be done while lying or sitting on the floor or while standing at the barre. Therefore, only a few words of general advice are offered here rather than an outline of specific stretching exercises.

**Reminders and Suggestions**   Be realistic about stretching. Remember that each body is different, so always stretch within your range of motion rather than by trying to emulate the flexibility of someone else's body. Remember that flexibility must be attained along with strength and endurance.

Allow the body to relax into the stretch. Forceful bouncing or reaching, which causes one set of muscles to tighten as another set is stretched, defeats limbering. All stretches should be done slowly and smoothly. To maximize the benefits, stay in the stretch for 30 slow counts, breathing slowly and evenly.

The correct position of the foot on the floor, the lift of the arch, and the alignment of foot with leg must not be sacrificed during stretches in a standing position. Do your own stretching. Relying on others to lift, bend, or push your limbs and torso can be dangerous. And, finally, do stretches only when the body is fully warmed up.

■ **Incorrect** positions

| Weight pushed back, spine swayed | Knees bent, pelvis released | Torso twisted, weight off center |

■ *Cambré* backward

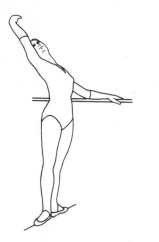

■ *Cambré* sideward

Coordinated movement flows into the space around the body

## MAKING PROGRESS

Far from being a boring preliminary to the rest of class, barre work is in fact an exciting, challenging, and rewarding introduction to ballet that leads to technical proficiency. Consider the barre rail as your "partner"; hold it gently and dance to it and with it. After class and before the day is over, try to review in your mind each exercise. Visualize the movements, remembering the sequences and the advice given by your instructor.

# CHAPTER 3

# *Ballet Technique:*
## Center Work

The following are some important questions that you will be able to answer after studying this chapter:

- What are the two most fundamental *port de bras*?
- How is *épaulement* used in exercises such as *battements* traveling forward and backward?
- What are the eleven positions of the body?
- What are the differences between a pose in *attitude* and a pose in *arabesque*?
- What are the names of six basic *pas de bourrées*? Describe them.
- What is meant by spotting for turns, and how is it done?
- What is the difference between a *piqué* and *a relevé*?
- How do you describe the direction of a *pirouette en dehors? En dedans?*

When barre work is completed, the mechanics of ballet technique are brought into the center floor. To the movements of the legs and feet are added movements of the head, carriages of the arms (*ports de bras*), and positions of the shoulders (*épaulements*), which bring artistic life to even the simplest ballet exercise. Using all these elements—the entire body—to create harmonious designs in space is the challenge of center work.

## DIRECTIONS OF THE STUDIO/STAGE

Ballet is taught as a performing art, even though 99 percent of all ballet students may never set foot on a professional stage. Positions and movements of center-floor work are based on the assumption that an audience is at the

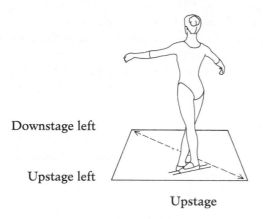

Audience
Downstage

Downstage left

Downstage right

Upstage left

Upstage right

Upstage

front of the room. At all times, the dancer/student must be aware of body line in relation to the eye of that audience.

The parts of the stage have directional names that also are useful in the studio: *Downstage* is toward the audience. *Upstage* is away from the audience. *Stage right* is to the dancer's right as the dancer faces the audience. *Stage left* is then to the dancer's left. These directional names remain constant, no matter which way the dancer faces. Much of beginning work is done facing the audience (a direction known as *de face,* although movement made toward the audience often is said to be done *en face*).

Usually, when center exercises are to be done facing a corner direction, they begin toward the downstage left corner and then are repeated toward the downstage right corner. When asked to face a corner direction, you should first imagine yourself standing in the center of a private stage about a yard square, then face the corner of that square rather than the actual corner of the studio. Align your shoulders and hips with the downstage corner of that imaginary stage square.

Your instructor may use a numbering system to designate the corners and the walls of the studio space. For example, downstage right may be corner #1; downstage left, corner #2; and so forth. As a learning aid, you can pencil in the numbers designated by your instructor on the diagram here.

## *PORT DE BRAS* (por duh BRAH)

Center-floor work often begins with *port de bras* ("carriage of the arms"), which refers not only to arm movements but also to groups of exercises for the arms. The term *corps et bras* ("body and arms") is in some ways more descriptive because the head, shoulders, and torso are very much involved, with energy for the arm movements coming from the dancer's back.

An infinite variety of *port de bras* is possible within the framework provided by the positions of the arms. Two fundamental exercises of *port de bras*, however, are the most essential and the most frequently used. They illustrate ballet's basic rule for arm movements: when the arms move from a low to a high position, they travel in front of the body through the position *en avant* (*bras avant*); when the arms move from a high to a low position, they travel outward through second position. These movements look deceptively simple, but, in the words of the great Soviet teacher Agrippina Vaganova, "*Port de bras* is the most difficult part of the dance, requiring the greatest amount of work and concentration."[1]

Again, variations of style exist, but the following descriptions outline the two basic exercises. Each of these *port de bras* can be repeated several times in succession and each sequence practiced to the other side as well:

■ *Port de bras* exercise 1

*Exercise 1*

1. The starting pose: Face downstage left in third or fifth position (right foot front), the arms *en bas* and the head inclined to the left and slightly lowered.

2. Raise the arms *en avant,* and, at the same time, lean the torso slightly forward from the waist.

3. Open the palms and fingers slightly and carry both arms to second position while the head turns and inclines to the right. During this movement, the torso can also lean to the right a small degree, and the eyes follow in the direction of the right hand. The hips and shoulders do not twist but remain in alignment facing the original downstage corner.

4. With breath, lower the arms and return the hands to the starting pose as the head simultaneously returns to its original position.

*Exercise 2*

1. The starting pose: same as in Exercise 1.

2. Raise the arms *en avant* as the torso inclines slightly forward and the head remains inclined to the left.

3. Continue to raise the arms *en haut* while the torso straightens and the head lifts and then inclines to the right.

4. Open both arms to second position, the palms and fingers opening slightly also, as the torso leans slightly to the right and the eyes follow in the direction of the right hand. The hips and shoulders do not twist.

5. Lower the arms and return the hands to the starting pose as the head simultaneously returns to its original position.

## Reminders

*Port de bras* exercises are done slowly and smoothly so that the movement flows through but does not stop in any one position. Take care that the hands stay centered on the body as they travel from the *bras bas* position to *bras hauts,* that the shoulders do not rise or twist, and that the fingers do not spread open.

## Suggestions

Feel that the *port de bras* is being initiated from deep within the body, rather than the hands just lifting to a position. When opening the arms to second position, sense the expansion of the chest and back. Feel the soft release as the arms lower.

This brief discussion of *port de bras* ends with a further observation from Vaganova:

> Only the ability to find the proper position for her arms lends a finesse to the artistic expression of the dancer and renders full harmony to her dance. The head gives it the finishing touch, adds beauty to the entire design. The look, the glance, the eyes crown it all.[2]

## CENTER EXERCISES AND *ÉPAULEMENT* (ay-pohl-MAH*n*)

Center work includes a group of barre exercises performed in center floor without the aid of the barre. Sometimes called *center practice,* these exercises

**54**

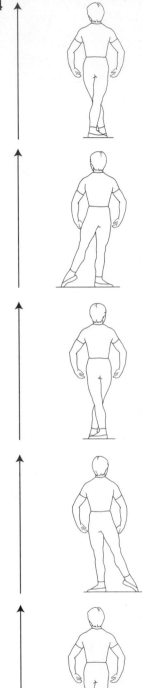

often are done by alternating feet—right/left/right/left. This quick shift of weight can help a dancer develop greater balance, coordination, and control. When traveling forward, an exercise usually begins with the right foot; when traveling backward, it usually begins with the left foot.

### Battements tendus

*Battements tendus* traveling forward and backward are an example of an elementary center-floor exercise. From fifth position with the right foot back, *battement tendu à la seconde* with the right foot; close with the right foot in front in fifth position. Repeat with the left foot. Continue in this way, alternating right and left legs eight or sixteen times. The exercise is then reversed so that the *battements tendus* close in fifth position back.

Beginning students generally practice these and similar exercises *de face*—that is, directly toward the front of the room. Later, an important embellishment is added, enlivening an otherwise flat appearance. It is called *épaulement*. Although this term literally means "shouldering," the exercise encompasses some slight movement of the head and upper body as well as the shoulders. The traditional rule for *épaulement* is: In steps that travel forward, the head and shoulders are aligned with the foot that closes front, the head turning slightly toward the gesture foot. In steps that travel backward, the head and shoulders are in opposition to the foot that closes back, the head inclining slightly away from the gesture foot.

Therefore, the exercise of *battements tendus* traveling forward using *épaulement* is: From fifth position right foot in back, extend the right foot *à la seconde* and, simultaneously, bring the right shoulder slightly forward of the left, with the head slightly turned to the right. The head and right shoulder are then aligned with the right or gesture foot. Close to fifth position front without changing the *épaulement*. The exercise is repeated with the left leg, so that the left shoulder is brought forward and the head is turned to the left.

The exercise of *battements tendus* traveling backward with *épaulement* is: From fifth position left foot in front, extend the left foot *à la seconde*

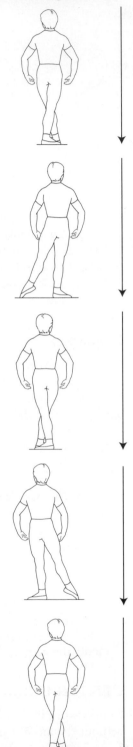

■ Traveling forward

and, simultaneously, bring the right shoulder slightly forward of the left, with the head slightly inclined to the right. The head and right shoulder are then in opposition to the left or gesture foot. Close to fifth position behind without changing the *épaulement*. The exercise continues alternating legs, the shoulders and head always in opposition to the gesture leg.

## Reminders

The degree and style of *épaulement* used is a matter of preference, but a general rule is to keep the hips facing directly front so that the action of *épaulement* is confined to the upper torso, shoulders, and head. Focus of the eyes may remain forward or move slightly toward the diagonal indicated by the forward shoulder.

*Épaulement* is not confined to center exercises. The principles of alignment and opposition are used constantly in *adagio* phrases, which are done later in the center. The final stage of instruction, the *allegro*, includes many steps that are improved greatly by the addition of a little shouldering action. However, students need a solid understanding of the mechanics of any step before embellishing it with *épaulement*.

## POSITIONS OF THE BODY

The classic line of ballet is built on the alignment of the body in space as well as on alignment within the body. There are eleven positions of the body in space, from which infinite variations of poses are possible. They are learned first with the extended leg at *pointe tendue* and later with the leg raised to 45 degrees and then to 90 degrees.

In the Cecchetti Method, eight of these positions are practiced in sequential order as a center-floor exercise. These eight positions are illustrated as though seen from the back so that the reader may practice the poses more easily. Usually, the gesture foot closes to fifth position after each pose before extending to the next position of the body.

## Facing Front

Beginning students quite soon are familiar with the three positions of the body that face directly front (*en face*), or toward the audience:

*À la quatrième devant* (ah la ka-tree-EHM duh-VAHn): The extended leg is in fourth position front; the arms are in second position; the head, hips, and shoulders face directly front.

*À la quatrième derrière* (deh-reeAIR): The extended leg is in fourth position back; the arms are in second position; the head, hips, and shoulders face directly front.

*À la seconde* (ah la suh-GOHnD): The extended leg is in second position; the arms are in second position; the head, hips, and shoulders face directly front.

■ *Croisé devant*  ■ *Quatrième devant*  ■ *Écarté devant*  ■ *Effacé devant*

### On the Diagonal

Once the front-facing positions are mastered, the student is introduced to poses on the diagonal. The terms for these poses, translated literally, are: *croisé* ("crossed"), *effacé* ("shaded"), *écarté* ("separated" or "thrown wide apart"), and *épaulé* ("shouldered"). Each can be done to the front (*devant*) and to the back (*derrière*). Stylistic preferences determine the height and degree of curve of the arms and the incline of the head and torso. The following descriptions represent one stylistic choice for these diagonal positions:

> *Croisé* (krawh-ZAY) *devant:* The dancer faces either downstage corner; the leg nearer the audience (the downstage leg) extends to fourth position front. The arm opposite that extended leg is *en haut,* and the other arm is *demi-seconde.* The torso and head incline slightly toward the low arm.
>
> *Croisé derrière:* The dancer faces either downstage corner; the leg farther from the audience (the upstage leg) extends to fourth position back. The arm opposite the extended leg is *en haut,* and the other arm is *demi-seconde.* The head and torso incline very slightly toward the low arm so that the dancer appears to be looking at the audience from under the high arm.
>
> *Effacé* (eh-fah-SAY) *devant:* The dancer faces either downstage corner; the leg farther from the audience (the upstage leg) extends to fourth position front. The arm opposite the extended leg is *en haut,* and the other arm is *demi-seconde.* The body leans very slightly back from the waist, and the head inclines toward the high arm.
>
> *Effacé derrière:* The dancer faces either downstage corner; the leg nearer the audience (the downstage leg) extends to fourth position back. The arm on the same side as the extended leg is *en haut,* and the

56

■ *À la seconde*      ■ *Épaulé devant*      ■ *Quatrième derrière*      ■ *Croisé derrière*

 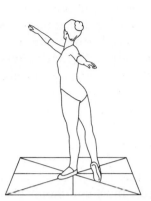 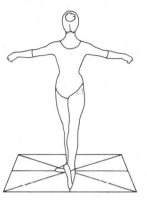 

other arm is *demi-seconde*. The body leans slightly forward over the supporting foot; the head turns and rises slightly toward the hand that is high.

*Écarté* (ay-kar-TAY) *devant:* The dancer faces either downstage corner; the leg nearer the audience (the downstage leg) extends to second position. The arm on the same side as the extended leg is *en haut*, and the other arm is *demi-seconde*. The torso is erect; the head turns and rises slightly toward the hand that is high.

*Écarté derrière:* The dancer faces either downstage corner; the leg farther from the audience (the upstage leg) extends to second position. The arm on the same side as the extended leg is *en haut*, and the other arm is *demi-seconde*. The torso and head incline slightly toward the hand that is low.

*Épaulé* (ah-poh-LAY) *devant:* The dancer faces either downstage corner; the leg nearer the audience (the downstage leg) extends to fourth position back. The arm nearer the audience extends forward, and the other arm extends backward. The torso turns slightly from the waist so that the back arm is slightly visible to the audience; the head inclines toward the front shoulder.

*Épaulé derrière:* This position is exactly the same as *épaulé devant*, except that the dancer faces either of the upstage corners.

## OTHER POSES OF THE BODY

*Attitude* and *arabesque* are two poses most frequently associated with ballet. As the reader readily can imagine by now, variations of these poses are practically unlimited, and differences of style do exist. Still, certain fundamental rules remain constant.

**57**

### *Attitude* (ah-tee-TEWD)

The ballet *attitude* is a pose on one leg, the other leg lifted, well turned out and bent at the knee with the lower leg and foot opened away from the body. Carlo Blasis, an early-nineteenth-century ballet master and author of important dance-technique manuals, considered the *attitude* to be the most elegant but the most difficult pose in dancing. He believed it to be a kind of imitation of the statue of Mercury, messenger of the gods, by the artist Giovanni da Bologna.[3] However, in today's technique, unlike in the Renaissance statue, the thigh and knee are lifted, well turned out, and level with, or higher than, the raised foot.

When the leg is lifted to the back, the pose is known as *attitude derrière*. Another variation calls for the leg to be lifted to the front, well turned out, the knee bent, and the foot raised as high as possible. This pose is known as *attitude devant*. These two *attitudes* most commonly occur in the *croisé* or *effacé* direction, with one arm raised *en haut* and the other opened *à la seconde*, usually referred to as *attitude position* of the arms.

**Reminders**  *Attitudes* require a well-turned-out supporting leg that maintains a strong verticality into the hip socket so that the body weight is balanced over the supporting foot. The abdominal muscles and spine lengthen upward so that the torso and pelvis do not lean to the side.

**Related Poses**  *Attitude à deux bras*—that is with both arms *en haut* (or *en avant*)—is an attractive alternative, especially helpful in stabilizing the *attitude* position. *Attitude à terre* is a pose frequently used to begin or end a movement phrase: Standing *en face* or *croisé,* bend the upstage leg, foot pointed on the ground either directly behind the supporting ankle or crossed behind the opposite shoulder with knees close together and arms in *attitude* position or some other pleasing shape.

Mercury

■ *Attitude croisée derrière*     ■ *Attitude croisée devant*     ■ *Attitude à terre*

## *Arabesque* (ah-ra-BESK)

Perhaps the ultimate pose in ballet is the *arabesque,* in which the body is balanced over one foot with the other leg fully extended behind. The arms also are extended, palms down, creating a long, symmetrical line from fingertips to toetips. Blasis surmised that the design and name were derived from ancient paintings, which in turn had been influenced by the Moorish and Arabic taste for architectural ornaments and embellishments.[4]

*Arabesques* are learned *à terre*—that is, the toes of the extended leg touching the ground. Later, as the leg is gradually raised *en l'air,* the pelvis responds by tilting forward in adjustment, the abdominal muscles remaining strongly engaged so that the weight is lifted out of the lower spine (lumbar vertebrae). At the same time, the torso lengthens upward and slightly forward through the upper spine (thoracic vertebrae) and head as the body weight centers over the ball of the supporting foot.

The arms are extended, rather than curved, with the fingers also extended and the palms facing the floor. Usually, the height of the arms balances the height of the leg, enabling an unbroken line to be drawn from the fingers of the front hand to the toes of the extended foot. Thus, the lower the leg, the higher the front arm, and, as the leg rises, the front arm moves into a more horizontal line.

Four basic *arabesques* are given here. The extended leg is pictured at different levels, *à terre* to 90 degrees, any of which may be done in any of the *arabesques.*

■ First *arabesque*

The dancer stands in profile to the audience; the leg nearer the audience extends to the back; the forward arm corresponds to the supporting leg; the other arm is taken slightly back of second position but without strain to the shoulder; the eyes focus over the forward hand.

■ Second *arabesque*

The dancer stands as in first *arabesque*, except the arms are reversed so that the forward arm is in opposition to the supporting leg; the head may incline toward the audience.

■ Third *arabesque* Cecchetti Method (or *arabesque à deux bras*)

The dancer stands as in first *arabesque*, but with both arms extended forward; the arm farther from the audience is slightly higher; the focus is between the two hands.

**Related Poses**   All the *arabesques* described can be done with a bend of the supporting leg. This pose, known as *arabesque en fondue*, frequently precedes or makes a transition to another movement. A common pose in later stages of training is *arabesque penchée* (pah*n*-SHAY), in which the leg is raised very high, causing the pelvis and torso to tilt well forward while still

The dancer faces the downstage corner with the upstage leg raised in *arabesque;* the forward arm is in opposition to the supporting leg; ribs, shoulders, and head focus toward the downstage corner.

■ First *arabesque en fondue*

maintaining the lifted shape of the spine in *arabesque*. The head and forward arm are low, counterbalancing the raised foot, which is the highest point of the pose.

**Reminders** In all *arabesques,* as the leg lifts to the back, it must be well turned out from the hip, which causes a slight rotation in the lower spine. At the same time, the supporting leg counters this pull by maintaining its outward rotation. Strong abdominal control through the waist, strength in the muscles of the lower back and in the hip rotators, and mobility in the hip flexors are all required to maintain the balance and the correct line of *arabesque*.

# CONNECTING MOVEMENTS

Connecting movements are those that link various poses, prepare for certain actions, move the dancer from one location to another, or any combination thereof. Although transitional in purpose, these steps enhance the flow of movement, helping to keep it vibrant rather than static. They are connecting movements in quite another sense as well: some of them developed from movements used in social and theatrical court dances in the seventeenth century, thus linking today's ballet to its aristocratic origins.

### *Glissé* (glee-SAY)

**Definition**   *Glissé* ("glided") has a sliding quality that relates it to *chassé* (see Chapter 4), a term by which it also is known.

**Description**   *Glissé* may be done forward, backward, or sideward, *en face* as well as on the diagonal. To perform forward or *en avant:* From a *demi-plié* in fifth position, slide the front foot forward to fourth position *demi-plié,* keeping the pelvis level and legs evenly turned out. Smoothly transfer the weight completely to the front leg, straightening the knees and extending the back foot to *pointe tendue derrière.*

**Reminders**   After the slide to *demi-plié* in fourth position, the transfer of weight to the front leg should begin before the heel of the back foot releases the floor. Smoothly coordinate the movements of the arms with the movements of the legs, moving the arms through *en avant* position during the slide before opening them to a desired position as the legs straighten.

**Suggestions**   Sense the torso pushing in the direction of the *glissé* and the arms opening forward and outward from the center of the body with energy. During the *glissé,* visualize the pose or position that is to follow so that the *glissé* is connecting with purpose to the next movement.

■ *Glissé* (or *chassé*) *en avant*

### *Tombé* (tohn-BAY)

**Definition**   *Tombé* (which means "falling" or "fallen") is any movement in which the dancer, having extended the gesture leg, falls forward, sideward, or backward into a *fondu* on that gesture leg.

**Description**   To perform *tombé en avant:* From fifth position *demi-pointes*, *dégagé* the front leg forward as the arms rise to a desired position. Fall well forward into a lunge on the gesture leg, usually opening the arms to another desired position. The back leg remains extended with the foot at *pointe tendue* or raised in the air.

**Reminders**   The falling action is soft and controlled, with contact to the floor being made smoothly through the entire foot (toe-ball-heel) into a *fondu*. The body is lifted upward out of the hips and through the waist as it centers immediately over the well-turned-out leg in *fondu*.

■ *Tombé à la seconde*

**Suggestions**   As when performing other connecting steps, use the breath to initiate the *tombé,* keep the energy flowing in the direction of the *tombé,* and visualize the movements that are to follow.

### *Piqué* (pee-KAY)

**Definition**   A sharp step in any direction taken directly onto the *demi-pointe* of a straight gesture leg. The brisk action reflects the literal meaning of the term—"pricked." The step is also called *posé* (poh-ZAY).

**Description**   To perform *en avant:* Facing downstage right with the right foot front in fifth position, *dégagé* the right foot forward to *effacé* as the supporting leg lowers into *fondu.* Push strongly from the supporting foot, and step well forward with a slight springing action onto the right *demi-pointe,* quickly lifting the left leg to a desired position such as *cou-de-pied, retiré,* or *arabesque.* Close the left foot to fifth position back.

**Reminders**   Emphasis should be on taking the center of the body well forward and directly onto the *demi-pointe* of the foot of the straight gesture leg. A *piqué* is not done with a roll-up or a *relevé* onto the gesture leg.

**Suggestions**   Perform each *piqué* as a picture, as though a photo could be taken capturing a perfect moment of balance. Initial practice can be a step onto the whole foot before attempting a step onto *demi-pointe.* Some usual positions for the raised leg in a *piqué en avant* include *sur le cou-de-pied derrière, retiré derrière,* and *arabesque.* It is wise to learn them in that order.

■ *Piqué en avant sur le cou-de-pied*

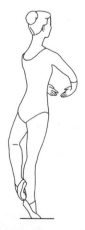

Instead of the finish to fifth position, the raised leg can lower in *fondu* directly beneath the forward foot, which then once more can extend in *dégagé* to continue a series of *piqués*. Or, from a *piqué* in *arabesque*, the raised leg can move forward into a *tombé*.

### *Pas de Bourrée* (pah duh boo-RAY)

**Definition**    The *bourrée* was a French folk dance form, court dance form, and musical form. The *pas de bourrée,* or "*bourrée* step," had dozens of variations in early-eighteenth-century dance technique. Today's ballet vocabulary contains considerably fewer, with six versions commonly appearing in elementary classes. Although the actual performance of the steps has changed, now, as then, the *pas de bourrée* involves three movements—either three shifts of weight, or two shifts of weight and then a closing to position.

**Description**    In general, if the preparation is a *dégagé*, the *pas de bourrée* will finish in fifth position *demi-plié*. If, however, the *pas de bourrée* begins with one foot raised in front or in back of the ankle, it usually will finish in a *fondu* with the other foot in a raised position. The first method is described and illustrated here:

> *Pas de bourrée dessous:* From fifth position, left foot front or back, *demi-plié* and *dégagé à la seconde* with the left foot (this is a preparatory movement). Draw the left foot to fifth position in back of the right foot as both feet rise to the *demi-pointes*. Immediately open the right foot to a small second position and step onto *demi-pointe*. Close the left foot front in fifth position *demi-plié*.
>
> *Pas de bourrée dessus:* After the preparatory *dégagé*, step in *front* and then to the side, and close the first foot in back.
>
> *Pas de bourrée derrière:* After the preparatory *dégagé*, step in back and then to the side, and close in back.

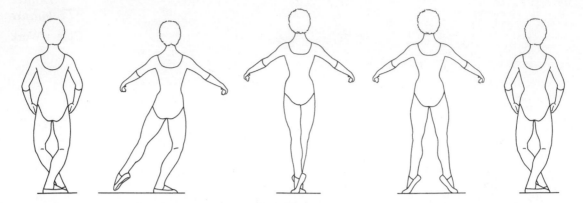

*Pas de bourrée devant:* After the preparatory *dégagé,* step in front and then to the side, and close in front.

*Pas de bourrée en arrière:* From *pointe tendue* in fourth position, right foot front, bring the right foot to fifth position front stepping onto *demi-pointe.* Immediately open the left foot, and take a small step backward onto *demi-pointe.* Close the right foot front in *fondu* as the left foot extends to *pointe tendue* in fourth position back.

*Pas de bourrée en avant:* Begin from fourth position back. Bring the foot to fifth position, step forward, and close back as the other foot extends to the front.

Both the *pas de bourrée en arrière* and *en avant* may start with a preparatory *dégagé* from fifth position, and they may finish in fifth position *demi-plié.* They are usually performed to the *effacé* or *croisé* directions.

**Reminders**   *Pas de bourrées* usually are performed quickly, with the three steps counted "and, a, *one*"—the accent on the last step. Therefore, keep the action light and the weight of the body well-lifted out of the legs.

**Suggestions**   Begin the practice of *pas de bourrées* slowly, giving a count to each step and stepping clearly into each position. Gradually increase the speed.

**Other Forms**   *Pas de bourrée piqué* means that the feet are picked up sharply to the height of the ankle or knee on each step. In *pas de bourrée fondu,* the second step is made in *fondu* rather than to *demi-pointe.* In more advanced training, *pas de bourrée* is done *en tournant,* either *en dehors* (turning outward with a *pas de bourrée dessous*) or *en dedans* (turning inward with a *pas de bourrée dessus*). Tiny running steps traveling in any direction are called *pas de bourrée couru.* They are done with the feet tightly crossed in fifth position on the *demi-pointes* (later on full point for advanced women students) or without turnout (in parallel position).

***Pas Marché*** (pah mahr-SHAY)

**Definition**  A walking step executed in an elegant, dignified manner.

**Description**  Steps are taken with the feet only slightly turned out. The weight is transferred smoothly through the foot, toes contacting the floor first. Each step can be preceded either by a very small *développé* or a low *dégagé* with the foot well extended. The heels scarcely touch the floor, the desired image being one of nonaffected assurance but decidedly not pedestrian casualness.

## TURNS

Most poses and steps can be done *en tournant,* or turning. They at once become more exciting to watch and more challenging to perform. Probably no aspect of ballet has received more analysis by teachers (or attention by students) than the *pirouette,* a complete spin on one foot.

Any turn demands a correctly aligned body whose feet, legs, and back have been strengthened by elementary ballet exercises. To this strong vertical balance is added the first principle of turning—the clear focus of the eyes on a fixed point and the quick snap of the head, called *spotting.*

### Spotting

For a turn in place, the gaze stays momentarily on a fixed point straight in front of the body as the turn begins. The head then leads the turn, arriving back at the fixed focal point before the rest of the body. This manipulation of the head and focus of the eyes allows the dancer to turn without becoming dizzy, and it contributes to the momentum for fast turns. The origin of the trick of spotting is not known. Erik Bruhn, one of the finest dancers of the twentieth century, suggested that it perhaps was "originally an accidental discovery which some dancer later embodied in his teaching and which eventually became a universally accepted practice."[5]

■ Spotting for turns

*Preparatory Exercise*

Students who find turning less than second nature (and many do) can become acquainted with spotting by revolving slowly in place while taking small steps on both feet. The focus remains on a fixed point to the front as the turn begins, and then the head snaps around to finish the revolution before the rest of the body. The head is erect, and the fixed focal point is on a line level with the eyes.

## Turns on Two Feet

Once the principle of spotting is understood, the student practices turns on two feet. These turns are done in place as *soutenus en tournant,* or traveling as *tours de basque* and *tours chaînés.*

### Soutenu en Tournant (soo-teh-NEW ahn toor-NAHn)

**Definition**    This movement, whose name means "sustained turning," most commonly is executed *en dedans,* or inwards.

**Description**    From fifth position, left foot back, slide the left foot to the side while bending the right knee (or *tombé* onto the right leg). Draw the left foot to fifth position front—either by closing straight in or by making a *demi-rond de jambe en dedans*—while simultaneously rising to the *demi-pointes* and turning right, thus facing the back of the room. (The left foot will be in front of the right.) Continue turning to the right on both feet until facing the front of the room once more, leaving the left foot in back in fifth position. The turn also is called *assemblé soutenu en tournant en dedans,* which implies a slight spring to the *demi-pointe* position. Reverse the movements to perform the turn *en dehors.*

■ *Soutenu en tournant en dedans*

**Suggestions**   The leg that opens and closes must stay straight. Open the arms to second position as the foot goes to the side; close the arms *en avant*, or raise them *en haut* by going through *en avant* position, as the turn is made.

> *Preparatory Exercise*
> The mechanics of these turns can be practiced at the barre as simple *battements soutenus:* Slide one foot *à la seconde* while the supporting leg bends; close in fifth position either *à terre* (heels on the ground) or *en relevé.* Later, half-turns can be practiced at the barre and in center, and, finally, the complete turn can be done in center.

### Tour de Basque (toor duh BAHSK)

**Definition**   *Tour de basque* (literally, "Basque turn") is also known as *petit pas de basque sur les pointes* ("little Basque step on the points"), reflecting a kinship with steps traditional to dances of the Basque people. (See *"Pas de Basque"* in Chapter 4.)

**Description**   From fifth position, right foot front, brush the right foot slightly off the ground to the front and then open it out to the side (*demi-rond de jambe en l'air*) while bending the left leg. Immediately step (*piqué*) onto the right *demi-pointe* in second position, and quickly close the left foot to fifth position front as the body makes one-half turn to the right. Continue turning to the right on both feet until facing the beginning direction once more, leaving the left foot in back in fifth position. Another turn can follow immediately to the same direction.

■ *Tour de basque*

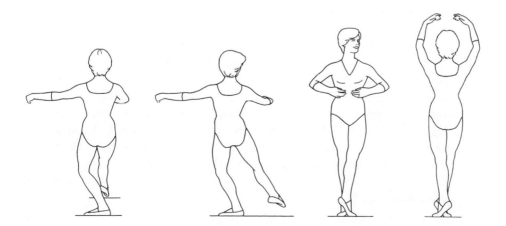

**Suggestions**    The crisp look of this turn is enhanced not only by the straight leg executing the *demi-rond de jambe* and *piqué* but also by the strong push from the floor and quick close to fifth position front by the second foot. As in *soutenu en tournant,* this turn is aided by the brisk closing of both arms from second position to a low, middle, or high position.

> *Preparatory Exercise*
> Before trying the turn, practice just the *demi-rond de jambe* and *piqué* to second position, closing the second foot quickly to fifth position front. Repeat the exercise immediately to the other side.

### *Tours Chaînés* (sheh-NAY)

**Definition**    Usually called simply *chaînés* ("chains, links"), these steps are a series of rapid, traveling turns also known as *déboulés* ("rolling like a ball") or *petits tours.*

**Description**    *Chaînés* are small, rapid steps done in succession, with a half-turn on each step and the feet close together in first position *en demi-pointes.* The turns are done traveling across the floor, usually on a straight diagonal line. Momentum for the turns is initiated by the first step outward and the opening of the arms toward second position; immediately, the pivot is made as the second foot closes to first position and the arms close either *en bas* or *en avant.* The energetic spotting of the eyes and snap of the head continues the momentum, but the arms remain closed as the series of rapid half-turns are done across the room.

**Suggestions**    Keep the height of the *demi-pointes* position consistent, and turn evenly on each foot, remembering that two equal half-turns make one full *chaîné* turn. Keep the hips and shoulders aligned so that the body turns as one unit, the legs straight and well turned out. Continue to lengthen the body upward as you turn.

> *Preparatory Exercise*
> Make slow turning steps in second position, keeping the arms in second position for better balance. Concentrate on the spotting of the head toward a fixed point in the direction of the turns and on making *even* half-turns straight across the room. Later, turn with more speed, with the legs closer together (first position, heels almost touching), the arms low, and the path a diagonal from upstage left to downstage right, then from upstage right to downstage left. If balance is lost or proper direction cannot be maintained, walk quickly out of the line of traffic and, if possible, begin again.

# TURNS ON ONE FOOT

After becoming acquainted with the turns that are done on two feet, students usually are introduced to the following traveling turn in which the dancer steps directly onto one foot for the turn. It is helpful to analyze it in four sections: preparation, initiative, turn, and completion.

### *Piqué (or Posé) Tour en Dedans* (pee-kay TOOR ahn duh-DAHn)

**Preparation**   For a turn to the right, extend the right foot forward while making a *fondu* on the supporting leg. At the same time, turn the head toward the right shoulder and raise *en avant* the arm corresponding to the forward leg and the other arm to second position.

**Initiative**   Keeping the right leg straight with foot pointed, swing it to second position (as in a *demi-rond de jambe en dehors*), and, with a strong push from the supporting foot, immediately face the right leg and step directly onto *demi-pointe,* knee straight. At the same time, open the right arm slightly and raise the left foot *sur le cou-de-pied derrière* (in back of the right ankle) or to *retiré derrière* (behind, or just below, the back of the right knee).

**Turn**   Without pause, execute a three-quarter turn *en dedans* to the right while closing the arms *en avant.* During the spin, the head faces briefly toward the left shoulder, then quickly resumes its focus over the right shoulder.

**Completion**   Lower the left foot into *fondu,* cutting directly under the right foot. At the same time, quickly extend the right leg forward, keeping the knee straight and the toes only a few inches above the ground, and open the left arm to second position. The pose now is the same as the preparatory one.

■ *Piqué tour en dedans*

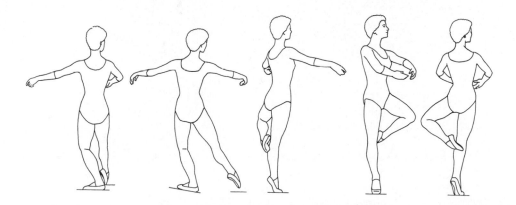

*Preparatory Exercise*

Review the description of *piqué en avant* in this chapter, and then practice a series of *piqués en avant* without turning. Place the raised foot *sur le cou-de-pied derrière* or *retiré derrière*. Finish each *piqué* by lowering the raised leg to *fondu*, cutting directly beneath the forward foot.

The following turns occur in place, rather than traveling. Although the complete turn may not be included in most beginning classes, exercises to help achieve the strength, balance, and form for them are a part of first-year-class material.

## *Pirouettes* (peer-oo-ET)

**Definition**    Literally, a "whirl," a *pirouette* is a complete turn or spin of the body on the *demi-pointe* of one foot. It is performed in place, rather than traveling. *Pirouettes* are performed by turning outward (*en dehors*) in the direction of the raised leg, or by turning inward (*en dedans*) in the direction of the supporting leg.

*Preparatory Exercises*

Before a complete turn is attempted, it is important to practice exercises that emphasize the correct form for *pirouettes* and the strength, balance, and coordination required.

**Exercises at barre**    A series of *relevés* can be practiced facing the barre, with time allowed for balancing: From a *demi-plié* in second, fourth, or fifth positions, *relevé* onto the *demi-pointe* of one foot as the other foot lifts quickly to *retiré devant*. A strong vertical lengthening down through the supporting *demi-pointe,* a level pelvis, and a well-turned-out *retiré* position are required. Close to a secure *demi-plié* in fifth position.

*En dehors*

*En dedans*

■ Preparatory exercise for *pirouette en dehors* from fifth position (as seen from the front)

**Center floor exercises for *pirouettes en dehors***   To practice coordination of movements of the arms with the legs: *Pointe tendue à la seconde* with the right foot as the arms open to second position, and close fifth position front in *demi-plié* as the right arm curves forward of the center of the body (*en avant*). With a push from both feet, *relevé* onto the left foot as the right foot lifts sharply to *retiré devant*, left arm joining the right *en avant*. After the balance in this position, the feet return to fifth position *demi-plié* as the arms remain in place or open outward toward the audience. Once these movements are mastered, the exercise can be practiced from a *demi-plié* in fourth position instead of from fifth. Later, a one-quarter turn outward in the direction of the raised leg can be made on each *relevé,* then half turns and whole turns can follow.

**Center floor exercises for *pirouettes en dedans***   To practice coordination of movements of the arms with the legs: *Pointe tendue* forward toward downstage left with the right foot. *Demi-plié* in fourth position, right arm *en avant* and left arm in second position. With a push from both feet, *relevé* onto the front (right) foot as the back (left) foot lifts sharply to *retiré devant*, left arm joining the right *en avant* and balance facing downstage right. Close to fifth position *demi-plié*, left foot front.

   The same exercise can be practiced from a preparation in fourth position with the back leg straight, full sole of the foot on the floor, and the weight over the front leg, which is in *fondu*. From there, open the arms to second position and the left leg to the side (*à la seconde*) at 45 degrees. Immediately *relevé* onto *demi-pointe* on the front foot, bringing the extended foot to *retiré devant,* and continue as in the previous exercise.

■ Preparatory exercise for *pirouette en dedans* (as seen from the back)

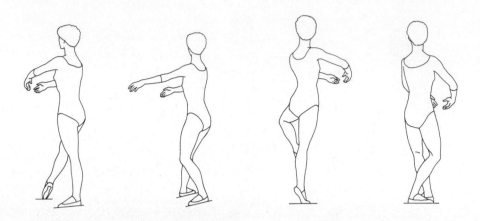

**Reminders**   For any *pirouette*, push strongly from the heels in making the *relevé*, keeping the hips in place as the knee is lifted to *retiré* position. When a full turn is made, be especially careful to maintain the outward rotation and alignment of the supporting hip. Press down into the supporting foot as the turn nears completion.

**Suggestions**   To help "put it all together" before a complete *pirouette* is attempted, try the following exercise: From a *demi-plié* in fifth position, right foot back and right arm *en avant, relevé* on both feet, and turn quickly to the right with the legs close together and the weight slightly more on the left foot. As the turn is made, bring both arms *en avant*, spot with the head, and finish on *demi-pointes* with the right foot front. Repeat to the other side.

■ Alternate preparation for *pirouette en dedans*

*Adagio*

**Definition**   Always an important feature of center work, *adagio* is a series of movements combining *port de bras,* exercises from barre work (such as *pliés, relevés, battements*), center exercises (such as *développés* to any of the positions of the body), the line poses of *arabesque* and *attitude* (often linked by connecting movements such as *pas de bourrée* and *tombé*), and turns (usually not traveling but in place). These movements are done slowly and as though without effort, reflecting the Italian term *adagio* ("at ease" or "leisure").

**Description**   In *adagio* sequences, the dancer must perform with coordination of the arms, legs, and head so that movement flows from one pose to another. A vital part of class in earlier times was the opportunity for each student to create individual combinations of movements (*enchaînements*) to develop a personal style. This also was a way to develop choreographic skills. The following are two ideas for putting together center-floor exercises to form an *adagio*.

> Two *battements tendus croisé devant* and two *battements tendus croisé derrière; dégagé* to *effacé devant,* fondu sur le cou-de-pied devant, *développé en relevé* to *effacé devant,* and *tombé* to first *arabesque fondue; pas de bourrée dessous.* Repeat entire combination to the other side.

> Preparatory exercise for *pirouette en dehors* (*pointe tendue à la seconde, demi-plié* in fifth position front and *relevé* bringing the front foot to *retiré devant,* and close fifth position front); preparatory exercise for *pirouette en dedans* (*pointe tendue à la quatrième devant, demi-plié* in fourth position and *relevé* bringing the back foot to *retiré devant,* and close fifth position front). Repeat *pirouette* exercises to the other side.

Repeat the entire combination, substituting *grands battements* in the first section and full turns in the second section.

**Suggestions**   Learn to observe and listen carefully when an *adagio* is explained. As the movements are demonstrated, try to memorize them quickly or imitate them, using full movements of the arms but minimal physical effort in the legs so that the muscles do not overtire (this practice is called "marking" an exercise). Next will come the chance to perform the movements as completely as possible, or "full out." If the class is divided into groups, observe carefully as other groups work, and learn from the corrections given them.

## MAKING PROGRESS

As you practice any center exercise, remember that the goal is to *dance.* Explore ways to make each movement a joy to watch. Remember to breathe and to lengthen through the entire body so that each pose seems alive rather than static or confined. Give thought to how you are making transitions from one pose or position to another so that even simple connecting movements are beautiful. Sustain the final position of a movement phrase or a turn. Remember that no movement goes unseen!

## NOTES

1. Agrippina Vaganova, *Basic Principles of Classical Ballet* (Leningrad, 1934), trans. Anatole Chujoy (New York: Dover, 1969), 44.

2. Ibid.

3. Carlo Blasis, *Code of Terpsichore* (London, 1828), republished by Dance Horizons (New York, n.d.), 74.

4. Ibid.

5. Erik Bruhn and Lillian Moore, *Bournonville and Ballet Technique* (London: Adam & Charles Black, 1961), 42.

# Ballet Technique:
## Allegro

Answers to these questions about ballet *allegro* are found in this chapter:

- What are the five basic ways in which a dancer can spring into the air? Name a ballet step that corresponds to each of those five movements.

- In what ways is *soubresaut* different from *changement de pieds*?

- In what ways is a *jeté dessus* different from a *jeté dessous*?

- Can you name two connecting or preparatory steps? Describe them.

- In what ways is a *grand jeté* in *arabesque* different from a *temps levé* in *arabesque*?

- What is a *révérence,* and how can it be done?

- Can you give an example of an *allegro enchaînement*? You should be able to compose and perform one using at least four different steps discussed in this chapter.

The lesson thus far has been a necessary prelude to the final, perhaps most important, part—the *allegro* (ah-LEH-gro). Taken from the musical term, *allegro* in ballet means the brisk, often rapid, action steps that include jumps and the connecting, auxiliary movements. These lively steps have been called the heart and soul of ballet, with their particular quality of elevation being its crowning glory. The performance of *allegro* is a true test of a dancer's skill, unmistakably revealed in the classical solo variations (dances in a ballet that correspond to the arias of opera).

How a dancer travels across the floor or into the air is the subject of the following pages. But first, it may be helpful to think of ballet *allegro* in very general terms.

# FIVE FUNDAMENTAL MOVEMENTS OF ELEVATION

A dancer may spring:

- From both feet to both feet (the basis of *temps levé sauté*)
- From both feet to one foot (the basis of *sissonne*)
- From one foot to both feet (the basis of *assemblé*)
- (Or leap) from one foot to the other foot (the basis of *jeté*)
- (Or hop) on one foot (the basis of *temps levé*)

All jumps, leaps, and hops require a bend of the knees (*plié*) for the push-off into the air and another *plié* after the jump to cushion the landing. In ballet, the landing *plié* from the first jump becomes the preparation for the next jump, thus linking the jumps together like the bounces of a ball. The knees and insteps of the feet act as springs; the jumps appear light and bouncy as though done from a springboard. This bouncy quality, known as *ballon* (bah-LOHn), gives the dancer the appearance of being airborne rather than earthbound. Indeed, in steps of very high elevation, the dancer seems to be suspended momentarily in flight.

Good *ballon* often takes years to achieve, but the following exercises can give a ballet beginner the sense of rebound from the floor as well as an introduction to the five fundamental movements of elevation. These basic movements are easiest to understand when they are performed without very much turnout.

### Preparatory Exercises

*Springs from both feet to both feet:* With the legs parallel (or with a very slight turnout), take very small jumps in place. The feet need not point fully, but the landing from each jump must be very soft, going through the toes, to the balls of the feet, and to the heels as the knees bend directly over the feet. This landing is fundamental to all the jumps that follow.

*Springs from both feet to one foot and from one foot to both feet:* With legs parallel (or with a very slight turnout), bend the knees and push off from two feet, landing on one foot; spring from that foot onto both. Do a series of these movements traveling across the room, forward or backward, as well as in place and alternating sides. (Most *allegro* steps can be done in many different directions.)

*Leaps from one foot to the other foot:* Take a slow run or lope across the room. Notice that the landing of the foot is from toe to heel, not heel to toe. This is true of all landings in *allegro*. Try to lope higher, covering less space forward but more space vertically.

*Hops on one foot:* These can be done in the same way as the first exercise but on one foot instead of on both feet, for a series of small hops, before changing to the other foot. They also can be done as a step-hop (a skip) across the floor, either forward or backward, with the arms swinging naturally. Try for higher elevation, with the knee of the bent leg lifted high in front and the other leg straight, the toes of both feet fully pointed in the air.

Combining several of these basic movements provides an introduction to *allegro* combinations, which later will form much of the work in the center. A sample combination of basic movements might be: three leaps forward (on the right, on the left, on the right), hop on the right, spring to both feet, spring to one foot, spring to both feet, spring to one foot. This combination should take eight counts, and it could be repeated across the floor. In an as-yet unrefined way, this is: *jeté, jeté, jeté, temps levé, assemblé, sissonne, assemblé, sissonne.*

## BASIC JUMPS

The first steps of elevation to be learned are basic jumps, which begin from and end on both feet—*temps levé sauté, soubresaut, changement de pieds,* and *échappé sauté.* These, and most other *allegro* steps, are best learned at the barre before they are attempted in the center floor. In many cases, preliminary exercises can precede the performance of the actual step—a kind of evolution helpful to the final understanding. The following general points should be kept in mind when performing these four jumps.

The preparatory movement must be a good *demi-plié*—knees bent directly over the feet and as deeply as the Achilles tendons will allow; the feet firmly on the ground at the big toes, little toes, and heels; the hips, ribs, shoulders, and head poised in dynamic alignment.

From the *demi-plié,* there is a strong push-off from the floor—the thigh muscles contract, and the knees straighten as the feet leave the floor by a firm push through the insteps and toes. In the air, the body is in alignment, abdominal muscles lengthened upward, the feet fully arched.

The landing from the jump must be smooth. Do not anticipate the floor (by relaxing the points of the feet) until the toes just touch the ground. Then roll down through the balls and soles of the feet to the heels, allowing the knees to bend into the *demi-plié* and keeping the pelvis from tilting forward.

When the jumps first are attempted, the arms usually are carried low—in first position or *demi-seconde,* sometimes in second position—and always supported from the center of the back. In most instances, the timing of the jump requires that the dancer be in the air on count "and," then return to the ground on count "1."

All *allegro* steps that follow are illustrated as seen *from the back.* The illustrated sequences read from left to right.

### Temps Levé Sauté (tahn leh-vay soh-TAY)

**Definition**   Literally, the term means "raised jumped movement." Sometimes called simply *sauté,* the movement is a spring from both feet ending in the same position from which it began.

■ *Temps levé sauté* in first position

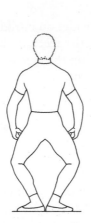
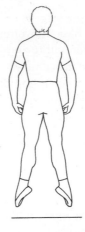
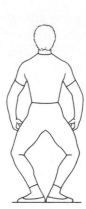

**Description**  This jump is learned in first position, later in second. It begins with a *demi-plié* in first position (or second). Push directly upward into the air. Then land in *demi-plié* as in the starting position.

> *Preparatory Exercise*
> *Relevés* finishing in *demi-plié* (see "*Plié*" and "*Élevé/Relevé*" in Chapter 2) done in first and second positions are basic to the understanding of *temps levés sautés* in those positions.

**Other Forms**  The exercise and the jump may be done in all positions of the feet and with simple variation in arm positions.

## *Soubresaut* (soo-bruh-SOH)

**Definition**  This step is aptly named: *soubre* ("sudden") *saut* ("jump or jumping"). It is, in effect, a *temps levé sauté* performed in fifth position.

**Description**  From *demi-plié* in fifth position, push directly upward into the air with the feet tightly crossed so that no space shows between the legs; land in *demi-plié* as in the starting position (the foot that began in front also finishes front).

> *Preparatory Exercise*
> Springing *relevés* done from fifth position (*sous-sus*, as described in "*Élevé/Relevé*" in Chapter 2) can introduce the tightly crossed position of the feet on the *demi-pointes*. In *soubresaut*, the position is the same, except that in the air the toes can be pointed.

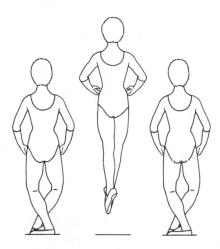

**Other Forms**    Although the basic *soubresaut* is done in place, the step often is performed traveling either forward or backward, usually with some lift of the arms.

A *grand soubresaut,* introduced in more advanced classes, resembles a *grand plié* in fifth position in midair: both feet are drawn up, toes are pointed, and knees are sharply bent.

## *Changement de Pieds* (shahnzh-mahn duh pee-AY)

**Definition**    Meaning "change of feet," this term usually is shortened to *changement.* It is a spring from fifth position to fifth position, landing with the foot that was in front now in back.

■ *Changement de pieds*

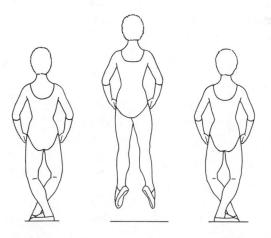

**Description**   From fifth position, right foot front, *demi-plié,* and push into the air, opening the legs slightly to first position. Land in fifth position *demi-plié* with the left foot front (taking care that the feet do not overcross the fifth position at the finish of the *changement*).

**Other Forms**   *Changement en tournant* is a complete turn in the air at the moment of the jump. These *changements* are learned first as quarter turns, beginning in the direction of the foot that was in front, with the body turning as one unit and the eyes focusing clearly in each new direction.

   *Petits changements* are those in which the toes barely leave the floor during the jump; the action happens more from the arches and ankles than from the knees and thighs.

   *Grands changements* are very high jumps and can be performed with the feet drawn up (as in *grand soubresaut*) or with the legs thrown apart (*écarté*). *Grands changements* are practiced at later stages of technical training.

### *Échappé Sauté* (ay-shah-PAY soh-TAY)

**Definition**   In this jump, the feet escape from a closed position to an open one, thus reflecting the meaning of the term—"escaped movement jumped."

**Description**   In *petit échappé sauté,* the jump is not high but is simply a small spring from a *demi-plié* in fifth position to a *demi-plié* in second position. The step is completed with another small springing jump returning to fifth position, usually with the foot that began in front finishing in back.

   The *grand échappé sauté* is a larger jump requiring more skill: From a *demi-plié* in fifth position, spring high into the air with the legs close together and feet well crossed as in *soubresaut,* arms *en avant.* Open the legs and arms

■ *Grand échappé sauté à la seconde*

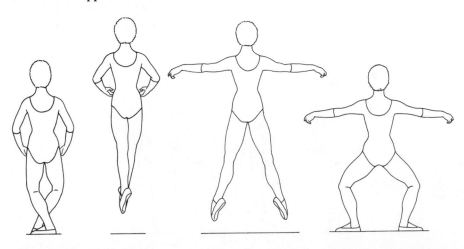

to second position in the air, then land in a strong second position *demi-plié* with the ankles well supported and thighs well turned out. Spring again into the air, the legs in second position. Draw the legs together before landing in fifth position *demi-plié,* usually finishing with the foot that began in front now in back and arms *en bas.*

**Other Forms**   *Échappés sautés* can be done to fourth position as well as second and with a finish on one foot in *fondu* instead of the return to fifth position *demi-plié.*

   *Échappés relevés* are done to the *demi-pointes,* without the spring into the air, as described in *"Élevé/Relevé"* in Chapter 2.

## MORE COMPLEX JUMPS: *PETIT ALLEGRO* STEPS

The following *allegro* steps, although considered elementary, require more coordination and considerable strength. They have many forms, from simple to complex, and thus they are practiced in every level of ballet class, from beginner to professional. Before discussing the basic forms of these steps, it is wise to review some terms that will be used in describing them. In these definitions, the gesture foot refers to the foot that is the first to rise, open, or otherwise leave the original position:

*Dessus* (duh-SUI): The gesture foot passes over (in front of) the supporting foot.

*Dessous* (duh-SOO): The gesture foot passes under (in back of) the supporting foot.

*Devant* (duh-VAHn): The gesture foot begins from and ends in the front.

*Derrière* (deh-reeAIR): The gesture foot begins from and ends in the back.

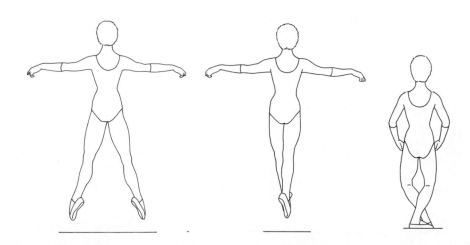

*En avant* (ah-na-VAHn): The step is executed in a forward direction, toward the audience.

*En arrière* (ah-na-reeAIR): The step is executed in a backward direction, away from the audience.

### Sissonne (see-SAWN)

**Definition**    *Sissonne* is a spring from both feet that finishes on one foot, and as such it represents the second half of a compound step called *pas de sissonne* in eighteenth-century dance technique. Today, if the gesture leg remains extended after the landing, it is a *sissonne ouverte* (oo-VAIRT), or open. When a quick return to fifth position is required, it is a *sissonne fermée* (fair-MAY), or closed.

**Description**    The most elementary form is *sissonne simple* (SAn-pluh) and is performed like a *soubresaut* but with a finish on one foot in *fondu,* the other foot pointed just above the supporting ankle, either in front (*devant*) or in back (*derrière*).

Most other forms typically travel sideward, forward, or backward and may finish *ouverte* or *fermée.* The body moves as one unit, the torso and arms established in a secure design during the spring and the landing. The following *sissonnes* travel to the side (*de côté*) with the gesture leg opening *à la seconde* at half height (*à la demi-hauteur*):

*Sissonne ouverte de coté:* From fifth position, right foot front, *demi-plié* and spring into the air from both feet, traveling slightly sideward in the direction of the front foot as the back leg extends *à la seconde;* land on the right foot in *fondu.* Pause in this position with the left leg

Query:
Should it also be côte in caption, 4th line from bottom, and 3rd line p.85?

■ *Sissonne ouverte de coté*

remaining raised, then close by sliding the foot through *pointe tendue* to fifth position.

*Sissonne fermée dessus:* Perform as *sissonne ouverte de coté,* but after landing in *fondu* quickly slide the left foot to fifth position front.

*Sissonne fermée dessous:* Travel sideward on the *sissonne* in the direction of the back foot, and quickly close the gesture foot behind in fifth position.

**Other Forms** Both *sissonne ouverte* and *fermée* may travel forward or backward in various positions of the body. A particularly pleasing version is *sissonne ouverte* traveling forward (*en avant*) in an *arabesque.* (See "Arabesque" in Chapter 3 for various *arabesque* positions.)

## Assemblé (ah-sahn-BLAY)

**Definition** This jump is a spring off one foot onto both feet. The term means "assembled" and refers to the bringing together of the legs in the air so that the landing can be made on both feet simultaneously.

**Description** *Assemblé dessus:* From fifth position, right foot back, brush the right foot to the side as the supporting knee bends deeply. Without pause, continue the *dégagé* movement until the right foot is off the floor. Push strongly from the floor with the supporting leg, maximizing the stretch of both legs in the air and the pointing of both feet. Assemble the legs in the air by bringing the right leg in front of the left. Alight simultaneously on both feet in *demi plié,* right foot front in fifth position. An opening of the arms outward from the body, motivated by a sense of breath in the torso, helps achieve the lightness required in this step.

■ *Sissonne ouverte en avant*

Shown in third *arabesque,* Russian school

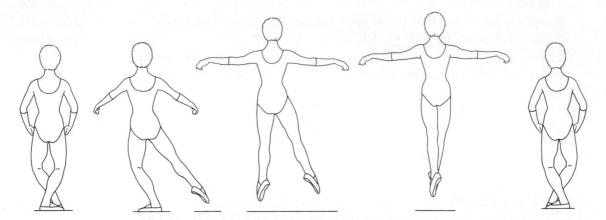

The following variations are described only briefly, the essential action of the legs remaining the same as in the *assemblé dessus*:

*Assemblé dessous:* The front foot brushes to the side and closes in back.

*Assemblé devant:* The front foot brushes to the side and returns to the front.

*Assemblé derrière:* The back foot brushes to the side and returns to the back.

*Assemblé en avant:* The front foot brushes forward and returns to the front.

*Assemblé en arrière:* The back foot brushes backward and returns to the back.

The *assemblés en avant* and *en arrière* require somewhat greater control, especially of the spine, and therefore are usually the last of this series to be learned.

### Preparatory Exercise

As a preparation for *assemblé dessus,* from fifth position, right foot back, *dégagé* to the side with the back foot as the supporting knee bends. *Relevé* high on the supporting foot, close the right foot front, and *demi-plié* on both feet in fifth position. From that same *demi-plié,* begin the exercise with the left foot brushing to the side, and so forth. Reverse the entire action as a preparation for *assemblé dessous.* The other *assemblés* can benefit from similar exercises, learned at the barre. As center exercises, they are particularly challenging.

**Other Forms**   *Assemblé porté* ("carried") is an *assemblé* that travels in the direction of the gesture leg, motivated by the impetus of that leg.

*Assemblé coupé* ("cut") occurs when the weight is already on one foot, the other foot in a position off the floor such as *sur le cou-de-pied derrière* following a *sissonne simple*. The spring into the air and the landing in fifth position are made without the usual brush of the foot on the floor.

A more advanced version, *grand assemblé*, is performed with the gesture leg brushing to full height, or *à la hauteur* (parallel to the floor). It often is performed traveling or turning.

### *Temps Levé* (tahn luh-VAY)

**Definition**   *Temps levé*, meaning "movement (or time) raised," is a hop on one foot with the other foot raised and held in any given position, unlike the *temps levé sauté*, which is a jump from both feet to both feet.

**Description**   Usually in beginning classes, the raised foot is placed just above the ankle of the supporting foot, either in front (*sur le cou-de-pied devant*) or in back (*sur le cou-de-pied derrière*). The ankle of the raised leg is fully extended and the toes pointed. From a strong *fondu*, the supporting leg pushes from the floor with elevation high enough for it to fully straighten, foot arched and toes pointed downward. The return to the ground is to that same leg, lowering smoothly into *fondu*.

> *Preparatory Exercises*
> *Fondus* and *relevés*, with the raised foot *sur le cou-de-pied devant* or *derrière*, can be incorporated in barre exercises to prepare for *temps levé*. They first should be practiced slowly, then with gradually increased speed, but always in moderation. Both this exercise and the *allegro* step are strenuous.

■ *Temps levé sur le cou-de-pied derrière*

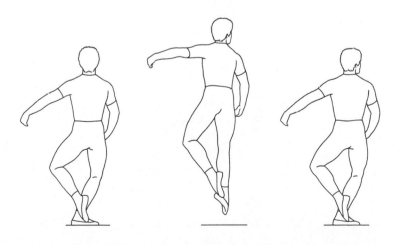

**Other Forms**   The position of the raised leg can determine the name of variations of this step, for instance, *temps levé en arabesque* and *temps levé en retiré* (discussed later in this chapter).

In the Cecchetti method, *temps levé* also can refer to a spring from fifth position finishing with one foot raised *sur le cou-de-pied* (*sissonne simple*, in other methods).

## Jeté (zhuh-TAY)

**Definition**   *Jeté* means "thrown." It is a spring or leap from one foot to the other, done with a strong brush or "throw" of the leg into the air.

**Description**   The most basic small *jetés* are the following two:

*Jeté dessus:* From fifth position, right foot back, *demi-plié,* and brush the back foot into the air as in a strong *battement dégagé à la seconde* while keeping the supporting leg in *fondu.* Immediately spring upward so that for a moment both legs are straight and both feet are pointed in the air. Land in *fondu* on the right foot just in front of the spot vacated by the supporting foot, which then points just above and in back of the right ankle. To continue in a series, brush the back (left) foot into the air from its pointed position at the ankle.

*Jeté dessous:* Perform as *jeté dessus,* but brush the front foot to the side, and finish the step with it in back, the other foot pointed just above and in front of the ankle.

The direction of movement for *jetés dessus* and *dessous* is up; they are thrown directly upward into the air and do not travel from side to side, even though the weight is transferred from one foot to the other on each *jeté.*

■ *Jeté dessus*

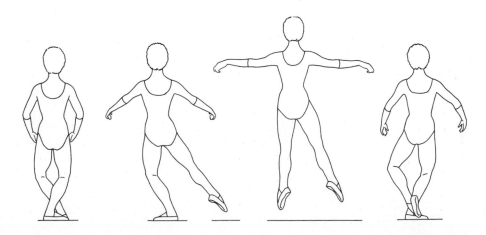

*Preparatory Exercise*

A preparation for *jeté dessus:* From fifth position, right foot back, *dégagé* with the back foot to the side while bending the supporting knee, *relevé* on the supporting foot, bring the right foot momentarily to fifth position front, and immediately lower onto it in *fondu.* When the transfer of weight is made, the left foot arches just above and behind the right ankle. Continue in the same manner, brushing the left foot to the side from its pointed position (now more like the action of a *battement frappé*). Reverse the entire action for *jeté dessous.*

**Other Forms**   *Jeté en avant* travels forward, initiated by a strong *dégagé* to the front. *Jeté en arrière* travels backward, with the *dégagé* brushing to the back.

The large *jeté* step, or *grand jeté,* is more appropriately a part of *grand allegro* (discussed later in this chapter).

## Pas de Chat (pah duh SHAH)

**Definition**   The term means "step of the cat" and implies the quick, catlike springing movement from one foot to the other that is characteristic of this step.

**Description**   Of the several styles of this step, the most elementary are the following versions, all of which travel directly sideward:

*Petit pas de chat:* From fifth position, right foot back, *demi-plié* and briskly raise the back foot, arched, to the ankle of the left foot. Immediately spring upward and to the side, quickly raising the left foot so that the toes of both feet almost touch in the air. Land in *fondu* on the right foot and quickly close the left foot to fifth position front in *demi-plié.* The body should incline slightly in the direction of movement.

■ *Petit pas de chat*

*Grand pas de chat:* Perform exactly as *petit pas de chat*, but raise the feet to the height of the knee (*retiré* position) and spring higher into the air with a sharp action from the thighs. Maintain a strong turnout, especially during the closing of the second leg into a secure fifth position *demi-plié.*

## CONNECTING STEPS AND PREPARATORY MOVEMENTS

Jumps are not always done one right after another. Instead, they often are linked together by connecting steps. Because these steps are done close to the ground, they give contrast to the high jump that will follow and prepare for and introduce the more exciting step. The connecting steps have another purpose—to carry the dancer from one spot to another. When done in a series and with *épaulement,* these relatively small and simple movements have a charm of their own.

### Glissade (glee-SAHD)

**Definition**    *Glissade* ("glide") is done close to the ground, with a brush of one foot along the floor, a shift of weight to that foot, and a slide into fifth position by the other foot. *Glissade* is considered a *terre à terre* ("ground-to-ground") step because the feet barely leave the floor.

**Description**    The following *glissades* travel to the side, beginning and ending with the same foot in front. The feet must not be lifted high off the floor, even though at one moment both legs are straight and both feet are fully pointed. The entire action of the step is timed "and 1," with the energetic close to fifth position on count "1." Performance should be light, with care taken to control the turnout, especially of the closing leg, so that the knees are well open and arches supported in the fifth position *demi-plié:*

■ *Glissade derrière*

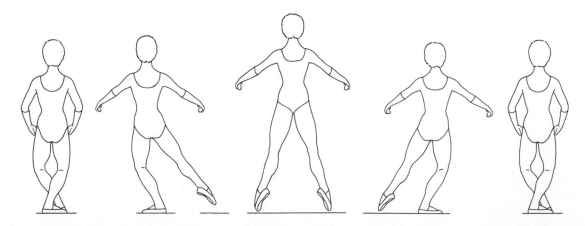

*Glissade derrière:* From fifth position, right foot back, *demi-plié*, and extend the back foot along the floor to the side, finishing with the foot fully arched and toes pointed a few inches off the floor, the left leg remaining in *fondu*. With a slight spring, shift the weight to the right leg in *fondu*, extending the left leg as the left foot points just slightly off the floor; quickly slide the left foot into fifth position front in *demi-plié*.

*Glissade devant:* Perform as *glissade derrière*, but begin with the front foot, which remains in front at the close.

In the following *glissades*, the basic action and timing of the legs are the same as just described, but they are done with a change of feet (sometimes called *glissades changées*, especially when done in a series):

*Glissade dessous:* Travel to the side, leading with the front foot, which finishes in back.

*Glissade dessus:* Travel to the side, leading with the back foot, which finishes in front.

### Preparatory Exercise

To learn the *glissade*, break the step down into four slow parts: From fifth position, *demi-plié* (count "1"). Extend one foot along the floor while the other leg remains in *fondu* (count "2"). Shift the weight onto the leading foot into *fondu*, and close to fifth position *demi-plié* (count "and 3"). Straighten the knees (count "4").

**Other Forms**   *Glissades* also may travel forward or backward *en face* or on the diagonals in *croisé* or *effacé*. The basic action and timing remain the same:

*Glissade en arrière:* Travel backward, leading with the back foot, which finishes in back.

*Glissade en avant:* Travel forward, leading with the front foot, which finishes in front.

Any of the above versions may be performed as an *adagio glissade*, that is, done more slowly, often with the transfer of weight on count "1" and the closing on count "2." Important here is the smooth transition, *legato* in quality, often used to link movements and poses in an *adagio* combination. (See "*Adagio*" in Chapter 3.)

## Coupé (koo-PAY)

**Definition**   *Coupé* means "cut." As a step, it has many forms, all involving one foot "cutting away" the other in order to replace it. Usually, the *coupé* occurs as a preparation for another step, but sometimes *coupés* are performed in a series, changing from one foot to the other.

■ *Coupé dessous sauté*

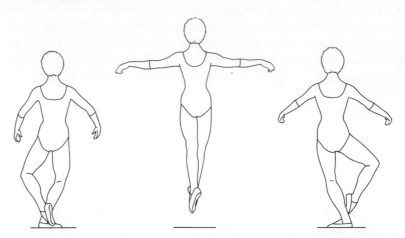

**Description**   *Coupés* are done *dessous* (one foot cutting under) or *dessus* (one foot cutting over) to replace the supporting foot. The movement may be done with a spring into the air or with a rise to the *demi-pointes:*

*Coupé dessous sauté: Fondu* on the right foot as the left foot arches just above and in back of the right ankle. Spring into the air just high enough to allow the right foot to arch, toes pointing downward, and land on the left foot in *fondu*, right foot arched just above and in front of the left ankle (*sur le cou-de-pied devant*). The action is reversed for *coupé dessus,* the front foot cutting over the back foot, which immediately arches *sur le cou-de-pied derrière.*

*Coupé dessous par terre:* From *pointe tendue* fourth position back, *fondu* on the supporting leg. Sharply draw the back foot to fifth position on the *demi-pointes, fondu* in place on the back leg as the front foot extends

■ *Coupé dessous par terre*

to fourth position front at *pointe tendue* or slightly off the ground. This version also can be reversed for *coupé dessus,* in which case the front foot cuts over the back foot. As an alternate method, from fifth position on the *demi-pointes* the leg can open with a small *développé.*

## *Chassé* (shah-SAY) *en l'Air*

**Definition**  Performed as a sliding movement, *chassés* ("chased") give the appearance of one foot chasing the other from its position. The term also is used for a *terre à terre* connecting movement made by a glide of the foot from fifth position *demi-plié* to an open position in second or fourth (see "*Glissé*" in Chapter 3).

**Description**  A *chassé* taken from fifth position usually begins with a preparatory spring into the air, similar to a *sissonne simple* or *temps levé.* From there, the smooth sliding action is achieved by gliding with the toes, rather than by stepping out onto the heel. When performing a series of *chassés,* the dancer should have the appearance of skimming across the floor. There are different styles of performing the step, but all *chassés* can travel forward, sideward, or backward. Two versions and two directions are represented here:

> *Chassé en l'air en avant:* Facing a downstage corner, *demi-plié* in fifth position, right foot front. Spring into the air, alight on the left foot in *fondu* with the right foot arched in front of the supporting ankle, the toes close to the ground. Immediately slide the right foot forward to fourth position, transferring the weight to the right leg in *fondu* as the left leg extends, foot pointing on, or close to, the ground. Spring forward into the air, immediately closing the left leg behind the right, alight in *fondu* on the left foot, and continue as described.

■ *Chassé en l'air en avant*

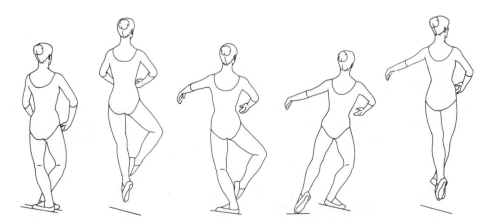

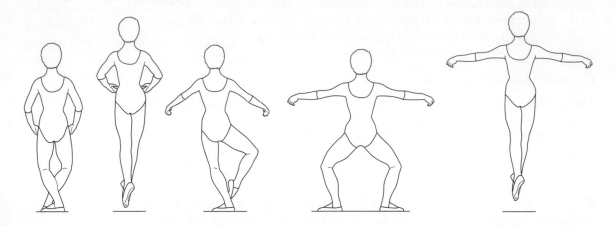

*Chassé en l'air à la seconde:* Facing downstage, *demi-plié* in fifth position, right foot front. Spring into the air, alight on the left foot in *fondu* with the right foot arched in front of the supporting ankle, the toes close to the ground. Immediately slide the right foot out to second position *demi-plié,* the weight evenly distributed on both feet. Spring into the air, traveling in the direction of the right leg and closing the left foot behind, legs straight and feet fully pointed. Alight in *fondu* on the left foot, and continue as described.

### Preparatory Exercise

Before attempting *chassés en l'air,* it is helpful to practice the movements as described but with *relevés* instead of springs into the air.

**Other Forms**  More advanced versions of the step include *chassé passé en avant,* in which the back foot slides through first position to fourth position in front. Another version, *chassé en tournant,* is performed with a turn in the air before the slide.

## ADDITIONAL CONNECTING STEPS AND PREPARATORY MOVEMENTS

Many connecting movements appropriate for use with *allegro* steps also are used with slower center work, for example in a sequence of *adagio* movements. Some of these steps have already been discussed in the previous chapter, such as *glissé, tombé, piqué,* and, especially, various *pas de bourrées.* And, paradoxically perhaps, many steps are appropriate for both *adagio* sequences and *petit* and *grand allegro* combinations, because they can be performed with differing degrees of dynamics.

Each of the following steps contains three transfers of weight. Each shift of weight usually occurs on each beat of a ¾ measure of music, such as a waltz rhythm.

## *Balancé* (bah-lahn-SAY)

**Definition**   The verb *balancer* can mean "to swing or rock to and fro." The *pas balancé* has three shifts of weight, usually performed in a waltz rhythm.

**Description**   *Balancé* is a step of many moods: Sometimes it is bouncy and performed with a light *jeté;* other times it is romantic and performed with a low glide along the floor. In all *balancés,* the legs must remain very turned out, and the lowering to *fondu* must be done softly. The following version is done *de côté* ("to the side") and usually begins with the back foot:

> *Balancé de côté:* From fifth position, right foot back, *demi-plié,* and extend the right foot to the side. With a slight spring, *tombé* over onto the right foot, bringing the left foot directly behind the right ankle (*sur le cou-de-pied derrière*). Shift the weight onto the left *demi-pointe,* bringing the right foot just off the ground. *Fondu* in place on the right foot, arching the left foot behind the right ankle (*sur le cou-de-pied derrière*). The *balancé* can then be repeated to the left side.

Movements of the arms (*ports de bras*) coordinated with movements of the head and shoulders (*épaulements*) can add a smooth, lyrical quality to the *balancé.*

**Other Forms**   *Balancés* may be performed *en avant* or *en arrière* ("forward" or "backward") in various positions of the body. They may be done *en tournant,* completing one half-turn on each *balancé.*

■ *Balancé de côté*

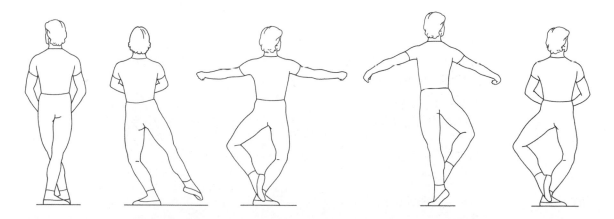

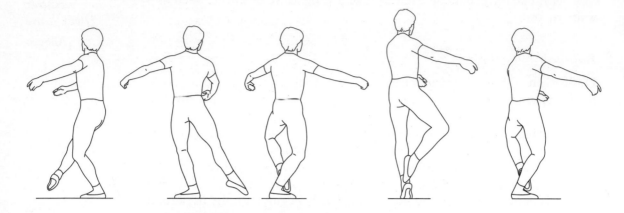

### *Pas de Basque* (pah duh BAHSK)

**Definition**   The "Basque step," commonly found in folk dances of many countries, takes its name from the Basques, a people of the Pyrenees region of southern France and northern Spain. In its simplest form, it is not unlike the *balancé,* except that the second movement always travels forward or backward.

**Description**   The *pas de basque* frequently begins facing one downstage corner and finishes to the other. It has many forms and stylistic variations: it may be large or small, and it may be jumped, glided, or turned. A variety of *port de bras* can be used in the following versions:

> *Pas de basque sauté en avant:* From fifth position, right foot front, *demi-plié,* and, with the right foot, execute a *demi-rond de jambe en dehors*

■ *Pas de basque glissé en avant*

(that is, extend the foot forward and then to the side) slightly above the floor. Spring to the side onto the right foot, bringing the left foot arched in front of the right ankle (*sur le cou-de-pied devant*). Step or *piqué* forward to *croisé* onto the left foot, and close to fifth position or *coupé dessous* with the right foot, arching the left foot in front of the supporting ankle (*sur le cou-de-pied devant*). The *pas de basque* then can be repeated to the left side. All movements can be reversed to perform the *pas de basque sauté en arrière*.

*Pas de basque glissé en avant:* From fifth position, right foot front, *demi-plié* and, with the right foot, execute a *demi-rond de jambe en dehors à terre.* Immediately shift the weight onto the right foot in *fondu,* extending the left foot *pointe tendue à la seconde.* Slide the left foot through first position *demi-plié* (some styles like it also to slide into fifth position) and forward into fourth position, taking care that the legs remain well turned out and the ankles supported, and remain in *demi-plié.* Shift the weight onto the left foot as both legs straighten. Slide the right foot into fifth position behind in *demi-plié.* The *pas de basque* can then be repeated to the left side, or all movements reversed for *pas de basque glissé en arrière.*

*Pas de basque glissé* can be useful as a preparatory step leading into another movement or as a connecting step between two other movements. Other such linking steps are described next.

### Pas de Bourrée Couru or Pas Couru (koo-REW)

**Definition**   *Pas couru* ("run") resembles a *pas de bourrée* because it is a compound movement made up of three quick steps, in this case performed as a smooth run.

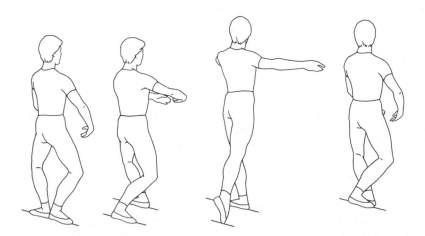

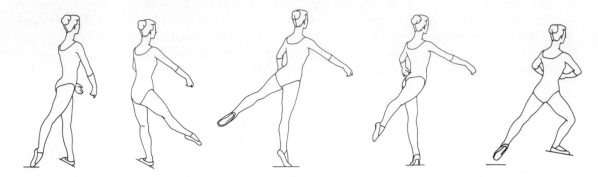

**Description**   To perform *pas de bourrée couru*, or *pas couru*, en avant: From a *pointe tendue croisé derrière* with the right foot, *fondu* on the front (left) leg as the right makes a small *développé* forward. With a push from the *fondu*, step well forward onto the right foot, quickly descending through the instep, and then forward onto the left foot. Without pause, step out again onto the right foot, this time into *fondu* as the impetus for the ensuing *allegro* step.

   The three forward steps (right, left, right) occur quickly without interruption as a three-step run, the final step having the strongest bend, or *fondu*. All the running steps are done with the toes descending first, not the heels, and with the body well forward toward the direction of the run. As the run begins, the arms can open outward to help start the momentum, then close quickly before the final step in order to extend in a desired position that enhances the *grand allegro* movement that follows.

## *GRAND ALLEGRO* STEPS

*Grand* ("large") *allegro* steps require more strength and cover more space, both into the air and across the floor, than the preceding ones. Thus, they are practiced after basic principles of *petit allegro* are understood, when the body is thoroughly warmed up, and usually toward the end of class. Probably no *allegro* steps are more fun to do or more exciting to watch than the following.

### *Grand Jeté en Avant* (grahn zhuh-TAY ah-na-VAHn)

**Definition**   The *grand jeté en avant* is a large, forward-traveling leap that is preceded by a preparatory movement, such as *pas couru, chassé,* or *glissade,* to give the necessary impetus.

**Description**   After an appropriate preparatory movement, one that finishes in a *fondu* on the forward leg with the torso reaching upward and slightly forward, thrust the back leg forward into a strong *grand battement*

*devant,* propelling the body into the air by the push-off from the forward leg, which is then thrust upward into a *grand battement derrière.* Both feet and legs are extended completely in the air, the body momentarily weightlessly airborne in a suspended pose.

Alight in the same pose, with the back leg and foot remaining extended in *arabesque* as the leading foot releases sufficiently to allow a deep *fondu* on the supporting leg. The torso, which has remained quietly lifted during the leap, is allowed to tip slightly forward from the pelvis upon landing in order to balance over the center of the supporting foot.

As a general rule, alignment of the shoulders with the rest of the torso is easier to maintain if the arms are extended in second *arabesque.* Therefore, *grands jetés* done with opposition—for example, if the right leg executes the *grand battement en avant,* the left arm is brought forward—are the most effective for early attempts. The fingers of the forward hand should be at, or just above, eye level and the eyes focused on some point slightly higher.

### Temps Levé en Arabesque (tahn luh-VAY ah-na-ra-BESK)

**Definition**   This movement is a hop or spring on one foot with the other leg extended in *arabesque* and is sometimes called *arabesque sautée.*

**Description**   To perform in first *arabesque:* Stand with the weight well centered over the right leg, the left leg extended straight behind at the desired *arabesque* height, the right arm extended forward, and the left arm opened to the side. Without otherwise altering the pose, *fondu* on the right leg, and push from the right foot into the air, quickly pointing the right foot and completely extending the leg. Alight on the right foot in a controlled *fondu,* maintaining the pose of first *arabesque.*

■ *Temps levé en arabesque*

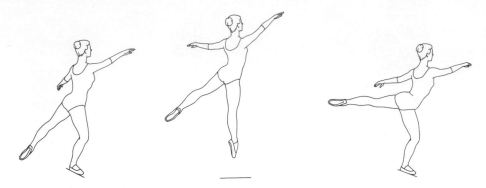

To perform a series of *temps levé* on the same leg, step forward on the left leg and then forward into a *fondu* on the right leg to repeat the action as just described. To alternate legs, precede each *temps levé* with a *pas couru* (three running steps), or simply execute as a step-hop on the right leg and then a step-hop on the left. Alternate the arms by passing them through the *en avant* position.

### Temps Levé en Retiré (tahn luh-VAY ahn ruh-tih-RAY)

**Definition**   A spring or hop is made on one foot with the other foot drawn up to *retiré* position.

**Description**   To perform in *retiré* position: Stand in *croisé* on the left foot with the right foot drawn up and pointed behind, in front, or to the side of

■ *Temps levé en retiré*

the supporting knee. With the right thigh well turned out and the arms established in a desired pose, *fondu,* and push into the air. Alight on the left foot in a controlled *fondu,* maintaining the *retiré* pose.

To perform this movement in a series on the same leg, step forward on the right leg and then forward into a *fondu* on the left leg to begin the *temps levé* action once again. To alternate legs, follow the general procedures described for *temps levé en arabesque.*

## BEATS

The broad term for steps with beats is *batterie* (bat-REE). Although classes in basic ballet usually do not include steps with beats, students in those classes may be curious about what is meant by "beats." Steps with beats are made as the calves of the legs open out and close back in, crossing in front and behind each other.

Once basic *allegro* steps are mastered, many of them are embellished, and some are performed exclusively with beats. These include such small steps as the *entrechats* ("braidings or interweavings")—jumps with rapid crossings of the legs in the air, *petite batterie.* Because both legs are active in movement, they are both counted; for example, in an *entrechat quatre,* because each leg makes two crossings, the step counts as four (*quatre*) beats. A few dancers (male) have managed five crossings—an *entrechat dix.* An uneven number, as in *entrechat trois* (three), usually indicates a finish on one foot or in an open position (second or fourth).

Beaten steps requiring higher elevation, *grande batterie,* include the *cabrioles* ("capers"), in which one leg is thrown into the air followed by the underneath leg, which beats against it, sending the first leg even higher into the air.

Exercises such as rapid *battements tendus* or *battements dégagés,* practiced at the barre and in center floor, are essential preparations for *batterie.* Two of the best center-floor *allegro* preparations for *batterie* are the following exercises:

### Temps Levés Sautés Battus en Seconde
(tah*n* luh-VAY soh-TAY bah-TEW zah*n* suh-GOH*n*D)

**Definition**   This series of jumps in second position is taken with a beat of the legs before each landing. The jumps can be high, as a preparation for *grande batterie,* or quick and small, as a preparation for *petite batterie.*

**Description**   To prepare for *grande batterie: Demi-plié* in second position, and push high into the air, fully stretching the legs and arching the feet. At the height of the jump, and with the legs well turned out, beat the calves together, right leg in front; open both legs and land in second position *demi-plié.* Repeat, beating with the left leg front. Continue for a series of *sautés,* alternating beats in this manner. In this exercise, it is important that the

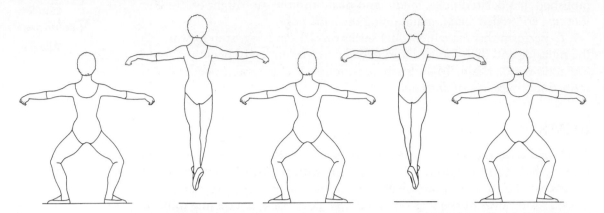

inner thighs initiate the beating action, so that the legs remain straight in the air; even though the calves must beat, the knees should not bend.

To prepare for rapid *petite batterie: Demi-plié* in a smaller second position, and spring slightly off the ground, extending the legs and sharply arching the feet but not necessarily completely straightening the knees. Immediately bring the legs together, crossing the right foot well in front so that both heels are visible as the legs beat from the base of the calves downward. Open both legs and land in a small second position *demi-plié*. Continue in a series of quick jumps, alternating the leg that beats in front.

## ALLEGRO COMBINATIONS

When several different steps are joined to be performed to a musical phrase, it is called a combination or *enchaînement* (ahn-shain-MAHn), literally, a "linking." *Allegro* combinations are the student's first taste of what it may be to dance—to perform one step after another, in time to music, with a definite beginning, middle, and ending of a movement and musical phrase.

In ballet class, combinations often are repeated to the other side or reversed. That is, if a combination travels to the right, it may then be repeated traveling to the left. Or, a phrase that moves forward may then be reversed to move backward. Quickly performing a series of different steps, and then repeating or reversing them, always has been essential training for a dancer's mind and muscles.

The following *petit allegro* combinations, made up of four of ballet's most basic steps of elevation, were found in a teaching notebook compiled by a ballet master in the 1830s.[1] Each combination is repeated to the other side and can be reversed as well. Note that the first step of combination 1 becomes the last step of combination 2, and so on:

1. *Jeté* (*dessus*), *assemblé* (*dessus*), *changement,* and *sissonne* (*simple derrière*)
2. *Assemblé, changement, sissonne,* and *jeté*

3. *Changement, sissonne, jeté,* and *assemblé*
4. *Sissonne, jeté, assemblé,* and *changement*

The following combination is an example of *grand allegro* that can travel across the floor: *Balancé de côté* to the right and to the left, *tours chaînés* to the right, *temps levé en arabesque* and *temps levé en retiré, tombé en avant, pas de bourrée dessous,* and *grand pas de chat.*

## COORDINATED MOVEMENTS

A combination, indeed any single step, requires coordinated arm and head movements if it is to be more than mere physical drill. Beginners learn the basic small jumps with the arms carried simply *en bas,* or in first position, the head straight. At that stage of learning, it is important to train the upper body, head, and arms not to react to the movement of the legs; flapping arms, jiggling shoulders, and a seesaw spine are to be avoided from the very beginning. But in steps such as *glissade* or *assemblé,* where the legs open out from the body, the beginner should open the arms also, usually to *demi-seconde.*

Later, steps of high elevation such as *grand échappé sauté,* large *assemblés,* and *sissonnes* benefit from arms (*not* shoulders) that rise to higher positions as the height of the jump is reached. A change of focus for the head and eyes, the use of *épaulement,* and the use of different directions of the body also add interest to *allegro* combinations in subsequent stages of training. Such coordination requires great skill and is the result of many classes, great patience, and determination to try and try and try, and then try once again.

## *RÉVÉRENCE* (ray-vay-RAHns)

The ballet class may end with a last flourish of jumps, or it may conclude with slow *pliés, relevés, grands battements,* or *ports de bras* to allow the students to wind down after working vigorously for an hour or more. In either case, the final movement of class is often the *révérence,* a bow or curtsy taken by teacher and class in appreciation of their mutual effort.

A *révérence* may range in form from simple to elaborate. For a woman, it is often a step to the side as the arms open to second position; the other foot is then brought behind the supporting foot, and the knees bend as the body leans slightly forward from the hips. A man may simply step forward, bringing the other foot close with the knee relaxed, arms remaining at the side as the head bows forward.

The *révérence* taken in class is not unlike the one a performer may take in acknowledgment of applause. Indeed, there often is applause after the class *révérence,* whereby the students formally thank the instructor and the accompanist for the lesson.

# Chapter 4

## MAKING PROGRESS

The visual excitement of watching a truly fine dancer comes, ultimately, from the dancer's look of oneness with the movement. Steps do not seem pasted on but as though they grew outward from the very core of the dancer. Tamara Karsavina, famous ballerina with the Diaghilev Ballets Russes and then revered teacher, offered this advice to students:

> Do not discard your "feel" of the movement as you do your practice tunic at the end of the class. Take it with you on the bus or the train; there is no extra fare for it. Remember that the mechanism of the dance becomes artistry only when it is inspired by feeling and that feeling perpetuated in your mind will pass into your movements.[2]

### NOTES

1. The ballet master was Michel St. Léon, former dancer at the Paris Opéra Ballet and father of the famous choreographer Arthur Saint-Léon (see "The Golden Age of Romantic Ballet" in Chapter 7).
2. Tamara Karsavina, *Classical Ballet: The Flow of Movement* (London: Adam & Charles Black, 1962), 15.

# The Ballet Body

In this chapter, you will learn about:

- Components of overall ballet fitness
- Somatic approaches toward achieving your movement potential
- Conditioning methods to maximize your endurance, flexibility, and strength
- Injury prevention and treatment
- Foot disorders and foot care
- Proper nutrition and weight management

The studio mirror reflects many shapes and sizes but seldom a perfect ballet physique, and this has always been true. Nevertheless, many a dancer has succeeded as a fine performer despite having a less-than-ideal body. For example, the glorious Soviet ballerina Galina Ulanova had a larger-than-usual ribcage; neither the legendary Anna Pavlova nor the sparkling Margot Fonteyn possessed perfect turnout of the legs; and the great *danseur noble* Erik Bruhn succeeded despite a large head that might have been judged out of proportion to the rest of his body.

As these famous dancers demonstrated, "talent" really translates into effective use of one's own individual body construction and use of one's intelligence to maximize those capabilities and to grow in artistry. Ulanova believed that "talent cannot exist without work," and she continued to attend ballet classes six days a week even at the peak of her career. "I shall never stop learning,"[1] she said—wise words for any student at any stage of training.

The following pages discuss ways to augment ballet training to enhance good health, prevent injury, and maximize individual potential.

# THE BALLET PHYSIQUE

For a long period in ballet's history, the shape and size of a dancer's body determined the type of roles he or she could perform, based on certain traditional notions of those roles (see "Eighteenth-Century Professionalism and Innovation" in Chapter 7). And rarely was a ballet dancer's skin any color but white. Today, however, studio enrollments and company rosters reflect "the fact that not all dancers are cut from the same piece of cloth to the same pattern. This is an encouraging shift: It allows the use of a greater number of artistic perspectives, as well as the ability to address the needs of new, larger, more diverse audiences."[2]

Ballet aesthetics, the rules and principles of beautifully balanced forms in space, translates for the dancer as the ability of the body to create a pleasing line. Therefore, a dancer's body needs a certain flexibility—in the spine to achieve an *arabesque* line and a fluid carriage of the arms; in the hip joints to allow an efficient turnout and extension of the legs; and in the ankles and feet for quick, articulate *allegro,* including soft landings from jumps. There also needs to be sufficient stretch in the muscles of the legs and the upper back to allow an easy flow of movement.

A dancer's body must be able to function reliably to have the strength and overall health and fitness to meet the day-to-day physical demands of ballet technique. Part of the task of ballet training is to develop the right combinations of both strength and flexibility. Each body is different, and therefore strengthening and stretching exercises must be undertaken within the individual capacities and limitations of each person's physique.

For example, a person with hyperflexed knees needs to work consistently and carefully on stretching the hamstring muscles at the backs of the legs. Stretching the hamstrings is *not* good practice, however, for a person with the opposite condition, hyperextended knees, which requires consistent, careful work in improving postural alignment. (See accompanying illustrations.)

Proper execution of ballet exercises and regular practice are fundamental for achieving strength, flexibility, and fitness. They alone are not always sufficient, however. The next few pages outline some things to consider for augmenting ballet training.

## FITNESS

Good dancers and good health are a necessary team. The four health-related components of physical fitness essential for ballet performers are:

- Cardiorespiratory endurance—strong lungs and a healthy heart that enable the body "to perform prolonged, large-muscle, dynamic exercise at moderate-to-high levels of intensity"[3]
- Muscular strength and muscular endurance—the amount of force that muscles need to produce movement as well as to halt or brake movement; to maintain a position, including correct body alignment; and to sustain repetitions of a given activity

Hyperextended knee—often accompanied by tilted pelvis, weight that is pushed
back on the heel, and locked knee

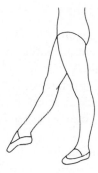

Knee brought into better alignment—often achieved by centering the pelvis,
shifting the weight forward over the center of the foot, and developing muscular
control to keep the knee stable

- Flexibility—"the ability to move the joints through their full range of
motion"[4]
- Body composition—the relative amount of fat and muscle in the body

Although ballet technique class, as a physical activity, develops these
four components of physical fitness in a moderate-to-high degree,[5] it cannot
meet all the conditioning needs of all dancers, who "need stamina to perform demanding variations, strength to lift other dancers, and flexibility to
achieve the desired line" that many ballet movements require.[6] In addition,
differences in individual body structure and restrictions in range of certain
types of movement sometimes require more specialized exercises. These include exercises that can change habitual movement patterns and strengthen
or stretch the appropriate muscle groups necessary for certain actions.

The dancer today has a number of approaches from which to choose for
specialized work. These methods not only can enhance the quality of movement for any level of dancer, but they also can be effective means of rehabil-
itating the body after injury. Some of the more popular choices are discussed

briefly in the following sections. Because these methods involve reeducating and retraining the body, their study should begin with a recognized expert in the particular method chosen.

## MIND/BODY APPROACHES

The term *somatics* frequently is used when referring to approaches that accept the importance of the interrelatedness of body, mind, spirit, and environment. It implies a holistic approach toward achieving one's potential. Importantly, somatic approaches help an individual tap into, and learn from, "the inherent wisdom of the body."[7] Brief descriptions of some of the somatic techniques that have found favor with dancers are included here.

### Alexander Technique

Muscle relaxation and freeing of tensions to achieve more efficient movement patterns and body alignment are integral to the Alexander Technique, developed by Frederick Matthais Alexander, an Australian actor. Central to his technique is the concept of "primary control," a term that refers to the correct use of the head and neck in relation to the entire body. "Forward and up" is the phrase used to achieve a sense of the head balancing effortlessly on the spine.

In the Alexander Technique, analysis of inefficient movement patterns can lead to inhibition of those faulty habits through visualizing correct movements and by carefully practicing basic actions such as sitting, standing, and bending. This analysis is done individually by a teacher giving verbal instructions and using a hands-on approach, communicating directly through touch to improve "the use of self."

Dancers using the Alexander Technique experience an ease in becoming placed up and over their legs and an improvement in coordination and in using their head, especially in spotting for turns.

### Bartenieff Fundamentals

The "Bartenieff Fundamentals" refers to a series of movement sequences aimed at developing more efficient movement patterns with particular attention given to movement quality. Integral to each movement sequence is finding how and where in the body the sequence should correctly begin. Proper initiation of a movement is crucial if correct neuromuscular action is to follow. The purpose and function of each movement sequence is clearly stated, along with instructions on how to perform the action as well as on what to avoid.

Developed by Irmgard Bartenieff, who trained in dance in Germany in the 1920s, the Fundamentals are important components of the Laban Movement Analysis system, created by Bartenieff's teacher, Rudolf von

Laban. Laban/Bartenieff Institutes of Movement Studies, located in the
United States, offer intensive one-year courses called the Certification Program in Laban Movement Studies.

Dancers find new insights into their own body alignment and movement
patterns using the Fundamentals sequences, which are premised on the belief
that posture is as individual as a signature: it reflects a person's internal feelings
and thus the individual body's unique "accommodation" to space.

## Feldenkrais Awareness

Breaking out of habitual movement patterns by increasing the ability to feel
and visualize movements is the goal of the body-reeducation method developed by Moshe Feldenkrais, founding director of the Feldenkrais Institute
in Tel Aviv, Israel, and currently taught by certified Feldenkrais instructors
in the United States.

At the Tel Aviv Institute, some one thousand "lessons" were devised,
each aiming at specific learning experiences, including the development of
deep or organic breathing patterns. Twelve of these lessons are given by
Feldenkrais in his book, *Awareness through Movement.* Feldenkrais students
are advised to do one lesson nightly before going to sleep, gradually increasing movement repetitions from ten to twenty-five times or more. In the
lessons, attention is focused on the smallest possible movements, requiring
the student to concentrate on minute signals from the body and thus increase body and movement awareness.

## Ideokinesis

*Ideo* (for "thought") *kinesis* (for "motion") is the name given by Dr. Lulu E.
Sweigard for her method of reeducating the body for more efficient movement and better balanced alignment. Ideokinesis involves mentally concentrating on visualizing a movement (such as a "perfectly" executed *grand
battement*) without physically performing it. Specific images, based on a
sound understanding of anatomy and biomechanics, are given by the teacher
for particular movement patterns. The student concentrates on these while
standing or simply lying in the Constructive Rest Position (CRP), a relaxing
position requiring no muscle effort. In her work with dance students at the
Juilliard School, Sweigard demonstrated that neuromuscular responses
could be improved and changed by using correct mental images.

## Massage

A massage session can be a relaxing treat for a healthy dancer as well as a
helpful treatment for an injured dancer. Types of massage vary from general,
light techniques to localized, deep-frictioning work. Massage therapy may
include exercises in breathing and in stretching and releasing.

CRP, the Constructive Rest Position designed by Dr. Lulu E. Sweigard, can help relieve muscle strain and enhance relaxation. By using visualization techniques in this position, one can then begin to affect skeletal realignment.

Massage can help relieve soreness, stiffness, and muscle spasm, and it can aid in recovery from injury by helping to stimulate blood circulation. After the injury is healed, massage can help break down scar tissue.

Today, some professional ballet companies have a masseur on their staff, who even travels with the company on tour to help the dancers meet the demands of an intensive performance schedule and to help them avoid injury.

## Yoga

In ancient Sanskrit, the word *yoga* means "union," specifically the union of body, mind, and soul. Yoga, as a system of physical postures (*asanas*), has evolved over thousands of years and comes from ancient Hindu philosophy promoting concentration and spiritual enlightenment.

It is estimated that some 18 million people in the United States practice some form of yoga exercise, and this includes many dancers, choreographers, and dance teachers. The form most common in the United States is hatha (meaning "physical") yoga, which emphasizes breathing, balance, and flexibility. There are different styles of hatha yoga with differing emphases on developing stamina, integrating muscle strength and relaxation, and improving alignment. And, there are hundreds of different *asanas,* or postures.

Hatha yoga classes often begin with breathing exercises and some type of warm-up exercise, followed by a series of *asanas,* each held for a few seconds or several minutes. These postures, correctly performed, can stretch and relax the body, helping to create a sense of inner well-being as well as to promote physical fitness. Classes usually end with a five- to ten-minute period of relaxation/meditation.

## CONDITIONING METHODS

The primary goals of conditioning for dancers are cardiorespiratory endurance, flexibility, and muscular strength and endurance. As with any exercise/fitness program, certain principles apply: maintain proper alignment of your body so that it can work efficiently; precede the workout with a gradual warm-up, and allow for a cooling-down, slowing-down, or stretching period at the end; gradually increase the amount of the activity; listen to the signals given by your body; and always be aware of the needs of your own physique.

## Cardiorespiratory Exercise

Aerobic exercise can improve a dancer's overall stamina by providing a varied progression of moderate exercise designed to give an adequate overload for the heart and vascular system. To be effective, aerobic exercise should occur at least three times a week. Gradually, the duration and intensity of the training can be increased, but always with careful consideration of individual needs.

Types of cardiorespiratory exercise best suited for dancers include brisk walking and swimming. Nonimpact aerobic-dance classes, usually one-hour sessions of continuous and vigorous activity, can offer benefits also, but dancers should be careful to select a class that offers safe and healthful workouts. Basic concerns should be:

- Does the class include a gradual warm-up at the beginning of the session?
- Are individual corrections given?
- Is proper alignment emphasized?
- Is there a cooling-down period at the end of the workout?

## Flexibility Exercise

All dancers desire flexibility so that they may have a wide range of motion, including high extensions. However, movement range around a joint or set of joints is highly individual, determined by one's genetic heritage, that is, how a joint is structured and the tightness of muscles, tendons, and ligaments that are attached to it. Within the framework of these given body attributes, muscles and their connective tissues are the keys to increasing and maintaining flexibility because they can be lengthened through regular stretching exercises. As was pointed out in "Stretches" in Chapter 2, these exercises should be done slowly and smoothly, relaxing into the stretch position and staying there for a minimum of thirty seconds. The pull of gravity and the exhalation of the breath will increase the stretch.

Dancers want to be able to move their joints freely, or with little resistance, during dance movements, but they must also be able to maintain stability. Therefore, flexibility must be functional. This means that strengthening must accompany stretching.

## Strength Training

Also known as weight training or resistance exercise, this type of conditioning increases and maintains lean-muscle strength. Strength training is most effective when it is performed slowly, moving through a joint's full range of motion against resistance. Such action is known as isotonic exercise, and it can be done using a person's own body weight (such as in sit-ups or push-ups), with weight machines, or with free weights (dumbbells and ankle weights).

A program of strength training can be designed to address specific areas of weakness in all parts of the body—arms, shoulders, chest, abdomen, back, hips, and legs. When beginners start with weight machines or free weights, they should work with a weight load that can be lifted or pushed fairly easily for five to eight repetitions. Breathing should be slow, taking three slow counts to exhale as the weight is lifted, then inhale just as slowly as the weight is returned to the starting position. Engage your abdominal muscles as you work, so that they are strengthened also. Gradually, the weight should be increased, always adding an amount that will cause muscle fatigue for the designated number of repetitions, but the repetitions need not be increased beyond a total of ten or twelve. Be sure to allow time to rest thirty to sixty seconds after the designated number of repetitions (referred to as a "set") before continuing for one more set or going on to another exercise.

As a general rule, strength-training sessions of twenty to thirty minutes two or three times a week is advised. Allow a day between each session so that the muscles can rest. Before your workout, remember to warm up and gently stretch the muscles you plan to strengthen; afterward, allow time to cool down and gently stretch again.

## Pilates Method

The Pilates Method refers to techniques of body conditioning, rehabilitation, and strength training developed by Joseph Pilates, a German-born pioneer in developing exercises performed on a mat and on a special apparatus, the "Universal Reformer." This versatile, horizontal bedlike machine slides on metal runners as the exerciser pushes or pulls against the machine's bars or straps. This and other types of Pilates equipment offer a variety of strengthening and stretching possibilities for working the entire body.

Pilates exercises are done with control and concentration, with special focus on the torso to strengthen the center of the body. "Once abdominal strength, a supple spine, and pelvic stabilization are achieved, the student then can be challenged with movements of the legs and arms."[8] This order of priorities is especially important for the dancer.

Pilates work can be tailored to meet the particular needs of each individual. It is important, therefore, to get instruction at a reputable studio and from an instructor with knowledge of kinesiology and, ideally, of dance.

## Floor-Barre Technique

Originated in New York City by dancer and ballet teacher Zena Rommett in the 1960s, Floor-Barre Technique adapts the technical vocabulary of ballet in exercises performed while sitting on the floor or lying on the back or side. The goals of the training include improvement of dance technique by development of better alignment, turnout, and extension.

Exercises for the legs and feet, performed in parallel as well as turned-out positions, emphasize alignment of all the joints involved. Torso, shoulder, and upper-back exercises combine breathing techniques and mental imaging to release tensions and increase flexibility.

As with the study of other conditioning methods, study of Floor-Barre Technique should begin with a recognized expert in the field. As a supplement, Rommett has prepared videotapes of classes for dancers of different technical levels (see "Selected Reading and Viewing").

Floor-Barre Technique also is used to rehabilitate the body after injury, but one of its benefits is to prevent injury in the first place. Building body strength and increasing awareness of proper movement are intrinsic to this practice.

## PREVENTING INJURY

Almost any form of physical activity, certainly one as demanding as ballet, raises the possibility of injury, and even a well-proportioned, well-conditioned body will suffer from strenuous movements or stretches if inadequately warmed up. The fundamental exercises at the barre have as one of their important functions, then, the systematic warming up of the body. When these exercises are neglected before a rehearsal or performance, or by a latecomer to class, injury is invited. Moreover, each barre exercise has its specific purpose, as was seen in Chapter 2. Incorrect or minimal performance of any of those exercises can result in aches and pains and sometimes serious injury.

The correct execution of each exercise is the dancer's fundamental safeguard against injury. Proper execution includes alternating movements of extension and movements of release. For example, in a *battement tendu,* the foot is extended along the floor until the muscles of the arches are contracted and the toes pointed for the fully extended position. In this position, the ankle is stretched tight, and the calf muscles are contracted. In returning to the closed position, the toes relax, then the arches and as the ankle and muscles in the leg release and the entire foot is placed on the floor.

Whenever possible, the weight should be momentarily transferred to both feet in a closed position. If this brief relaxation is omitted, cramps may occur along the sides or arches of the feet; when the relaxation is systematically omitted, the muscles in the calf and thigh may cramp. Eventually, those muscles will become hard and bulky and will lack the essential elasticity for ballet.

The order of exercises at the barre also can prevent a muscle-bound look. Exercises are done to all directions; that is, *grands battements* done to the front, which contract the quadricep muscles of the thigh, are countered by *grands battements* to the back, which stretch those muscles. *Relevés,* which tighten the calf muscles, are followed by *demi-pliés,* which relieve that tension.

In beginning ballet classes, teachers usually find it more appropriate to convey the desired outcome of a movement than to analyze the elaborate patterning of the groups of muscles involved. They demonstrate and give a general description for the correct execution of a movement or pose, believing that ballet:

> Has its own technique of definite and exact movements. *If these movements are performed correctly, the correct muscles will work.* If the movement is not performed correctly, wrong muscles will come into play. . . . The dancer cannot begin by trying to find out which muscles to use. The right effort will eventually ensure right muscle work.[9]

More specific information can be provided and assimilated as students advance in their training. Many university-based dance programs include courses in kinesiology especially geared to an understanding of human movement as it relates to dance. Kinesiology courses incorporate the study of anatomy (structure of the body), physiology (function of the body), and sometimes biomechanics (principles and laws of mechanics, usually using quantitative data, as applied to the function of human movement). The practical benefits of kinesiology include improving movement efficiency and learning how to avoid injury.

## INJURIES AND AILMENTS

"If it hurts, it's good for you" is not good advice; pain may well be the body's warning to cease a certain activity. Following is a brief discussion of some injuries and ailments that can occur to dance students.

### Cramp

A sudden muscle cramp during class should be a vivid reminder to warm up properly, to drink adequate amounts of fluids, and to guard against the buildup of tensions during exercises (for instance, when possible, return the weight to both feet between movements that use one leg only). A cramp can be relieved by immediate gentle stretching of the cramped muscle, accompanied by massage. Soreness may result, but if the cramp is *fully* relieved before work is resumed, there will be no serious damage.

### Muscle Soreness or Stiffness

Sore or stiff muscles, fairly common complaints from students who are not used to practicing ballet exercises regularly, can be a kind of "sweet pain," seldom long-lasting or in any way debilitating. The best remedy is to increase circulation by stretching and exercising the muscle lightly again as soon as possible and by applying heat. Prevention of soreness, or its often-accompanying stiffness, includes sufficient warming up and gentle stretching, and then an adequate warming down, such as end-of-class *battements, pliés,* and *ports de bras* exercises (the dancer's equivalent of a racehorse's walking routine following the race).

## Muscle Strain

Dancers often display a stoical pride in ignoring or minimizing nagging pains that should alert them to the possibility of a serious injury. One such injury, called a strain, is a tearing of muscles and, in severe cases, tendons as well, usually occurring anywhere from the hips down. The common causes can be structural weakness, previous injury or severe illness, overuse, or incorrect execution of an exercise (sometimes the very first exercise at *barre*, the *plié*). A strain produces stiffness, tenderness, and pain. Swelling can occur too, but it can be minimized if the following procedures are observed:

1. **R**est      Immediately cease using the injured area.
2. **I**ce      Apply ice compresses for fifteen minutes to the injury and to an area well above and below it. Repeat every few hours for thirty-six to forty-eight hours.
3. **C**ompression      Between icings, apply pressure by snuggly wrapping the injured area with an elasticized bandage.
4. **E**levation      Elevate the injured area above the level of the heart.

This **R-I-C-E** procedure can be supplemented with anti-inflammatory medications such as ibuprofen. Moist heat can be applied after all possibility of swelling is gone, usually at least thirty-six hours after injury. Activity should be resumed slowly and after pain and swelling have disappeared.

## Ligament Sprain

A sprain is damage to ligaments of a joint and occurs most frequently in the ankle joint but can sometimes occur in hip or knee joints. A violent stretch or twist or fall can produce a sprain but so also can incorrect knee-to-foot alignment during jumps or overly zealous attempts to turn out the feet beyond the range permitted by the hip joint. The injured joint will be very painful and sometimes impossible to use. To achieve a speedy recovery, swelling must be controlled as quickly as possible. Immediate treatment should include the **R-I-C-E** procedure just described (rest, ice, compression, and elevation), then immobilization of the joint to avoid further tearing of ligament fibers. Any such taping or bandaging should be done by, or in consultation with, a specialist. Uninformed treatment can be injurious.

## Bone Dislocation and Fracture

The same preliminary treatment also applies to such other serious injuries as dislocations (a bone thrown out of joint) and fractures. Although it is relatively rare for a dancer to break a bone, it is relatively common for a dancer to have stress fractures. These tiny changes in a bone's structure usually occur in the feet or along the shin area and can be a result of dancing on a hard floor, overwork, inadequate rest, or faulty technique. Stress fractures usually heal themselves with several weeks of rest. Ignoring the problem and continuing the activity that caused the injury may transform a tiny crack into a complete fracture.

## Bruises

The most debilitating bruises for dancers are ones that occur on the ball of the foot or under the heel. Poorly executed exercises, such as *battements frappés* in which the foot is pounded rather than brushed against the floor, or incorrect landings from jumps can result in a bruise (contusion). Dancing on hard surfaces or just the intrinsic shape and structure of one's foot also can contribute to these injuries. The **R-I-C-E** procedure should be followed. Later, gentle stretching and application of moist heat may be applied.

## Shinsplints

The most common definition given of shinsplints is a minor tearing of the muscle attachments from the tibia (shinbone), resulting in soreness, pain, and swelling below the knee on the inner side of the front of the leg. Not only dancers but also anyone can get shinsplints if the arches of the feet are not supported properly by the muscles and ligaments in the feet, thus causing pronation of the feet when they are bearing weight. Landing incorrectly from jumps (heels off the floor and/or without a *demi-plié*) and dancing on a hard floor can lead to shinsplints.

Preventive tactics include careful prebarre warm-ups that emphasize gentle stretching of the calf muscles and foot flexors such as *demi-pliés* and *relevés* performed with turnout or in parallel position.

Another recommended exercise is the following:

> *Exercise 1*
> Press the heels to the floor, and, while keeping the legs and back straight, lean forward to take hold of a wall or the barre; remain in this position sixty seconds.

After class, a repetition of this exercise is advised, plus the following stretch:

> *Exercise 2*
> Stand on one leg and bend the other leg back at the knee, taking hold of that foot and keeping the knees near one another. Adequate space should remain between the heel and the buttock to protect the knee. Hold for sixty seconds; repeat with the other leg.

Stretching exercises to help prevent shinsplints.

Pain from shinsplints can be severe, and the usual treatments, though not always effective, are ice applications (to help reduce swelling) and then moist heat and rest. Occasionally, a half-inch-thick sponge rubber pad worn inside the heel of the shoe gives relief; arch supports or tape around the shins may be advisable in particular cases. Dancers subject to shinsplints should consult a physiotherapist for specific exercises to help strengthen the muscles involved. If pain and local tenderness persist, they may signal a stress fracture.

## Tendinitis

Tendinitis is an inflammation of a tendon, its connective tissue, or its sheath, the latter normally secreting a protective lubricant. If this lubricant is defective, then pain may result after repeated motions involving a given tendon. Overwork of the connecting muscle or a severe blow to a tendon may cause tendinitis, or the cause may be idiopathic—that is, unknown. Unfortunately, the Achilles tendon, connecting the back of the heel and the calf muscles, is particularly vulnerable to inflammation, especially for dancers who have a shallow *demi-plié*.

The first sign of tendinitis usually is a constricted, burning sensation that becomes more severe as the tendon cools following cessation of exercise. Swelling may accompany the pain, and the dancer will find it difficult to *relevé* or point the foot.

The most effective treatment is rest—a hard prescription for most dancers to follow—but if it is ignored, the tendon problem may continue much longer than necessary. Because the application of heat may provoke more pain, ice may be more satisfactory but so also may contrast baths of hot and cold water in some cases. Certainly, a physician should be consulted when pain and swelling are acute. Taping of the tendon by a specialist or heel lifts inserted in the shoes may be effective, along with rest.

## Knee Injuries

Persistent pain, redness, or swelling in the region of the knee are warning signs of a significant problem, perhaps a sprain, tear of the ligaments around the knee, or tendinitis. Other serious symptoms are a tendency for the knee to lock, to give way suddenly, or to be unable to straighten fully, any one of which may indicate a cartilage tear or the slipping of the patella. An orthopedic physician should be consulted immediately for accurate diagnosis and treatment.

Research has shown that women are more vulnerable to knee injuries and chronic knee pain than men. A number of factors may be involved, one of which is that women tend to have wider hips than men. This can cause the thigh bone (femur) to descend at a more inward angle, which, in turn, can distribute uneven weight on the knee joint. Vulnerability to stress on the knee ligaments and wear and tear on the cartilage may result.

The inherent alignment of the hip joint to the knee joint can't be changed, but much can be done to prevent injury, including practicing ballet exercises correctly and avoiding hazardous compromises. A knee is strongest when straight, therefore *rond de jambe à terre* practiced incorrectly with a relaxed knee invites stress to the surrounding ligaments. Closing to a tight fifth position *demi-plié* and then straightening the knees in that position can result in a twist to the knees, especially if true outward rotation is not occurring at the hip joint. "Sitting" in a *grand plié* or allowing the knees to fall inward when rising out of a *plié* also contributes to stresses on the knee joint.

## Back Ailments

Back pain most common to dancers is caused by muscle strain, accentuated by rotary or bending movements of the back. A female dancer may experience such strain in the lower back when incorrectly attempting a high *arabesque* by hollowing out the low lumbar area rather than distributing the extension throughout the spine. A male dancer may find he has pain higher in the back as a result of lifting his partner when the lift was made off balance without his center of gravity over his feet or when fatigued. Muscle spasm in the back may be a signal of such hazardous activity.

For back pain associated with muscle spasm, warm whirlpools or baths can be effective because of the antigravity effect of the water. Application of ice, massage, and gradual stretching may give relief. If strain has occurred, rest is the best remedy, followed by carefully selected back exercises. For chronic back pain, hot pads, hot showers, and saunas can be helpful, but they are not curative.

A ruptured disc can occur from incorrect bending or lifting. Here, the pain usually occurs quite low in the back, down the legs, or both, because the last two discs are the ones most commonly affected. Correct diagnosis between disc problems and muscle strain is sometimes difficult and requires considerable medical experience.

## Clicks, Snaps, and Pops

Painless clicks, snaps, or pops in the joints of the hips, knees, or ankles are often disturbing to students, who wonder whether they are doing something wrong. The answer, usually, is no; a click may merely indicate a bone rubbing against an unyielding tendon or ligament.

A snap or pop may be due to a thickened capsule around a joint; sometimes it may indicate the joint is poorly aligned. However, a painful click in the knee may signal cartilage damage. Any noisy joint that *hurts* should be checked by a physician.

## FOOT CARE

A dancer's foot must be strong as well as flexible, offering stability for balance as well as efficient propulsion for movement. And dancers want a foot that arches and points easily and beautifully! Individual variation in the shape and structure of the foot has an effect on how each dancer meets these goals. The foot's inherent (and inherited) shape must be respected during ballet training, but correct training can improve both appearance and function.

No part of the body must meet as many demands from ballet as the feet; therefore, it is important to attend to their care and to be alert to any problems that may occur.

### Daily Care of the Feet

Healthy feet must be clean. They should be thoroughly washed and carefully dried, especially between the toes. An absorbent foot powder should be used if the feet perspire. Tired feet can be revived by baths of contrasting temperatures—hot to cold to hot and so on. Long soaking should be avoided because it can cause cracks between the toes. Elevation of the feet can offer respite by reducing the amount of blood in the extremities.

### Foot Disorders

**Flat Feet**   The clinical flat foot is weak, has no arch, and will never serve a dancer. However, a flexible foot may appear to be flat when bearing weight but will show an arch when weight is removed. Such a foot must be disciplined not to roll when assuming ballet positions. This muscle conditioning sometimes produces discomfort along the inner border of the foot. It is not serious, but when it persists, a few days' rest is advised. When work is resumed, care must be taken to stay always within the correct range of turnout. Special muscle-strengthening exercises may be recommended, including many *battements tendus* to develop the set of short muscles on the underside of the foot.

**Bunions**   Different types of bunions can occur at stress points, usually at the base of the big toe but sometimes at the little toe. The body develops calcium deposits at the point of stress, where the toe shifts position, or both. The foot that has a tendency toward bunion formation (often determined by looking at the feet of parents or siblings) will, in all probability, develop one in intensive ballet training, although careful training often ensures correct functioning of the foot in spite of its abnormal appearance. Extreme care should be given to the selection of proper-fitting ballet shoes (see "Clothing" in Chapter 1) and sensible, well-fitting street shoes. Moist heat applied before class and ice afterward may alleviate some discomfort from an angered bunion, as may anti-inflammatory medication (nonprescription ibuprofen pain relievers).

## Minor Foot Ailments

Professional dancers assume great fortitude toward blisters, corns, and other occupational foot nuisances, which, of course, are encountered by many people who have never danced a step in their lives (ill-fitting hose or street shoes can be a source of trouble for any pair of feet).

Dance students usually exist on a very limited budget, spending most of what extra money they have on ballet lessons and ballet shoes. Professional treatment of foot problems is a luxury in which the student seldom indulges, unless and until a problem becomes acute. Some practical suggestions are offered here for the prevention and treatment of minor disorders that may occur.

**Blisters**   Caused by excessive friction on a given area, blisters are best prevented by protecting the skin, that is, minimally, by wearing ballet tights with feet (not ankle-length tights unless adequate socks are worn). Additional aids are gauze pads, moleskin, or adhesive bandages, placed on the vulnerable site before the blister appears. Tender feet can be toughened by regular applications of tincture of benzoin and pampered by systematic use of talcum powder rubbed around the toes.

A small blister need not be opened (thereby inviting the possibility of infection) but simply protected by a doughnut-shaped pad, the center of which can be filled with petroleum jelly. If a sizable blister occurs and interferes with daily activities, the area should be cleansed with an antiseptic and the blister carefully drained—opened with a sterile needle that has been boiled or held in a flame—but without removal of the blister cap. The wound then should be painted with iodine and covered with a sterile gauze pad. Blisters that have been unroofed—that is, the overlying skin removed, thus exposing a tender area—heal more slowly. They must be carefully treated with an antiseptic and covered with a sterile pad to avoid the greater possibility of infection.

**Corns and Calluses**   Corns and calluses are a thickening of the outer layer of the skin, the body's protective response to excessive pressure or friction on the feet.

Corns usually occur on the top of the foot, usually at the toe joint. The skin may slightly thicken or it may develop into a hard bump.

The prevention of corns is ultimately the elimination of the pressures that cause them (sometimes improper footwear). If the problem persists, the least that the victim can do is wear simple pads of moleskin, adhesive felt, or foam that are designed to disperse the pressure from the area. Horseshoe-shaped pads that do not cover the corn itself should be used in preference to circular ones, because the flesh eventually will work through the hole when the latter are used.

Sometimes, a soft corn can develop between the toes as a result of excessive pressure. Precautions include foam-rubber wedges or bunches of lamb's wool placed between the toes.

Calluses spread on the bottom of the foot or along the outer edges. A mild build-up of tissue can be reduced by a simple abrasive such as a callus file or pumice stone. Applying moleskin patches or soft pads may help to reduce the friction that causes the callus. Cracks or fissures in a callus can best be prevented by keeping the feet clean, by limiting the callus buildup, and by using a lubricant such as petroleum jelly or baby oil. If a callus spreads across the ball of the foot, it usually indicates a problem with the metatarsal bone and should be diagnosed by a physician specializing in podiatry.

**Toenail Problems**   Long toenails can cause trouble for dancers because of the snug fit of their ballet shoes. Therefore, most dancers keep their toenails cut very short. Proper nail trimming should conform to the contour of the toe but never down into the corner of the nail.

Ingrown nails, usually occuring at either edge of the big toe, may be caused by improper nail trimming, excessive pressure, injury, or an inherited tendency. Soaking the foot in warm water several times a day and placing a small amount of lamb's wool beneath the toenail edge can give some relief. An ingrown nail can become painful and lead to infection, so it is wise to have it checked by a podiatrist.

An abnormally thick nail can be caused by injury, pressure, or fungal infection. If the nail is not infected, it can be treated by trimming, filing, or grinding. Eventually, it may loosen and drop off. Surgical removal of part or all of the nail may be required if pain persists. Never try to remove a nail by yourself.

**Fungal Infection**   Fungal infection, the cause of athlete's foot, also can be the cause of foot problems such as thickened or ingrown nails. Oral or topical antifungal medications can help the fungus from spreading. Certain individuals apparently can have a tendency for fungal infection, and, once infected, the potential is always present. A doctor should be consulted if fungus is suspected.

**Warts**   Warts are caused by a viral infection that has invaded the body through small breaks or cuts in the skin. A common form, a plantar wart, occurs on the bottom of the foot and often grows in clusters but may appear elsewhere on the foot. Warts can be mistaken for corns or calluses, so it is wise to have them examined by a podiatrist or dermatologist.

The discomfort from a wart on a weight-bearing area of the foot can be a very real concern for a dancer. Depending on the size and location of the wart, a specialist may treat it with topical medication, with curettage (removal with a tiny, spoon-shaped instrument), or with laser treatment. Warts are contagious, so avoid going barefoot in studio dressing rooms or showers. Protection against infection includes keeping the feet clean and dry.

## EATING HABITS

Dancers are concerned with the importance of creating a certain image on stage, where lights and costumes have the effect of adding pounds to the body. Dance students rightly conclude that steps of elevation and pointe work are much easier to perform and are less stressful to the anatomy when the body does not carry excess weight. But in their zeal to stay thinner than would seem necessary by most ordinary standards, dancers and dance students sometimes ignore the fact that their bodies were designed for purposes other than dancing. And they often ignore the fact that each body is different, requiring an individualized approach to weight management. The demands and expectations made of each dancer's body require necessary nutrients every day to produce good health, consistent energy, and a sense of well-being.

### Diet

Diet, to the dancer, should mean a habitual way of eating so that the body maintains itself with maximum energy and efficiency. An overweight or underweight condition deserves the attention of a professional who can prescribe a particular, corrective diet based on many factors, including height, sex, age, metabolic rate, and bone structure.

No dancer or dance student should attempt a self-prescribed crash diet (which often leaves one tense, tired, and prone to illness and injury) or rely on tricky diet pills to control appetite artificially (weight thus lost usually is regained as soon as the pills are stopped). Fad diets, although frequently the subject of dressing-room conversations ("I eat *nothing* but yogurt and celery"), are not the answer either, because no single food contains anywhere near the fifty essential nutrients required for a healthy body.

### Eating Disorders

Eating disorders are serious issues of great complexity. Two types of eating disorders sometimes associated with a dancer's obsession with thinness are anorexia nervosa, a type of self-starvation, and bulimia, characterized by eating great quantities of food followed by laxative abuse, self-induced vomiting, or both. A variety of causes are now recognized as possible contributing factors to these eating disorders—psychological problems and environmental pressures as well as genetic and cultural background. Psychological therapy and, more recently, drug therapy are used to treat these disorders. It is important to remember that:

> [A]ny dancer suspected of having an eating disorder should be approached with concern and caution, with the understanding that you are dealing with a potentially volatile situation. . . . If you find you must confront someone because of a probable eating disorder, it is best to consult an eating disorders professional beforehand on how to approach the situation. Despite good intentions, confrontations can do more harm than good if handled improperly.[10]

Psychological counseling services at a university, medical clinic, or hospital can be consulted for advice.

## Proper Nutrition

A person subject to listlessness, frequent illness, and a generally low energy level may be suffering from poor nutrition. Just consuming a certain number of calories every day is no guarantee of good nutrition. Calories are the measure of energy released by the food a person eats, and the amount differs according to the kind of food. But any food should also provide a variety of substances—nutrients that are essential for the building, upkeep, and repair of tissues and for the efficient functioning of the body. According to their use, nutrients are classified as proteins (for body maintenance and growth), carbohydrates (for the most efficient energy fuel), fats (for some energy fuel and essential vitamins and fatty acids), and specific vitamins and minerals (for transformation of energy and regulation of metabolic functions).

Like other people who participate in active physical effort, dancers can observe a very direct connection between what is ingested into their bodies and their performing condition. Of particular importance is the maintaining and replenishing of body fluids:

> Drinking adequate fluid is essential for top performance. Body fluids have important jobs: fluid in the blood transports glucose to the working muscles and carries away lactic acid; urine eliminates waste products; sweat dissipates heat via the skin. If you lose too much sweat, and don't replace your fluids, you reduce your ability to provide adequate circulation to muscles, internal organs, and body surface. This not only hurts performance but can also endanger health.[11]

Besides water, fluid intake should include juices such as orange juice and drinks such as lemonade. Remember that beverages containing alcohol (beer, wine) or caffeine (coffee, tea) cause increased urination and thus can have a dehydrating effect.

Smoking is especially harmful for dancers because it is directly linked to cardiovascular disease (disease of the heart and blood vessels), lung cancer, and bone-density loss. A dancer must have a healthy heart, strong lungs, and firm bones; therefore, a dancer must be a nonsmoker.

The optimum daily amount of vitamins and minerals is often revised by health officials as new research brings new evidence to bear. In addition, individuals have differing needs, so a prescription that is appropriate for one person may not be at all appropriate for another.

It is thought that women may need additional iron in their diet because of the loss of blood during menstruation. But it should be remembered that vitamins and minerals occur naturally in foods and that vitamin and mineral supplements are no substitute for natural food. A well-balanced, nutritious diet is essential, and it may be totally adequate for the body's vitamin and mineral needs. Best results come from eating grains, beans, fish, and fresh fruits and vegetables.

Recent diet research places greater emphasis on the energy-producing qualities of carbohydrates than on the more traditional protein sources. Thus, a preperformance meal of pasta with fresh vegetables and fruit is more beneficial than one of steak.

Dancers and dance students often are forced into unusual eating schedules. Ideally, their preclass or preperformance meal should be eaten three hours before the activity to allow time for digestion and absorption of food. Because this timing is not always possible, several light meals a day (eaten one to one-and-a-half hours before the dance event) may be preferable.

## Food for Thought

Dancing doesn't demand a perfect body; you can dance well if you have "a feeling for movement and music, a sense of rhythm and good coordination."[12] As an adult, you are still growing; muscle size and bone strength increase as you exercise and will continue to do so. The image of the thin, frail-looking dancer of the 1960s and 1970s has changed; dancers now are larger, healthier, and more individual looking. Individual expression is important; the goal of dance training is the discovery and development of your individual quality and capacity for movement. As an adult, your age and experience, your sense of self and body awareness, can contribute to the mind–body adventure of beginning ballet study.

### NOTES

1. Albert E. Kahn, *Days with Ulanova* (New York: Simon & Schuster, 1962), 4, 8.
2. Richard Philip, "Ideals," *Dance Magazine,* September 1998, 7.
3. Thomas D. Fahey, Paul M. Insel, and Walton T. Roth, *Fit and Well: Core Concepts and Labs in Physical Fitness and Wellness,* 3d ed. (Mountain View, Calif. Mayfield Publishing, 1999), 23.
4. Ibid., 24.

5. Fahey et al. (160) classify ballet (meaning here, center-floor combinations) as high in developing flexibility and muscular endurance but only moderate in developing cardiorespiratory endurance, muscular strength, and body composition.

6. Gigi Berardi, *Finding Balance: Fitness and Training for a Lifetime in Dance* (Princeton, N.J.: Dance Horizons/Princeton Book, 1991), 97.

7. Sally Sevey Fitt, *Dance Kinesiology,* 2d ed. (Schirmer Books, 1996), 304.

8. Susan McLaw, "The Pilates Method of Body Conditioning," in *Dance Kinesiology,* 2d ed. (Schirmer Books, 1996), 315–16.

9. Celia Sparger, *Anatomy and Ballet* (London: Adam & Charles Black, 1982), 10.

10. Robin D. Chmelar and Sally S. Fitt, *Diet: A Complete Guide to Nutrition and Weight Control* (Princeton, N.J.: Princeton Book, 1990), 111.

11. Nancy Clark, "Nutrition, Fluids, Dehydration, and Thirst Quenchers," *Dance Teacher Now,* September 1991, 19.

12. Ellen Jacob, *Dancing: A Guide for the Dancer You Can Be* (Reading, Mass: Addison-Wesley, 1981), 39.

# The Ballet Profession

In this chapter, you will learn about the broad range of ballet-related careers, including:

- The world of professional ballet
- Nonprofessional performing opportunities
- Teaching careers in public and private institutions
- Uses of dance film, video, and computer technology
- Literary pursuits in dance history, research, and criticism
- Scientific fields of dance therapy and medicine
- Business and production areas

The world of ballet encompasses many fields of interest in addition to the obvious ones of teaching ballet technique and creating and performing dances. Many of those other ballet-related fields are viable career opportunities for an adult beginning ballet student, whereas a career as a ballet teacher, choreographer, or professional dancer is probably an unrealistic goal.

A college freshman who begins the study of ballet must realize that at a comparable age most students who aspire to a career in professional ballet are already accomplished technicians, having had seven or eight years of training, and many are already employed by a professional company. Adults who begin ballet training in their early thirties must understand that many professional dancers consider retiring from the stage by age forty. What sort of life do these artists live, whose careers begin and end so early?

As a student of ballet, it is important to have some background information and understanding about the world of professional ballet. Therefore, this chapter begins with a glimpse into that world and then will introduce other ballet-related vocations.

# PROFESSIONAL PREPARATION

As a rule, by age seventeen or eighteen a student with aspirations for a professional career in ballet will have reached an advanced level of ballet technique and, immediately after graduation from high school, will enter a professional ballet school, if not there already. Students benefit from having their talents appraised by people in the profession and from seeing themselves in close comparison with the products of the professional schools. By taking classes from a school associated with a company, students know when company replacements are needed, when auditions are scheduled, and when the school faculty thinks they are ready to take the audition.

There are other routes. A student can write to a company to request an audition, or sometimes auditions can be arranged when a company visits a city while on tour. Members of a touring company may spot a talent in a local studio; many companies conduct regular summer workshops that can serve as showcases for aspiring performers. Some students may instead elect to enter a university that offers a major in ballet and performing opportunities in campus-based or local companies.

An aspiring performer is advised to have an up-to-date résumé consisting of basic personal information and a succinct one-page summary of dance training and performing experience as well as any scholarships and awards. A videotape of class work, performance, or both should be prepared, if possible.

But the surest way into the more prestigious professional ballet companies is through the professional school associated with a given company. Companies like to mold their dancers into a common style and groom their soloists for the many roles in the repertory. Therefore, they give preference to a talented eighteen-year-old who can be enrolled in their professional school rather than to an equally talented twenty-two-year-old who has already finished training elsewhere. Many companies, such as the National Ballet of Canada and the New York City Ballet, oversee the entire preparatory period, from beginning children's classes to preprofessional ones. Graduation performances often are exciting concerts that are reviewed by critics; at this time, some lucky graduates receive an invitation to join the resident company.

Because the performing years are short, the ballet business must be entered early. Twenty years of dancing is considered a reasonable period for peak performance, even though stars may continue to enchant audiences well beyond that limit, as did Margot Fonteyn, Galina Ulanova, Alicia Alonso, and Rudolf Nureyev. Even so, statistics have shown that most company dancers are under age thirty.

A traditional gateway to membership in a company has been by audition, the format being a "regular" ballet class. Any audition requires patience— patience to wait one's turn, trying to keep muscles warm and enthusiasm at a high pitch while others are being judged; patience to stand for interminable minutes in a line next to other eager bodies, all the while being critically surveyed and evaluated according to the immediate, undisclosed needs of the company; patience to wait for another audition or possible openings in the company later on if a first audition is unsuccessful.

An audition requires a certain protocol. Mamas, teachers, and friends should be left at home. Stage makeup should not be worn; an audition is not a performance. Applicants should be dressed neatly and simply, as for a ballet class. They should come to the audition fully warmed up, able to dance the first combinations as well as possible, for there may never be a chance for later ones. The applicant should do exactly what the choreographer asks without adding personal variations. Following precise instructions quickly is a requisite for the professional theater. It is a good idea to be prepared to perform a short solo or variation.

Nervousness is to be expected. But a body that has been well trained will not be destroyed by butterflies in the stomach. The carriage of the arms, the shape of the legs, the flexibility of the spine, the arch of the foot will remain, even if accompanied by a tense face or wobbly balance. The judges are professionals, but they, too, once had to audition for a first time, and they can recognize talent, training, and performing potential beneath a nervous skin.

Unfortunately, talent, good training, a reasonably attractive face, and a well-proportioned body are not guarantees of success at an audition. The supply of dancers with those qualities usually is much greater than the availability of positions in professional ballet companies. Dancers often attribute their success (or more usually their lack of success) to politics (whom one knows) and luck (being in the right place at the right time).

## JOINING A COMPANY

The dancer who is successful at an audition will enter a relatively small, intimate community. Most American ballet companies have fewer than thirty dancers, and some "chamber" ballet companies have only six to ten dancers, even though the "big two," American Ballet Theatre and New York City Ballet, have close to 100 on their rosters. A company is headed by an artistic director—usually a choreographer, perhaps the chief one of the troupe—who, in consultation with the business administration of the company, makes all final decisions—repertory, promotions, hiring, firing. The company may have associate or assistant directors. There will be a ballet master or mistress whose duties include rehearsing ballets and giving classes to company dancers.

The new member of the company will begin a daily regimen that, by most ordinary work standards, is strangely cloistered and far removed from the "real" world. Each day begins with class, a period of hard physical work. Every dancer, no matter how experienced, must do daily *pliés, battements,* and *ronds de jambe.* It is a humbling experience, for without the taxing daily exercises, no dancer's body will retain the strength and precision necessary for ballet performance, nor will technique improve.

## BALLET REHEARSAL

The class systematically warms up the dancer's body for the rehearsal period, which often follows directly. A dancer may spend two to five hours daily in rehearsals (sometimes more, for which overtime compensation is generally paid), and these rehearsals may be called with little prior warning; dancers regulate their lives by notices on the rehearsal bulletin board.

At a rehearsal for a new ballet, the choreographer is in charge and is given the power to cast and compose the ballet of his or her choice. These decisions must, of course, meet with the approval of the company director, but choreographers are entrusted with a great deal of power. How does one compose a dance? Ask a choreographer, and receive a very personal answer; one method may work for one choreographer and quite another method for the next. Even the same choreographer may use different strategies with different ballets or dancers. The music for the ballet or the idea of the ballet may have whirred around in the choreographer's head for weeks, months, or years, but a first rehearsal sometimes produces only the most tenuous promise of what will develop. Some choreographers arrive at a rehearsal with notepads full of explicit details for gestures, movements, and floor patterns; others prefer to experiment there, letting chance happenings or even accidents suggest movement possibilities. All must respond to the particular qualities of the dancers assembled for their ballet. Even if the choreographic process appears random, it usually is following the broad, basic structure of the dance, because it has been viewed time and time again in the mind of the choreographer.

Almost without exception, choreographers for professional ballet companies are former dancers themselves, and most of them therefore learned the craft of choreography by apprenticeship, watching a master choreographer at work while they participated as dancers in the creation of a new ballet. This background enables choreographers to draw on a large movement vocabulary, which they then are able to demonstrate. One choreographer may expect the cast to imitate movements exactly; another may merely indicate the desired movement in the barest outline, preferring to see how the dancers continue and fulfill the movement. A rehearsal can be an exciting creative experience for all concerned.

Once the details are worked out for each dance sequence, they are practiced over and over again. Some choreographers never change a single step once it has been set, but others redo, throw out, and start again. During rehearsals for a new ballet, a dancer learns to keep several versions of one sequence in memory—a prodigious task, because the same dancer will have roles to remember, rehearse, and perform in many other ballets. Beginning students are wise to cultivate dance "memory" as they are learning dance technique: try to reconstruct an entire class by memory; practice doing this every day while the experience of dancing is still fresh. Eventually a dancer's muscles provide a memory storehouse; the muscles seem to respond without conscious mental effort.

Human memory, the oral tradition, and danced demonstration have been the methods by which choreography from a previous generation, or from a preceding season, is passed along to the dancers of the next. But today, more and more use is being made of videotape and dance notation to record choreography. (See "Recording Dance" later in this chapter.) A videotape library of a company's repertory is vital to speeding up the rehearsal process. A dancer new to a part may be shown a videotape of a given ballet and told to learn a particular role before attending a next rehearsal. Ultimately, a skilled dance notator is a valuable asset for the preservation and transmission of a company's repertory in a more detailed form than that provided by videotape or film.

Another valuable member of any ballet company is the rehearsal pianist, who may sit for hours replaying the same short passage of music until a choreographic problem has been solved and the sequence learned by the dancers. When a reliable pianist is not available, a choreographer may rehearse with a tape recorder. Or, if music is being composed especially for the ballet, the dancers may hear only counts at rehearsal. Because of ever-increasing production and rehearsal costs, a complete orchestral score may not be heard before the first stage rehearsal.

In all cases, counting of the musical bars or phrases is done in great detail by dancers and choreographers alike; very, very seldom is any movement improvised on the ballet stage. Even large crowd scenes in some of the classical ballets are planned down to minute details of who goes where and when and how. Stage rehearsals are tedious but necessary parts of the dancer's life. Before the initial performance of any ballet, it must be seen on stage, costumes must be danced in, lighting plans must be tried, and the orchestra must be rehearsed with the dancers.

Companies that tour extensively, usually the smaller companies, learn to adapt to all kinds of theater conditions. They are likely to find a differently proportioned stage at every stop—wide and shallow, narrow and deep, square, semicircular—and theaters with skimpy wings making leaping exits hazardous at best. New stages call for adjustments, and sometimes particular movements will need to be modified or changed, but these revisions are worked out before performance, not during it.

A dancer's sense of space becomes finely tuned. Relationships to other dancers must be kept, and distances from the sides or front or back of the stage must be preserved. This sense of space is not accomplished with a yardstick or the counting of floorboards, although visual aids can include such visible features as marks taped to the stage floor and an auditorium's lighted exit signs, aisles, or openings into the wings. But through their training in ballet classes and their experience during rehearsals, dancers learn to relate quickly to distances and to remember spatial patterns.

Occasionally, a company on tour will arrive at a new theater with insufficient time to rehearse the evening's performance fully. The best they can do is to "block" the dances on the new stage; the dancers walk through their parts and, by means of a kind of elaborate hand and finger sign language, indicate the steps that later will be performed in those spots.

## BALLET PERFORMANCE

Backstage, the stage manager, or the *regisseur,* tries to oversee the preperformance activity that, to a visitor, may resemble chaos. Stagehands lug equipment, scenery, and props. Lighting technicians preside over a maze of wires and towers (light "trees"). Wardrobe ladies, mouths full of pins, may be making last-minute alterations. Each person does his or her specific job; union regulations forbid the overlapping of backstage tasks. Amid the dust and drafts and commotion, the dancers, bundled in layers of warm-up attire, go through barre exercises, holding onto any wall or chair or ladder available.

Where is the magic that will soon be seen on stage? It is slowly forming in the minds and muscles of the dancers. The ritual of warming up is one of several that prepare the dancers for performance and preoccupy the nerves. Makeup is another. Dancers cover their everyday faces with carefully applied stage makeup more elaborate than that used by other stage artists, because it must stand up under the rigors of fast movement, varied lighting, and profuse perspiration.

For women there is another ritual—that of preparing pointe shoes. Each dancer personally sews on the ribbons of her shoes and breaks in each pair according to her own method—ranging from simply walking around in the shoes, to soaking them in water, to slamming a door on them (when off the feet, of course). The "box" of the shoe is in reality only several layers of cloth held together by a strong glue. The rest of the support comes from a leather sole and shank. Pointe shoes break in easily, and their life is short. A ballerina may use a new pair of shoes for each act of a ballet; a member of the *corps de ballet* may have to make do with only one new pair a week. Fortunately, shoes are provided by most companies, and they are handmade by skilled artisans who build each pair of shoes according to a mold of each individual dancer's foot.

As curtain time approaches, the dancers help zip or hook each other into their costumes. Hairdos are given a final layer of spray. Toe-shoe ribbons are checked for the twentieth time (a loose ribbon is a dancer's nightmare). *Demi-pliés* and *battements tendus* keep pace with the flutter in the stomach. Nervousness can attack the dance novice and dance veteran alike, but most, probably all, pride themselves on being troupers. They know that their nerves are bringing their bodies to the high pitch necessary for performance.

## LOOKING AT THE BALLET

What does the audience see as the curtain opens? The merely interested but ballet-uneducated public will immediately see movement with a capital *M*, for that is the prime of ballet. They will see living sculpture created by a lifted leg and an outstretched arm—and the spaces framed by those limbs that become important designs in themselves. Members of an audience may not know whether a movement is done correctly, but they can sense its quality. Fellow humans are dancing, often expressing human feelings in dramatic situations, and the emotions and muscles of the audience have an empathic response. Costumes and stage designs help set the appropriate scene; lighting underscores the appropriate mood. Above all, the music is linked to the spectacle on the stage. Some, or all, of these elements are employed—even in a so-called abstract ballet—to carry the audience along a choreographer's intended path.

Among the members of the audience are the dance critics, who usually have the advantage of having seen a great many ballet performances, thereby gaining some yardstick with which to assess one ballet evening or one ballet trend with another. They know that the repertory of most companies typically represents three or four types of ballets: revivals of, or excerpts from, nineteenth-century European or Russian story-ballets (such as *Giselle* or *Swan Lake*); early-twentieth-century one-act ballets from various Ballets Russes companies (such as *Les Sylphides* or *Gaité Parisienne*); works by leading choreographers of the mid-twentieth century (such as *Serenade* or *Theme and Variations* by George Balanchine); and contemporary ballets that may have been composed by the director of a given company. An acquaintance with ballet history (see Chapter 7) is essential for an informed opinion from a critic or a patron of the ballet.

Reviewing the New York dance scene, critic Marcia B. Siegel observes:

> Seeing is a very selective, individual and concrete process, and it means more to me than opinion. . . . Each separate dance experience carries its own unique and momentary life, but to consider *only* that singular evening's lifetime, it seems to me, is to deny evolution, to deny civilization.[1]

A dancer can inevitably and almost instantly sense an audience's approval or disapproval, its involvement or its boredom. Audience reactions can change during the course of an evening, and it is the performer's particular pleasure to change indifference to enthusiasm. An audience's support, with appropriate laughter or hushness, is intoxicating to the performer, who may receive the final tribute of applause in a state of outward calm but inward jubilation.

## AFTER THE SHOW

Coming down from the high emotional pitch of a performance is not easy. A dancer may long to repeat the whole show immediately. The body is warm and loose, the nerves are calm, the unknown has been faced and conquered. Now, one could really perform! No thrill, physical or spiritual, could compare with those moments of power onstage—pity the person who is not a dancer!

Backstage, chatter is almost exclusively about the performance that has just ended—what did or did not go well. The dancers, unwilling to let go of the magic they have created, must nevertheless get back to reality. Costumes must be hung, faces must be cleansed of all makeup, bags must be packed.

The dancer's body, which has just spent several hours fluctuating between near exhaustion and instant recovery, cries out for food and fluids. The dancers head for home or to a late-night restaurant or to a reception that a local organization may have prepared in their honor. Deprived of stage makeup and colored lights, the dancers look appallingly pale and much smaller than they did on stage. But these people are athletes, even though they are trained to conceal all effort, and when the night's work is finished, they need to replenish their bodies with nutritious food.

Dancers realize that they live in a separate world. They grew up in ballet classrooms; they were socialized in studio dressing rooms and rehearsal halls. As professionals, their six-day-a-week schedule permits them little time for interests or friends outside the dance profession; it even permits them little sunshine. They are like hardy indoor houseplants who thrive under artificial lights—of the theater.

Reflecting on the dancer's commitment, Robert Weiss, a principal dancer with New York City Ballet, said:

> It's a very funny profession. . . . You get into it at such a young age. . . . It's not only a profession, it's a way of life. . . . Despite all the problems, mental and physical, the company politics and all that stuff, there's a reward in dancing that's indescribable. It's just different from any of the other performing arts—the mental and physical coming together. And when everything is right—two or three times a year, maybe—well . . . there's no other feeling like it, and you remember that, and you'll do almost anything to feel that again.[2]

Onstage, dancers are magicians; offstage, they tend to be supremely disciplined, practical, punctual people. The "fairy princess and prince charming" leave the theater, returning home (or back to hotel rooms) to do the inevitable evening laundry of sweaty leotards and tights. They look forward to such simple luxuries as a hot bath and a night's sleep as few others can appreciate. Is this a "real" life? What of the future? Next year or the next? The tired dancers focus on tomorrow. There is class to take at ten-thirty in the morning.

## NONPROFESSIONAL CIVIC AND REGIONAL COMPANIES

The traditional route to the professional ballet stage just described is not realistic for the adult beginner, but performing opportunities sometimes exist in nonprofessional companies throughout the United States. Certain repertories may call for more mature dancers who may not necessarily need advanced levels of technique. The annual holiday performances of *The Nutcracker* ballet, a significant percentage of any ballet company's annual revenue, offer roles for dancers of many levels of technique.

Serious amateur dancers have benefited from the establishment of civic ballet companies, a movement begun in 1941 by Dorothy Alexander in Atlanta, and, gradually, local ballet companies began to work together to sponsor performances and dance festivals. In 1963, the National Association for Regional Ballet (NARB) was established, also with inspiration from Alexander, to promote high performing and teaching standards through mutual communication, sharing of membership resources, and annual regional performance festivals.

By 1981, NARB had a membership of 100 companies. A few years later, it was reorganized as Regional Dance America (RDA) and continued its work and even expanded to include a choreographic training program and the first national festival, which was held in Houston in 1997.

A few regional companies, such as the Atlanta Ballet, have attained professional status; that is, they have met federal guidelines for minimum wages for at least thirty weeks a year as well as maintained annual budgets of a certain amount. Many other professional companies have dancers who grew up in the regional ballet movement. And ballet training is one of the usual requirements for performers in most modern dance companies and musical-theater productions.

## OTHER BALLET-RELATED CAREERS

The increasing popularity of dance in general, since the "dance boom" of the 1970s and 1980s, has created the need for knowledgeable experts in numerous

College dance degree programs prepare students for a variety of dance careers. Pictured here in 1989, in *Leap* 912, a modern ballet by Sandra Noll Hammond, are University of Hawaii students Jaye Knutson, Chris D. C. Ramos, and Cornelius Carter. Today, Ramos performs and choreographs in New York City; Knutson and Carter are members of university dance faculties.

ballet-related fields, now located in many parts of the country besides the large dance centers of the east and west coasts. The following pages offer information on some of those opportunities.

## Teaching and Choreography

Teaching and choreographing are two traditional nonperforming careers. Both require an intensive dance background but not necessarily a professional performing one. University and college dance curricula vary, but most offer courses in choreography ("composition classes"), creative movement for children, and teacher training ("methods or pedagogy classes"). Teacher training courses usually are geared toward public school teaching (dance has enjoyed a significant increase in elementary and secondary schools) and college programs (where a master's degree is routinely expected for a faculty appointment, especially in lieu of professional dance experience).

Career preparation for private studio teaching has been haphazard in the United States, because there are no certification or licensing requirements. Yet the challenges of running a commercial studio, whose roster may reflect preschoolers to senior citizens, call for a careful program of study:

> Whether offered by a university, a conservatory, or a professional studio, such a program should require studies in a variety of dance techniques with special emphasis on teaching beginners and preschool creative movement. It should require instruction in preparing course outlines spanning a greater number of development years than most public school or university teachers face when dealing with the progress of a single student. Curriculum planning would need to identify long-range goals as well as detail the construction of daily, monthly, and yearly class plans, which allow for physically sound and emotionally satisfying progression in technique and also some initial experience in composition for the student. Selection of accompaniment, improvisation, creating combinations and studies for different levels to achieve specific technique goals, educational theory and instructional methods, child development, psychology, anatomy or physiology, choreography, production, studio organization, administration, promotion, business practices, and financial management should all be a part of the studio teacher's preparation. A little advice on dealing with stage mothers and some basic professional ethics would not be amiss.[3]

Ballet teachers in higher education have an organization, CORPS de Ballet International, which promotes ballet excellence in college dance curricula and fosters interchange between the professional and the academic dance worlds.

## Recording Dance

Recording dance, either by special notation or by videotape and film, is an expanding field that offers great benefits to both the dance world and the community at large. Its purposes are:

To preserve masterworks for future generations; to increase the availability of the work beyond its immediate performance; to provide accurate tools for stylistic and structural analysis by the historian, critic, and researcher . . . ; to furnish students and choreographers with material for study. Anthropologists, ethnologists, and sociologists look at recorded movement for clues to the work habits and folk dances of other cultures.[4]

And, as discussed earlier in this chapter, it can facilitate the dance-rehearsal process.

Skilled technicians, sensitive to the special requirements of the dance, are needed for preserving dance on film, or most especially on videotape, as well as for compiling tapes for instructional use. Thus, today the field of videography is a promising area for the dance specialist.

As a method of accurately recording dance for purposes of analysis and reconstruction, however, film or tape usually must be augmented by notation. Many notational methods have been tried since the fifteenth century. Today, the two notation systems most used are Labanotation (developed by Rudolf Laban and first published in 1928) and the Benesh method, also known as Choreology (developed in England in the 1950s).

A number of college dance programs offer courses in notation. Special training programs frequently are offered by the Dance Notation Bureau in New York City, which also secures work for many notators (those who write down movement in a notation system) and reconstructors (those who restage a notated dance). The use of computerized equipment and new software for notation make this an exciting, innovative field. Relatively recent national organizations dedicated to "assuring dance a life beyond performance" include Preserve Inc., SAVE AS:DANCE, and the National Initiative to Preserve America's Dance (NIPAD).

## Computer Technology

The expanding world of computer technology has opened up other fields for a dance specialist with computer expertise. Some of the uses of computer technology in dance include:

Notation, choreography, CD-ROMs, course structuring, videoconferencing, digital artifacts and databases, motion sensing, motion capture, distance learning, autonomous agents, robotics, avatars, web dances, Internet performance, collaborative projects, marketing, advertising, and interactive environments, both real and virtual.[5]

## History, Research, and Criticism

Developments in the uses of computer technology have given impetus to the field of dance history, an endeavor that combines research, writing, and performance with knowledge of music, art, theater, social customs, and dance. A Renaissance or Baroque dance scholar is called on to teach at early-music workshops and festivals; to lecture at events sponsored by art museums and libraries; and to reconstruct historical dances (or choreograph in a historical style) for theater companies and for college departments of dance, music, or drama. A specialist in nineteenth-century social dance, such as dance-historian Elizabeth Aldrich, often is hired to stage dance scenes in period films.

Ballet companies interested in reviving long-lost works have employed dance researchers and reconstructors to restore important dances to today's stages. For example, the Joffrey Ballet added to its repertory the 1847 *pas de six* from *La Vivandière,* choreographed (after Antonio Guerra) by Arthur Saint-Léon and reconstructed by Ann Hutchinson Guest from Saint-Léon's own notation system. Such activity has helped establish respect for dance scholarship within the professional dance world.

Educational academies have encouraged reconstruction projects, such as the 1991 performance at the Juilliard School of Vaslav Nijinsky's 1912 ballet, *L'Après-Midi d'un Faune.* Students were given Labanotation transcriptions of Nijinsky's own notated score, from which they read their own part in preparation for rehearsals.

Training of dance writers, researchers, and critics is beginning to be found on more college campuses. The establishment in 1982 of the first U.S. graduate program in dance history and theory (at the Riverside campus of the University of California) is but one example. Certain dance courses, such as dance history and dance ethnology, are accepted as arts and humanities options for general college requirements. The Congress on Research in Dance, the Dance Critics Association, and the Society of Dance History Scholars help promote dance as an area for research, as do similar organizations in Great Britain and continental Europe.

Dance scholars must have access to libraries. Of particular value are the dance holdings at the Harvard Theatre Collection; the San Francisco Performing Arts Library and Museum; the National Museum of Dance in Saratoga Springs, New York; and the Library of Congress in Washington, DC. Most impressive of all is the Dance Collection of the New York Public Library, located in the Performing Arts Research Center at Lincoln Center in New York City. Vital to these institutions are their knowledgeable dance librarians, who sometimes are people with prior experience as dance students and performers.

The catalogues of many library collections now can be accessed on the Internet and most have websites. Several of those institutions with significant dance holdings have formed an alliance, the Dance Heritage Coalition, to enhance their accessibility to scholars. (For listings of some websites, see "Selected Reading and Viewing.")

Dance criticism in local and international newspapers and periodicals, once the part-time work of writers from other professions (music, theater, sports), now is produced by a number of writers whose background includes training in dance. One such critic is Octavio Roca of the *San Francisco*

Jaye Knutson, Kathryn White, and Laurie Lowry, while students in various master's degree dance programs at the University of Hawaii, performed *Entrées pour les princesses,* a suite of dances reconstructed and staged by Sandra Noll Hammond from the 1829–1830 notebooks of dancing master Michel St. Léon—a project that combined history, research, notation, and training in early-nineteenth-century ballet technique.

*Chronicle,* who studied at the Academia de Ballet Alicia Alonso before earning degrees in philosophy at Emory and Georgetown Universities. In distinguishing the work of a dance critic from other types of dance writing, Roca said:

> Talk of whether or not a dance is socially relevant or politically useful is all very nice, but the real question is whether a dance is good or bad.
>
> Being able to tell the difference, dance by dance, is a critic's responsibility. And that means separating competence from incompetence, acting from acting out, professional polish from mere good intentions, art from dross or worse.
>
> Finding a common bond between your [audience] experience and mine [critic] makes criticism possible. It is also what makes it an immensely satisfying calling.[6]

Alyssa Darrow trained in ballet at the Marin Dance Theatre in San Rafael, California. She graduated with a BFA in Dance from California State University, Long Beach. Now a member of the California Ballet in San Diego, she also is beginning the certification program to become a trainer in Pilates Technique.

## Dance Therapy and Medicine

Among areas of growth in the field of dance-related activities are dance therapy and dance medicine, little-known professions prior to the 1940s even though dance and healing have been associated since ancient times. The American Dance Therapy Association (ADTA), founded in 1966, defines dance therapy as the therapeutic use of movement to further the emotional and physical integration of a person. Those who may benefit are "individuals who require special services because of behavioral, learning, perceptual, and/or physical disorders; and rehabilitation of emotionally disturbed, physically handicapped, neurologically impaired, and the socially deprived of all ages, in groups and individually."[7] Both graduate and undergraduate degree programs in dance therapy allow academic specialization in this field, with workshops and special courses offering additional preparation. The ADTA has annual conferences, as well as regional seminars and workshops, and publishes the *American Journal of Dance Therapy.*

Dance medicine, a term that first appeared in 1979 at an international medical symposium, encompasses the attention and care given to dancers by medical physicians, some of whom are hired by professional dance companies to treat and rehabilitate dancers after injury. For example, the Cincinnati Ballet is associated with a performing-arts medicine program that offers a range of services in general conditioning, injury prevention, and rehabilitation.

Dance medicine now has a growing body of literature—research publications, textbooks, and, since 1997, its own scientific journal, the *Journal of Dance Medicine and Science,* which is the official publication of the International Association for Dance Medicine and Science. Through scientific research, testing, and publication, the field of dance medicine has increased our understanding of basic ballet principles—for example, the order and repetition of barre exercises.

Many people who have studied dance have gone on to train as specialists in various conditioning methods, such as yoga or Pilates Method, and in somatic approaches, such as Alexander Technique or Bartenieff Fundamentals. (See Chapter 5.)

## Administration, Management, and Marketing

Arts administration, management, and marketing are areas of increasing need and diversity as companies, festivals, and programs seek funding and bookings, coordinate arts events and publicity, and deal with legal and budgetary matters. Training programs in arts management and administration include workshops as well as degree programs at universities, but many posts, because of their varied requirements, require on-the-job training.[8]

Marketing, or how to "sell" ballet, may be the key to finding new ways to win new audiences and to energize those already dedicated to the art. In times of economic downturn or uncertainty, there is ever-greater need for new and creative ways to showcase the performing arts. These challenges require personnel who understand a particular locality and its dance organizations. As Clive Barnes, a senior dance critic and consulting editor for *Dance Magazine* said, "All marketing is local."[9]

## Production

Obvious performance-related fields include such vital areas as stage and theater design; costuming and lighting; and music accompanying, composing, arranging, and conducting. The skilled technical director or stage manager, who can oversee these diverse aspects of production, is highly prized.

## Volunteer Assistance

Every dance organization benefits from well-informed, dance-loving people who serve on a company's board of directors, on a school's guild, or in a host of other service capacities connected with ballet production and education. The energy, ideas, and enthusiasm of such people provide invaluable assistance to the entire field of dance. Not the least important in this category are the informed, sympathetic members of the audience who regularly attend and support dance concerts. All of these volunteers deserve a sincere bow of gratitude from the dance community. Again, to quote critic Octavio Roca:

> The phenomenal thing about ballet—in every sense of that very useful term—is that it takes two to give meaning to the phenomenon. There is no unmediated, essential truth in ballet. The truth of a ballet arises not in a vacuum but in public, in real life, in the magical moment when the audience witnesses the dancers in motion.[10]

## POSTSCRIPT

As this brief discussion illustrates, there is more to the dance field than dance. But no matter what ballet-related vocation (or avocation) is pursued, it is pursued best by persons who have had some dance training. So the first rule of preparation for any of these careers is: buy some basic dance equipment (see "Clothing" in Chapter 1), enroll in the best school available, and study ballet technique diligently (and perhaps other dance techniques as well). Make a habit of attending dance performances. When possible, join local or campus performing groups and participate (onstage or backstage) in theater productions. Observe master teachers conducting technique, composition, or improvisation classes. Observe choreographers conducting rehearsals. These years of preparation can occur along with other training or other jobs because such dance classes, rehearsals, and performances frequently take place in the evening or on weekends. Even when dreams of being a professional dancer are not the goal, one can pleasurably (and perhaps even profitably) take part in the world of ballet. Class just may begin at seven-thirty in the evening!

## NOTES

1. Marcia B. Siegel, *Watching the Dance Go By* (Boston: Houghton Mifflin, 1977), xvi.
2. Quoted in the *Los Angeles Times,* 11 June 1981.
3. Mimi Marr, "Where Do They Go When the Dancing Stops?" *Dance Magazine,* September 1975, 64.
4. Linda Grandey and Nancy Reynolds, "Recording the Dance," in *The Dance Catalogue,* ed. Nancy Reynolds (New York: Harmony Books, 1979), 194.

5.  Lisa Marie Naugle, "The Body As Interface: Using Computers in Dance," *Proceedings*, Society of Dance History Scholars, June 1998, 135.

6.  Octavio Roca, "Love at First Sight: Ballet Speaks to Each Audience Member in a Personal Way," *San Francisco Chronicle*, 16 August 1998, E3.

7.  Kayla Kazahn Zalk, "Dance Therapy: The Oldest Form of Healing and a New Profession," in *The Dance Catalogue*, ed. Nancy Reynolds (New York: Harmony Books, 1979), 205.

8.  An example of the complex, specialized nature of running a large ballet company is revealed in the following news item about a 1992 tour by American Ballet Theatre: "For a touring company as large as ABT, however, with its 76 dancers and 45 traveling staff members, there's no way to leave New York City without first purchasing 1,500 airplane tickets and bringing along six portable computer terminals, 5,000 pairs of shoes, 900 to 1,000 costumes, 300 wigs, $5,000 in cosmetics, a washer and dryer, to say nothing of 50 gallons of liquid detergent and 40 gallons of fabric softener." (*San Francisco Chronicle*, 17 January 1992.)

9.  Clive Barnes, "Rethinking the Zeitgeist," *Dance Magazine*, December 2002, 126.

10. Roca, "Love at First Sight."

# Ballet History

In this chapter, some of the things you will learn about are:

- The development of theaters for dance
- The first dancing masters
- The development of the five positions of the feet
- The first accounts of barre work
- The development of *pointe* work and *pas de deux*
- Court ballet, ballet-pantomime, romantic ballet, and classical ballet
- Changes in ballet costumes
- Leading dancers, choreographers, and teachers
- Important ballet productions
- The development of ballet in the United States

One of the intriguing questions that dancers today might like to ask dancers of the past is, "How exactly did you dance?" Ballet dancers of today may well wonder about the origins and evolution of the dance technique and style they are expected to master in today's classrooms and to perform in contemporary theaters.

Accounting for the past is not an easy task in the dance realm. Of all the arts, the art of movement is the most ephemeral—disappearing almost as it occurs, leaving few and inexact records of its brief glory. "Ballet is now . . . now is when it happens" was a familiar saying of choreographer George Balanchine, founder and first artistic director of the New York City Ballet.

Much of ballet's history, especially its technical and choreographic history, has been lost for lack of a generally accepted and precise recording device. Unlike students of opera, drama, or painting—who can study and practice from scores, scripts, or canvases that may be hundreds of years old—dance students have to rely almost exclusively on personal contact with practitioners of their art. What did the dancing masters of the past teach their pupils? Seeking that answer has become the focus of much recent research in dance history and is the theme of this brief survey.

## A TRADITION BEGINS

To trace the tradition of instruction from dancing master to pupil inherited by today's ballet instructors and students, we begin in the fifteenth century with the appearance of a new aid for an old art—the first dance instruction book. Sometime around the 1440s, a professional dancing master wrote down what to dance and how to dance it, thus allowing later generations to recreate, with substantial understanding, technique and choreography that is now more than 550 years old.

Like manuals by subsequent authors, this treatise,[1] by Domenico da [from] Piacenza (a city in what is now northern Italy), did not forecast the future but described the inherited dance tradition of its own time. Thus, it is possible that Domenico's dances represent an even earlier tradition, and it is certain that he did not expect his dances to be connected to a then unknown genre, classical ballet. Nonetheless, historian Ingrid Brainard pointed out that Domenico's choreographies include two miniature dance dramas, perhaps "the first two real ballets."[2]

## BACKGROUND TO THE TRADITION

Without instruction books, a discussion of dance prior to the fifteenth century can be only speculation, advised by careful study of dance artifacts such as evidence from musical scores, literary references, artistic depictions, clerical diatribes against dancing, philosophical advocacy for dancing, and a host of other secondary sources.

We know, for instance from cave drawings, that ancient peoples, sometimes costumed as animals, employed dance in a variety of ways. Judging by tribal dances today, movements were well organized and could be rhythmically complex, humorous as well as serious.

Egyptian tomb paintings depict solemn religious dancing of funeral processions patterned on the legend of the devoted Isis mourning for her beloved husband-brother, the god Osiris. Also portrayed are exuberant, acrobatic secular entertainments associated with those rites.

This dual nature of dance—ennobling and intoxicating—was evident in Greek culture also, whether associated with gestures of the noble chorus in the great dramatic tragedies or the rowdy, satirical dances of comedies and satyr plays. Greek dancing cannot be reconstructed with any certainty—despite the many visual sources, such as sculpture and vase decoration, documenting the integral place of dance in Greek life as private entertainment, communal activity, or religious ritual.

Western theatrical dance has reflected, from the sixteenth century onward, Greek influence in thematic material and in costuming. Western education in the nineteenth and twentieth centuries championed the benefits of dance to health and harmonious physical development, as did the ancient Greeks. The choice of *orchesis* (Greek for "dance") as the name of college dance clubs underscores that connection.[3]

Greek theaters (*theatron*, "place for seeing") have had their influence as well. They were outdoor amphitheaters, rising along a concave slope of a hill in a three-quarter circle of seats above a level, circular performance area called an *orchestra*. Behind that circular area, and opposite the spectators, was the *skene*, a structure whose facade provided a background, perhaps a temple, for the play, and whose interior served as a dressing area for the performers. Principal characters appeared from a central doorway, and entrances on either side provided other access.

As the Romans began conquering the surrounding countryside, they copied or adapted aspects of Greek drama and theater, but the result was a gradual decline in the close relationship that dance had enjoyed with song, verse, and dramatic expression in the earlier Hellenistic period. For an empire of peoples sharing no common language, for audiences who preferred exciting and colorful spectacles to classic dramatic forms, Roman theatrical fare developed danced interpretations emphasizing movement and gesture rather than verse and song. Highly skilled pantomime artists (*panto*, "all"; *mime*, "acting out") enjoyed great wealth and considerable political power.

Roman outdoor theaters were huge and opulent. The stage, raised about 5 feet high, could be as much as 300 feet long and 40 feet deep. The simple *skene* of Greek theaters became highly decorated facades whose columns and statuary could dwarf the performers. The orchestra area was reduced to a semicircle, used less for dancing than for seating important spectators or, on occasion, even flooded for performance of water spectacles.

A preference for spectacle over content saw the great pantomime artists gradually replaced by *mimi* specializing in lewd farces. These increasingly lascivious popular entertainments, along with circus games and gladiatorial combats, were denounced by early Christian moralists.

## DANCE IN THE MIDDLE AGES

Even as the Church fathers preached against dancing as a form of bodily pleasure that impeded preparation for the spiritual afterlife, Christian theologians frequently employed dance imagery to extol the harmony of the universe and of the soul with that universe.

The period from the fifth to the fourteenth century (from the decline of the Roman Empire to the beginning of the Renaissance), known as the Middle Ages, was not devoid of earthly dance. A variety of entertainers—jugglers, acrobats, conjurers, minstrels, and dancers—were familiar sights at medieval fairs, marketplaces, and village greens. Of these entertainers, the minstrel, who sang and played an instrument, was a kind of voice for society in the absence of theaters and before the invention of the printing press.

In France in 1330, journeymen jugglers and minstrels decided to form their own guild, following the example of other trades and in recognition of their increasing popularity as entertainers for an aristocracy growing in wealth and worldliness.[4] Chivalry influenced social life, including the taste for art songs and refined social dances. Thus, "minstrels and jugglers had progressively relinquished their monkeys and their bears, concentrating on refining their skills as dancers and choreographers to suit the demands of a more polished and sophisticated society."[5]

By the early fifteenth century, a distinction was made between those musicians who played a treble fiddle and instructed dancing and those who played a bass fiddle in a band. Both the minstrel-dancers and the band members remained within the same guild, headed by the "king of the violins."[6] Indeed, the violin, played by the dancing master himself, continued to be the instrument for accompanying dance classes and ballet lessons until the twentieth century.

## SOCIAL AND THEATRICAL DANCES OF THE RENAISSANCE AND EARLY BAROQUE PERIODS

We return now to Domenico da Piacenza, author of the earliest extant dance-instruction manuscript. Like his French counterparts, Domenico was skilled both in music and dance. The content of his manual, like that of many in the next centuries, gives us an idea of the skills and duties expected of dancing masters at court. For instance, they were theoreticians: "Dancing is the synthesis of movement and space and music . . . if you do justice to these elements, the result will be true dancing." But if not, Domenico went on to say, you will not be more than a "mere stamper of the feet."[7]

Besides giving daily dance instruction to their noble patrons, dancing masters, regarded as experts on proper social behavior, also taught correct ballroom manners, including how to dress properly, how to bow correctly, and how to handle one's gloves, hat, fan, or sword with ease. All were requisites for advancement in courtly circles. We might call this elegant, effortless-looking deportment the "courtesy of grand manners," an attribute still reflected today in the posture and bearing of the classically trained ballet dancer.

The dancing master was expected to devise new dances for the ballroom and for court festivals, where he might also perform along with his noble pupils. Choreographies were documented in a variety of ways: explanations in prose, shorthand symbols, and initial letters or abbreviations of step names. One of the choreographic forms that developed was the *ballo,* a dance piece for a specified number of dancers, featuring frequent changes of musical rhythm and sometimes possibilities for dramatic expression.

Italian festival art developed the *intermezzi,* spectacular musico-dramatic interludes inserted between the acts of lengthy plays. Originating in the late fifteenth century in Ferrara, the *intermezzi* came to include elaborate mechanical marvels of scenic effects; brilliantly costumed actors, singers, and dancers; and the coordinated efforts of poets, composers, designers, and choreographers.

During the sixteenth century, thematic material for the *intermezzi* (usually four to six in number) became more unified and sometimes related directly to the play. Their chief purposes, however, were to edify and entertain the spectators and to enhance the prestige of the host. Perhaps the most elaborate examples were the *intermezzi* of 1589, devised to accompany the comedy *La Pellegrina* ("The Pilgrim"), one of the entertainments among the wedding festivities in Florence for Ferdinando de' Medici and Christine of Lorraine. Overseeing the entire production was Emilio de' Cavalieri, a composer, organist, voice teacher, dancer, choreographer, administrator, and diplomat! His choreographic instructions for the final *ballo* (for four women, three men, and a singing chorus that also moved) have survived, providing a rare example of sixteenth-century theatrical dance.[8]

The step vocabulary used by Cavalieri can be understood from published descriptions of similar movements by other Italian dancing masters of the period, notably Fabritio Caroso and Cesare Negri.[9] Their treatises include choreographies for dozens of social dances (Negri also has a few theatrical ones), written in prose form, and their music, written in lute tablature. Typically beginning and ending with a gracious *riverenza* or bow, the repertory includes examples of the *balletto*, a couple dance with several sections in contrasting rhythm.

One of the more elaborate formats begins with an introductory passage, perhaps a stately *pavana* in duple meter (two or four beats to a bar of music), followed by a triple-meter *gagliarda,* in which first the gentleman does a solo of leaps, beats, and jumps and then the lady performs a variation in a more restrained yet lively manner. Then, a brisker *saltarello* for both dancers leads to the finale, the exuberant *canario* with toe-heel brushes and stamps in intricate rhythms.[10]

This structure for a sixteenth-century *balletto* for a *cavalière* and his lady is not unlike that of the ballet *pas de deux* for a *danseur* and ballerina. Beginning as it does with an *entrée* and *adagio* for the couple, the *pas de deux* proceeds to exciting variations performed first by the male dancer and then by his partner and is brought to conclusion in the lively coda for both. The technique is markedly different, however. Renaissance dancers did not point their feet or turn out their legs. Dancing side-by-side or face-to-face, partners seldom touched except for an occasional holding or tapping of hands. Indeed, only movements for the legs were described in this period. Their intricacy, however, required practice, and Negri's illustrations show a courtier holding onto a table and a chair, the better to execute his leg movements.

Court choreographers may have borrowed ideas from groups of itinerant entertainers, practitioners of *commedia dell'arte* ("comedy of skill") that originated about the mid-sixteenth century. Often parodying court behavior, these professional actors were skilled musicians and dancers as well. Their

Handsome dance manuals such as *Le gratie d'amore* ("The graces of love," 1602), by Cesare Negri, document the highly developed dance technique of Italian courtiers, who practiced intricate legwork while holding on to pieces of furniture.

dynamic quality and popular stock characters, such as Harlequin and Columbine, appear as frequent influences in ballet's technical and artistic history, but documentation of their early dances does not remain.

Lost, too, are the genuine early folk dances of peasants, artisans, and villagers, for the material in the dance manuals reflects only the practice of the courts and upper classes. Yet, through the years, folk and national dances have been lively sources for ballet choreographers to call on. Some traces of early folk dances may be found in dance descriptions published in 1589 by Thoinot Arbeau, a canon in the Roman Catholic Church.[11] Neither a dancing master nor employee of a royal patron, this scholarly churchman nevertheless wrote an important instruction book of dances standard with the gentry and nobility of the French provinces.

Far less complex than the Italian repertory, some of the dances that Arbeau described may have an even more humble background. Performed with simple steps and hops in a circle or chain formation by several couples, the *branles* may be descendants of the medieval *carole* or *chorea*. Another dance described by Arbeau, the *volta* ("turning"), is distinguished by its hearty turns in which the gentleman lifts his partner.

Arbeau's book emphasizes courteous social behavior and correct execution of dance technique, including proper positions of the feet and legs. Bearing faint resemblance to ballet's positions of the feet, Arbeau's positions are illustrated showing only slight turnout. He believed that although "the degree [of turnout] is left to the discretion of the dancer . . . the natural rotation of the leg will not permit it to exceed a right angle."[12] Similar positions were used for fencing, which, along with dancing and riding, was a requisite accomplishment for any gentleman.

More sophisticated dances were typical of the French royal courts where they were featured in lavish entertainments organized to celebrate royal events, as well as to reinforce royal political prestige. Costly festivals of several days' duration often included banquets, water shows, fireworks displays, and balls. Composite entertainments of verse, music, dance, and decorations were devised to highlight the occasion. Italian dancing masters, employed by the French monarchy, became increasingly important to oversee these complex performances, which developed into the genre known as *ballet de cour* ("court ballet").

An elaborate example was the 1581 production of the *Balet Comique de la Royne*. The title of the ballet (literally, "The Queen's Comedy-Ballet" and now usually spelled *Ballet Comique de la Reine*) was chosen more for the "beautiful, tranquil, and happy conclusion than for the quality of the personages, who are almost all gods and goddesses, or other heroic persons."[13]

The plot was unfolded by a succession of verses, songs, and dances that gave a certain dramatic unity to the production. The libretto, the music, and several engravings of the elaborate costumes and pageant cars (somewhat like parade floats, pulled by several men) were published, but alas, not the choreography. Some description survives of the final dance, however, a *grand ballet* in which ladies of the court performed:

> Forty passages or geometric figures . . . sometimes square, sometimes round, . . . then in triangles accompanied by a small square. . . . At the middle of the Ballet a chain was formed, composed of four interlacings, each different from the others. . . . The spectators thought that Archimedes could not have understood geometric proportions any better than the princesses and the ladies observed in this Ballet.[14]

In Italy by the 1580s, permanent theaters were being built, adaptations of earlier Roman designs, with perspective painting added to the stage. Inclined ramps connected the stage to the floor of the auditorium, and all three areas could be utilized for performance. In France, however, entertainments such as the *Ballet Comique* occurred in the center floor of large rooms of a palace. Royal dignitaries sat at one end of the hall, and performers and decorative pageant cars entered at the opposite end. Along the sides were raised galleries accommodating many hundreds of spectators watching the dance patterns unfold.

The English equivalent to the Italian *intermezzi* and the French *ballet de cour* was the court masque, usually based on a mythological or allegorical theme adapted to extol the virtues of the monarchy. Enhanced by scenic wonders and poetic verses, masques offered a succession of songs, speeches, and dances performed by elaborately costumed members of the court. Noble, serious characters of the masque proper were contrasted with

Members of the aristocracy took part in elaborate court entertainments featuring dancing in intricate geometric patterns, as in this scene from the first *intermezzo* of *La Liberazione di Tireno e d'Arnea* ("The liberation of Tyrsenus and Arnea," 1617) held in the Medici theater of the Uffizi Palace in Florence. Note the variety of performance levels—auditorium floor, ramps, stage, and suspended scenery.

demons, furies, and nymphs in antimasque sections of the production. Members of the audience were invited to join the masquers in general dancing, called revels.

Social dancing by the entire assembly frequently terminated theatrical evenings in Italy and France as well. A favorite English form was the country dance, a lively circle or longways dance for several couples at once. Choreographies and music for these pleasurable dances were collected and published in 1651.[15] The English love of dancing is apparent in the many references to dance by Shakespeare in his plays, such as in *Henry V* when Bourbon declares, "They bid us to the English dancing schools and teach lavoltas, high and swift corantos."

However, during the Commonwealth following the overthrow of the monarchy in 1640, theatrical activities and court masques in England were suspended. Italian taste turned to the development of opera, an outgrowth of the *intermezzi*. But in France, the ballet was to enter an important new phase.

## BIRTH OF THE CLASSICAL BALLET

Louis XIV (1643–1715) brought *ballet de cour* to its most brilliant phase. The king, himself a nimble dancer who appeared in court ballets over a period of eighteen years and continued daily dance lessons for many more, excelled as patron of the arts. In bringing together and encouraging first-rate composers, choreographers, dancers, designers, and poets, the royal dancer-patron-impresario intended that court functions would provide a diverting occupation for his courtiers and an impressive display of French cultural magnificence for all Europe.

An early and crucial appointment was that of Jean-Baptiste Lully as composer responsible for the music for court ballets. Having learned to play the guitar in his native Italy, Lully arrived in France as a young teenager and soon showed prowess as violinist and dancer, attracting notice by the court. He danced alongside the young Louis in an elaborate fête, the *Ballet de la Nuit,* in which the fourteen year old king first appeared in the role of Apollo, the sun god. A sumptuous example of *ballet à entrée,* the production had four acts, each with a separate plot, composer, and numerous *entrées* ("entrances") interspersed with spoken lines.

Typically, most dancers were members of the court. Gradually, as Lully was granted more control, court productions became more integrated unities, and professional dancers, including women, assumed more roles. One virtuoso dancer (and accomplished violinist as well), Pierre Beauchamps, was to have an important place in ballet's formative years.

Beauchamps made his debut as a choreographer in 1661 in the *comédie-ballet, Les Facheux* ("The Bores"), a new theatrical form created by Jean-Baptiste Poquelin, better known by his stage name, Molière. Given only two weeks to mount the production, Molière and Beauchamps, who also composed the music, decided to use dance as a means of enhancing the actual development of the plot and to encourage dancers to be more expressive in their dancing, as well as to join the actors in gestures and poses during the action of the play. It was a course they followed in other productions, *Le Bourgeois Gentilhomme* ("The Gentleman Citizen," 1670) being probably best known today, but seldom performed now with its music or dance possibilities.

In 1661, the year of Louis XIV's ascension to absolute power, the king showed his commitment to improve the quality of dancing by establishing the Académie Royale de Danse. Thirteen of the most experienced dancing masters were appointed to set artistic standards for teaching and training dancers for court ballets. Also, they were granted independent power to license teachers, a privilege violently opposed by the musicians' guild, to which dancers had belonged for three centuries.

Creation of dance specialists was deemed timely, however, as ballets took on greater theatrical aspects. One of these aspects was the moving of ballet productions from the ballroom floor onto a raised stage. Establishment of the proscenium arch as a stage frame enhanced the use of hidden machines to shift scenes quickly. Such a theater, the Palais Royale, was given over for performances by the Académie Royale de Musique, a performing institution (later known as the Paris Opéra) established by Louis XIV in 1672 to be headed by his protégé, Lully. Beauchamps, by now director of the dancers' academy, was appointed dancing master to the music academy.

During the seventeenth century, theatrical productions receded behind the confines of the proscenium stage, as in this performance at Versailles in 1674. Performers were well aware of the royal personages seated directly opposite stage center. This "comedy in music," *Les Fêtes de l'Amour et de Bacchus* ("The Festival of Love and Bacchus," first presented in 1672 and revived at intervals until 1738), was based on a text by Molière, with music by Lully and dances by Beauchamps.

Performers, no longer surrounded by their audience, needed to rely less on symbolic formations of large groups and more on the agility and design of an individual body watched by spectators out front. Precise movements and poses required more codification of the step vocabulary. The establishment of the five positions for the feet, still foundational for today's ballet technique, is credited to Beauchamps, who "found that nothing was more important to maintain the body in a graceful attitude and the steps in a fixed space than to introduce these five positions."[16] Basic to their design was turnout of the leg, already a requirement for "a handsome carriage of the leg . . . regarded as a necessity of elegant bearing" among seventeenth-century nobility and gentry as well as dancers.[17] The angle of turnout, when heels touched and toes turned outward, was about 90 degrees. Complete 180-degree turnout was still a century away.

Preservation of choreography continued to be a problem, and Louis XIV requested Beauchamps, who had become the monarch's personal dance instructor, to devise a method of notating dance movement. By 1700 the long-awaited notation system was completed and published, not by Beauchamps, however, but by another choreographer, Raoul Anger Feuillet. In his treatise, symbols rather than words indicate positions, steps, and the various movements of the dance—*plié, élevé, sauté, cabriole, tombé, glissé, tourné*—and the symbols are aligned along the choreographic figure or pattern of each dance.[18]

The French terminology of the Académie Royale de Danse became, and has continued to be, the standard for the rest of the Western ballet world, but the execution of the various steps has, in most cases, changed considerably. Nevertheless, by means of the notation system and helpful manuals from the early eighteenth century, the charming dances of that period can be reconstructed with considerable accuracy. For the next twenty-five years, annual collections of dances were published and eagerly sought in order to learn the latest ballroom dances, thus preparing for the coming social season, and to keep up with what was happening in theatrical dance. More than 350 notated dances exist from the Baroque period and can be reconstructed today.

*la Bourgogne*

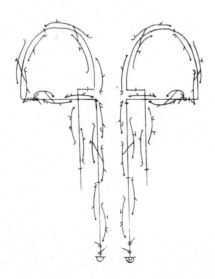

*Chorégraphie*, the dance notation system published by Feuillet in 1700, was widely used to record dances in the first decades of the eighteenth century. This is the opening section of a *dance à deux*, one of the many dances published along with that first volume of dance notation. Along the track, which shows the pattern the dancers make in space, are the symbols showing the kinds of steps the dancers make. The tiny lines intersecting the track correspond to the musical measures at the top of the page.

The New York Baroque Dance Company is frequently invited to perform in revivals of eighteenth-century operas, such as this production of *Orfeo et Euridice* (1761) by the German composer Christoph Gluck. Artistic director and dancer Catherine Turocy bases her choreography and staging on careful research of eighteenth-century dance, music, costumes, and stage practices.

Dance technique of both amateur and professional shared many characteristics, differing in the degree of difficulty and dramatic expressiveness expected for stage performance. Judging by the elaborate choreography for esteemed performers, the technical level for ballet was indeed high. Movements for the hands and rules for opposition of arms to legs became standardized. Indeed, such were the regulations and influence established by the Paris Opéra throughout Europe that it is not surprising to learn there were rumblings of discontent.

## EIGHTEENTH-CENTURY PROFESSIONALISM AND INNOVATION

Stage dancers were now professionals, but their strictly codified movement and costuming continued to reflect their courtly heritage, as did their stage productions. One highly popular performance vehicle of the early part of the century was the opera-ballet, a musical production of singing, dancing, and scenic display, not unlike the court *ballet à entrées*. But some innovative dancers and ballet masters envisioned dramatic dance performances without dependence on either words or song to relate a scenario. Such experiments took place outside the Paris Opéra domain.

In 1717, John Weaver, an English dance master and theoretician, attempted a wholly danced drama, the *Loves of Mars and Venus,* as a revival of practices "from the Ancients, in Imitation of their Pantomime."[19] Also in London, a visiting young French dancer of exceptional expressive ability, Marie Sallé, broke several traditions: she challenged the male dominance in choreography by composing the ballet *Pygmalion* (1734), in which she dared challenge standard costuming as well, appearing "without pannier [hoops around the hips], skirt, or bodice, and with her hair down. . . . Apart from her corset and petticoat, she wore only a simple dress of muslin draped about her in the manner of a Greek statue."[20] Sallé's efforts were toward achieving greater realism and expression in ballet. Her rival for favor among the highly vociferous ballet fans was Marie-Anne de Cupis de Camargo, a highly skilled technician who excelled in steps of virtuosity that, until her time, were usually associated with male dancers.

Prior to the French Revolution, a typical eighteenth-century ballet costume for a male dancer included a plumed headdress and a *tonnelet,* or wired skirt, not unlike the ballet tutu later worn by female dancers. For women, a tightly laced corset, a long skirt held out by wire frames at the hip or along the petticoat, and heeled shoes were deemed suitable for any role.

Of the many ballet masters who challenged the status quo, only Jean Georges Noverre made the effort to publish his complaints and suggestions. In 1760, he urged dancers to:

> Renounce *cabrioles, entrechats,* and overcomplicated steps . . . away with those lifeless masks . . . take off those enormous wigs . . . discard the use of those stiff cumbersome hoops. . . . Renounce that slavish routine which keeps your art in its infancy . . . gracefully set aside the narrow laws of a school to follow the impressions of nature.[21]

Even as he quarreled with much of his dance heritage, Noverre, a student of the elegant "god of the dance," Louis Dupré, did not wish to reject all that had gone on before. For instance, "In order to dance well," he said, "nothing is so important as the turning outward of the thigh."[22] But for Noverre, movements of the legs, no matter how brilliant, were only a part of true dancing, where "everything must speak; each gesture, each attitude, each *port de bras* must possess a different expression."[23]

Noverre elaborated his ideas as ballet master in Stuttgart, later in Vienna, and finally as ballet master at the Paris Opéra, a position he had long coveted.

The climactic scene of Noverre's dramatic *ballet d'action, Jason et Medée,* is shown in a satiric drawing published during its 1781 London season. Gaetano Vestris, celebrated dancer of the noble style, staged the London version and danced the role of Jason, the faithless husband.

Noverre created some 150 ballets during his long career, but none survive. He disdained notation, but in any case the old Feuillet system, adequate as it was for earlier divertissements, was not able to accommodate the innovations of *ballet d'action* (later called *ballet-pantomime*) in which a dramatic plot was conveyed entirely in movement and gesture.

However, a gently comic ballet by one of Noverre's outstanding pupils, Jean Dauberval, has survived. *La Fille Mal Gardée* ("The Ill-Guarded Girl") was produced in Bordeaux just two weeks before the outbreak of the French Revolution in July 1789. This timely ballet featured peasants as heroes and depicted real-life situations using a dance style that blended the academic technique of the time with folk-dance elements. The ballet soon enjoyed success on stages from London to St. Petersburg, and it still is performed today, notably by Britain's Royal Ballet, in versions true, though not to Dauberval's original steps, at least to his carefully constructed plot and delightful characters.

The wearing of masks to help portray characters, a tradition of ancient origin, was abolished by 1772, allowing facial expression to become more important. Fashion implemented by the French Revolution replaced cumbersome courtly dress and rigid corsets with lighter, more flowing costumes based on Greek and Roman drapery. Greater freedom of movement, especially for the upper body and arms, allowed gesture to become "more natural," a goal of the dance innovators.

Dance technique as well as style had been affected by changes in costume. For women especially, shucking of the long hooped skirts allowed freedom of leg movement previously impossible, plus the possibility for supported *adagio,* for now their partners could get close enough to hold them. Charles Didelot, a student of Dauberval, extended the concept of partnering, including simple lifts and movements that emphasized strength for the male and lightness for the female. By an ingenious system of almost-invisible wires, his lightly clad dancers could be raised, lowered, or flown across the stage, an apt device for his highly popular ballet *Flore et Zéphyre* (1796), the love story of a nymph and the breeze of the West Wind.

But having discarded heeled shoes in favor of heelless sandals or slippers, dancers were achieving a new elevation on their own. Outstanding for his sensational jumps, beats, and turns was Auguste Vestris, son of the celebrated Gaetano. Unlike his father, who epitomized the elegant, noble style of his teacher, Dupré, Auguste excelled in dazzling virtuoso displays of skill.

The Paris Opéra had long endeavored to enforce strict observance of three distinct dance styles, including designation of proper physique for each. For the noble style, a dancer's structure should be stately and well proportioned because he would be destined for serious, heroic roles, for gods such as Apollo (or Venus, if a woman). The *demi-caractère* dancer could be of medium height, still elegant but adept at a variety of virtuoso styles appropriate for lesser gods such as Mercury or *Zéphire*. The comic or grotesque dancer could be of indifferent stature, even thickset, but necessarily strong.

Appearing in London in the 1781 season was Gaetano Vestris's son, Auguste, whose technical virtuosity could not be denied even by this English caricature. Through his dazzling performances as a youth and his long career as a teacher, Auguste Vestris exerted a great influence on the development of ballet technique on the eve of the romantic period.

These roles were of a rustic or pastoral nature and could include steps and dances characteristic of various national or folklore sources. Steps of almost acrobatic nature, the specialty of comic or grotesque dancers, were documented in 1779 by Gennaro Magri, including the "apparently supernatural" balance of Antoine Pitrot on "the tip of his big toe."[24]

But, as in the case of Auguste Vestris, who became an influential teacher in the early nineteenth century, such distinctions of the old order were beginning to break down, just as steps and styles were evolving toward a different form. What was yet lacking was the artistic impetus to make use of these newly developing skills.

## THE GOLDEN AGE OF ROMANTIC BALLET

An artistic push did come along; the romantic movement was felt in ballet no less than in literature, music, and painting. For ballet, it was a liberation from strict thematic and technical conventions of previous eras. Basic subjects of romanticism came from the perceived conflicts between beauty and ugliness, good and evil, spirit and flesh. With themes juxtaposing realism

Newly installed gas lighting enhanced the Paris Opéra premiere of Meyerbeer's opera *Robert le Diable* ("Robert the Devil," 1831), especially this ballet scene, in which the ghosts of nuns rise from their graves to lure Robert. Featuring Marie Taglioni in choreography by her father, the opera's ballet scenes were early examples of the romantic era's fascination with the supernatural and exotic, more fully realized by the Taglionis' *La Sylphide* the next year.

and fantasy, mortal with supernatural, romantic ballet wanted it—and had it—both ways: to be a vehicle for a real drama and a showcase for masters of technique.

The aerial flights provided by Didelot's wires were ideal for the spiritual creatures of the new ballets, but dancers wished to create ethereal illusion by their own movements. Because it was the woman who was cast in the role of unattainable supernatural creature, it was she who desired to dance on the least possible earthly surface, the very tips of her toes. But wishing alone would not make it so. "Paradoxically, Romanticism may have stressed irrational and spontaneous behavior, but the mastery of a structured and rational training method was needed to portray such behavior on stage."[25]

Such a method had been evolving since the last decades of the previous century, especially in classes at the Paris Opéra Ballet School and in various Italian centers of opera and ballet.[26] But not until 1820 was there a published account of ballet technique as we recognize it today, including the first outline of the structure of a ballet class. The author of this text, a young

**159**

Amalia Brugnoli was among the first to dance on the point of her foot, performing "very extraordinary things," according to Marie Taglioni, who saw her in 1822. Brugnoli, shown here with her husband, dancer–choreographer Paolo Samengo, also studied and danced with Carlo Blasis, whose school at La Scala produced many of the extraordinary technicians of nineteenth-century ballet.

dancer named Carlo Blasis, later developed a rigorous method of training at the Ballet School of La Scala in Milan.[27]

As described in more detail by his disciple, Giovanni Léopold Adice,[28] Blasis's barre work included, in the order given, 48 *pliés,* 128 *grand battements,* 96 *petits battements* (like *battements tendus* today), 128 *ronds de jambe à terre* and the same *en l'air,* 64 slow *petits battements sur le cou-de-pied,* and 120 rapid ones. These were "preliminary" exercises, to be repeated in center floor before going on to the rest of the lesson!

Blasis's illustrations show dancers in complete 180-degree turnout and legs extended to hip-level but, surprisingly, no dancer on full pointe. Yet prints from the turn of the nineteenth century depict a few dancers poised on the extreme points of their toes. But pointe work as such was not generally in use, nor was its revolutionary nature fully realized.

In 1831, E. A. Théleur, an English dancer and teacher who trained in France and Frenchified his name from Taylor, indicated several movements that could be done either "on the balls of the feet or the tips of the toes." His book was the first ballet instruction text to actually show illustrations of women on toetip, and it was the first published attempt to devise a new system of dance notation in the nineteenth century.[29] Like Blasis before, Théleur asserted that heels should never leave the floor in *pliés* and advocated the correct maximum height of the leg as hip level.

More detailed information about *enchaînements* for ballet classes and student performances, as well as solos and *pas de deux* for theatrical presentation, are contained in the teaching notebooks (1829–1836) of Michel St. Léon (né Léon Michel), a dancer who retired from the Paris Opéra Ballet in 1817. As his notes clearly describe, women as well as men were expected to perform multiple *pirouettes à la seconde,* and men as well as women would on occasion rise onto the points of their toes.

To prepare for her debut in 1822, Marie Taglioni trained arduously six hours a day with her father, Filippo, who, as teacher and choreographer, was one of the early leaders of the romantic movement in ballet. Marie Taglioni epitomized a newly developing style: her delicate *piqué* to full pointe replaced the deliberate rise to half-toe of the previous century; one leg extended slightly backward became a waist-high *arabesque* and, with the other foot poised *en pointe,* a symbolic yearning to soar upward. To the previous emphasis on *terre à terre* steps ("ground-to-ground," meaning the feet scarcely leave the floor) was added the *ballonnée* style with its high and effortless-appearing jumps and leaps.

To show off his daughter's superb skills, Filippo Taglioni created many ballets, including his masterpiece, *La Sylphide* (Paris, 1832). In the soft glow of gaslights, Taglioni, as the Sylphide, clothed in a full skirt of the lightest gauze reaching to mid-calf, seemed to float about the huge opera house stage with her soaring, silent *jetés,* her incredibly smooth movements, and her delicate balances. The theme and setting of *La Sylphide* and the costume, technique, and personality of Marie Taglioni ushered in the golden age of romantic ballet (1832–c.1845) and created a style still popular today. One of the most frequently performed ballets in America has been *Les Sylphides,* a neoromantic storyless ballet created by Michel Fokine to the music of Chopin seventy-six years after *La Sylphide.*

A ballerina is never without rivals, and one of Taglioni's most successful challengers was Fanny Elssler, a Viennese beauty whose specialty was theatricalized folk or national dancing, done with the sparkle and precision of a highly skilled ballet dancer. Her greatest success was in the cachucha, a Spanish dance in Jean Coralli's ballet *Le Diable boiteux* ("The devil on two sticks," 1836). Spanish influences had been felt in social and theatrical dancing since the Renaissance; nineteenth-century ballet dancers routinely performed theatricalized folk dances from many regions and most could play castanets.

When Taglioni accepted an invitation to dance in St. Petersburg, Elssler remained in Paris to enjoy the role of undisputed star of the Opéra. Two years later, in 1840, Elssler crossed the Atlantic for a three-month American tour that was extended to two years. Audiences in New York, Philadelphia, and Baltimore rivaled each other in their adulation for Elssler and her fiery dances; Congress adjourned for her performances in Washington.

The spiritual Taglioni and the sensual Elssler split the artistic world of ballet fans into two passionate factions, reminiscent of the Sallé–Camargo rivalry a century before. But another ballerina came along who offered the

Fanny Elssler charmed audiences in the United States as well as in all of Europe with her passionate dancing, especially in this Spanish-style solo complete with castanet playing. This portrait accompanied the New York publication of the sheet music for that dance.

public *both* qualities, moreover in the same ballet; she was Carlotta Grisi, and the ballet was *Giselle,* first performed in 1841.

The dual role of Giselle—a peasant girl in Act I, a ghostly Wili in Act II—challenges dancers to this day. Coralli did the choreography, with solo passages for Mlle Grisi composed by Jules Perrot, one of the few male dancers of the romantic era to receive much attention from the public or press, although his contributions to *Giselle* went unacknowledged at the time.

An American dancer, Mary Ann Lee, traveled to Europe to study and then returned to dance *Giselle* in Boston in 1846. Her partner was George Washington Smith, the first American *premier danseur.* Their contemporary, Augusta Maywood, extended a European visit to a lifetime career, becoming the first American dancer to achieve fame and fortune abroad.

The ballerina had become the undisputed star of the ballet stage. Four of these talented, temperamental ladies were persuaded to dance together in London in 1845. Their short ballet, *Pas de Quatre,* was a masterpiece of choreographic diplomacy by Perrot, who managed to display the individual skills of the dancers without offending the pride of any one of them. It was agreed that Taglioni should be awarded the place of honor, the final variation of the ballet. The others, after tempestuous argument on the day of the performance, finally agreed to appear in order of their age: first, the young Danish dancer Lucile Grahn, who excelled in *pirouettes,* then Carlotta Grisi, followed by Fanny Cerrito, an Italian dancer of uncommon speed and brilliance.

Jules Perrot's plotless divertissement *Pas de Quatre* (1845) cleverly displayed the individual skills of four of the greatest ballerinas of the romantic period, shown here in the pose with which the ballet began and ended. Surrounding Marie Taglioni are Carlotta Grisi, Lucile Grahn, and Fanny Cerrito.

These and other ballerinas continually expanded the limits of ballet technique. They rivaled male dancers in the size of their leaps and the speed of their footwork. They danced more and more on the tips of their toes, an achievement requiring tremendous strength in soft slippers. A little darning around the point of the shoe, a little cotton batting inside, and ribbons

**163**

tied tightly around the ankles offered the only assistance to Taglioni and others of her era.

The delicately pale, unworldly romantic ballerina was, in fact, a far stronger technician than her robust, voluptuous eighteenth-century predecessor. For the first time in the history of Western theatrical dancing, females, now *en pointe,* replaced males as the dominant stage performers. However, two male dancer–choreographers of the period deserve special mention: Auguste Bournonville, developer of the Danish repertory, and Arthur Saint-Léon, creator of *Coppélia* and a system of dance notation.

Bournonville studied with Auguste Vestris. Through his many ballets still performed today by the Royal Danish Ballet and by his documentation of ballet technique, Bournonville is responsible for keeping alive much of the French ballet tradition. His version of *La Sylphide,* not Taglioni's, is the one usually seen today. Bournonville should not be accused of plagiarism; adapting someone else's ballet, without necessarily giving credit to the originator or using the original musical score, was a common practice in both the eighteenth and the nineteenth centuries.

Saint-Léon's international career was also typical of dancers and ballet masters of the time. He worked in London, St. Petersburg, Rome, Brussels, Milan, and Vienna as well as his native Paris. Somehow he found time to

The tradition of the ballet classroom, passed along from teacher to student, is celebrated in August Bournonville's homage to one of his teachers, Auguste Vestris. This scene is from Act I of Bournonville's *The Conservatoire or A Marriage Advertisement* (1849), performed by Royal Danish Ballet dancers Rose Gad and Christina Olsson as the students and Lloyd Riggins as their approving ballet master.

publish, in 1852, a system of dance notation.[30] Easy to decipher, his notation and descriptions give vivid examples of classroom exercises closely related to the earlier tradition described by his father, Michel St. Léon, and by Blasis and Théleur, including *grandes pirouettes* and multiple beats.

Among the very few notated dances of the first half of the nineteenth century are the *Gavotte de Vestris,* an already famous duet by the time Théleur notated it, and a *pas de six* from *La Vivandière,* one of Saint-Léon's popular ballets and the only example of his choreography he succeeded in recording. Sad to say, most of the great romantic ballet repertory has been forgotten, and the rest has survived only through fallible memory.

In the second half of the nineteenth century, the great opera houses of Europe relied more and more on spectacular vehicles tailored for the talents of a star ballerina. Smaller provincial theaters, unable to satisfy public taste for such elaborate fare, gradually ceased sponsoring new ballet productions, thus drying up a traditional source for inventive choreography. The lack of fine roles for male dancers and public preference for female dancers resulted in women taking male roles *en travestie.* For instance, the role of Franz in Arthur Saint-Léon's ballet *Coppélia* (1870) was originated by the shapely Eugenie Fiocre, a tradition for that ballet that continued well into this century.

London, once an ardent sponsor of the finest ballets at Her Majesty's Theatre, began to relegate dancing to divertissements during intervals between other acts at the Alhambra and Empire music halls. In Copenhagen, Bournonville managed to preserve the artistry of the romantic period, avoiding excesses he observed elsewhere: the "unending and monotonous host of feats of bravura," the "obvious lascivious tendency that pervades the whole choreographic movement," "the heroines of the ballet [who] continuously appear in the same more or less spangled costume."[31] His comments referred to the Russian repertory of the 1870s, before it entered a period of brilliant successes that in many ways marked the glorious culmination of the romantic era.

## EMERGENCE OF BALLET IN RUSSIA

The Russian theater had long relied on foreign talent for its ballet, beginning in the eighteenth century with imported French ballet masters and with exponents of *ballet d'action* from Vienna. At the start of the nineteenth century, Charles Didelot came to St. Petersburg, revolutionizing teaching methods and establishing the foundation of the Russian school. His work was continued by his fellow countrymen Jules Perrot and Arthur Saint-Léon.

Still another Frenchman, Marius Petipa, was to have the greatest effect. Arriving in St. Petersburg in 1847 at age twenty-five, he was to become *premier danseur* and then ballet master of the Imperial Ballet. By the end of his remarkable fifty-six-year career in Russia, Petipa had created close to sixty ballets and so nurtured native Russian talent that his adopted country, and in due time the world, was convinced that the very best in ballet meant Russian ballet.

A Petipa production meant evening-length ballets of several acts, fantastic stage effects, and fairy-tale plots related through pantomimic gestures by characters whose natures were revealed through their dances. Diversity during the long evening was achieved by alternating acts having naturalistic settings, which might include lively comic or folk-dance-inspired passages, with acts having supernatural locations, perhaps a dream sequence with enchanted, winged creatures.

Beautiful symmetry characterized a Petipa ballet—groups of four, eight, thirty-two, or more lovely women moving in ingenious patterns. Dance passages often were repeated three times, then brought to an appropriately bravura finish. The hero and heroine usually performed only in the nobler, classical style, and their *pas de deux* was the highlight of any given act. With Petipa, the *grand pas de deux—adagio,* variations, and coda—achieved a level of artistry that is still much admired, remaining technically challenging as well.

The term "classical ballet" has come to mean ballets that have the refined choreographic structure and bravura dance technique developed during this period in Russia. Some of this repertory was preserved in a system of notation devised by Vladimir Stepanov and later used to mount the ballets in the West. One of these, *The Sleeping Beauty,* first produced in St. Petersburg in 1890, was perhaps Petipa's crowning achievement. Its scenario was meticulously outlined by Petipa for Tchaikovsky, whose score is considered one of the finest.

It would be unfair to leave the impression that Marius Petipa singlehandedly made Russia the ballet capital of the world, for he had help from many sources. His talented but humble assistant, Lev Ivanov, was responsible for choreography of *The Nutcracker* and for Acts II and IV of *Swan Lake,* two other ballets with music by Tchaikovsky that probably are the most popular works associated with ballet from the 1890s. Christian Johannsen, a pupil of Bournonville who was already a leading dancer with the Imperial Ballet when Petipa first arrived, later became one of the finest teachers of its school.

In the latter part of the century, the Imperial Theatre was host to a galaxy of Italian stars, products of the Blasis tradition of rigorous schooling. Among them were Virginia Zucchi and Pierina Legnani, whose amazing skills (including Legnani's sensational thirty-two *fouettés*) were carefully studied and then emulated by Russian dancers. Another technical wizard from Italy, Enrico Cecchetti, became an invaluable teacher in Russia before bringing his influential method of instruction to the West.

By the 1890s, the Imperial Theatre School was producing native dancers as glorious as the foreign artists who had so long monopolized the Russian ballet spotlight. Imagine the excitement of classrooms where pupils such as Anna Pavlova, Tamara Karsavina, and Michel Fokine came, from childhood on, for their daily lessons. A class of perfection was established for such outstanding artists of the school. Nicolas Legat succeeded his master, Johannsen, as instructor, and accounts of his teaching were published by one of his pupils, André Eglevsky, later a soloist with the New York City Ballet.[32]

The dynamic partnership of Margot Fonteyn and Rudolf Nureyev, shown here in the "Black Swan" *pas de deux* from Petipa and Ivanov's *Le Lac des Cygnes* ("Swan Lake," 1895) combined the English and Russian ballet traditions to the delight of Western audiences during the 1960s.

Ballet at the Imperial Theatre (renamed the Maryinsky; later known as the Kirov) was the pride of the czars, whose purse generously funded it. Productions at the lesser-renowned Bolshoi Theatre in Moscow grew in importance under the leadership of Alexander Gorsky. (Paradoxically, after the Russian Revolution of 1917, both the Bolshoi Ballet and the Kirov company became sources of great pride for the Soviet regime.)

By the end of the nineteenth century, dancers and audiences had grown accustomed to a kind of ballet ritual revolving around bravura technique. A slightly stiffer ballet slipper was developed that allowed the ballerinas to try more and more difficult steps on pointe. Male dancers regularly performed eight or more *pirouettes* and multiple *entrechats* of the legs while in the air. Solo dances stopped the show, and the excitement was so great that even a ballerina's entrance was greeted with applause. Indeed, she was an impressive sight, with diamonds sparkling from her head, ears, and neck. No matter what her role or the theme of the ballet, a ballerina wore jewels from her private collection (usually gifts from titled admirers) and a full-skirted, tight-waisted costume (*tutu*) that reached to just above her knees. Soloists were allowed to insert their favorite steps into the choreography; they danced along with the music but some considered it an incidental element.

Noverre would have written a manifesto scolding such absurdities just as he did in his own time, almost 150 years before. As it happened, a young Russian dancer and choreographer, Michel Fokine, picked up the pen in 1904 and urged the ballet administration to work for more harmonious productions in which music, decor, costume, and dance would blend in a meaningful way. He decried the gymnastics that had crept into ballet at the expense of a sensitive interpretation of a chosen theme. He believed a mood or story line should be understandable through the dance, rather than be dependent on passages of pantomime.

Soon after, Isadora Duncan, a free-spirited American dancer, visited Russia and greatly impressed Fokine, Gorsky, and others with her expressivity, her sensitivity to music, and her revolutionary appearance—bare feet, unbound hair, and flowing Grecian tunic. Although the Russians did not wish to emulate Duncan's contempt for the classical ballet, some believed innovative ideas like hers would bring freshness into the static situation in Russian theaters. But management did not approve of suggestions in this direction (Marius Petipa had retired by 1903, but traditions established during his reign continued). Subsequently, a group of Russian artists, including Fokine, determined to bring ballet into the twentieth century and to transport their ideas and talents out of Russia for the rest of the world to appreciate. It was a challenge, and it proved to be their glory.

## THE DIAGHILEV BALLETS RUSSES

The one performance in all ballet history that most dancers wish they could have seen occurred in Paris on an evening in May 1909. It was the European debut of the Ballets Russes, the birth of a new era in ballet. Instead of one full-length ballet, the program consisted of several distinctly different offerings, each with its own dance style. The dancing seemed born of the music; the coordinated costumes and stage decor set the proper mood—it was "total theater," the dream of Michel Fokine brought to reality by a company of young Russians.

At the helm of this historic troupe was Serge Diaghilev, artistic director and impresario extraordinaire. Although skilled in neither painting, music, nor dance, he had the capacity to discover and inspire the greatest talents in each of those areas, and he longed to prove the talents of his countrymen—to themselves and to a Europe that had heretofore considered Russia a rather barbaric land.

Diaghilev knew the choreographic potential of Fokine, who was eager to have his ballets staged without the restrictions imposed by the Maryinsky management. The ballets that Diaghilev selected for the Paris season included *Le Pavillon d'Armide,* evoking the gracious style of the court of Louis XIV; *Cléopâtre,* a dramatic vision of ancient Egypt; *Les Sylphides,* a suite of dances in romantic style and costume; and the savage Polovetsian dances from the opera *Prince Igor.*

Collaborations were started with St. Petersburg painters for sets and costumes. Igor Stravinsky was asked to arrange some of Chopin's music for *Les Sylphides.* The Russian theaters agreed to release Fokine and a number of other dancers to go with Diaghilev during the months when they were not working.

No one has ever assembled a finer roster of dancers, some of whom became legends in their own lifetimes. Leading *danseur* was Vaslav Nijinsky, possessor of an incredible elevation, a magnetic stage personality, and an acting ability that matched his fabulous dance technique. Heading the list of ballerinas was Anna Pavlova, who seemed to epitomize the Fokine philosophy. She had an uncanny ability to use every part of her exquisite body to create a magical image of motion and stillness that seemed beyond the range of mere bones and muscles. Among the other stars of that first Paris season were Tamara Karsavina, Vera Fokina (wife of Michel Fokine), Adolph Bolm, and Mikhail Mordkin.

They set out on an unprecedented adventure, meticulously and extravagantly guided by Diaghilev, even to the redecoration of the Théâtre du Châtelet and the seating of the most attractive influential people for that first audience. The season was a triumph.

As the Paris press trumpeted every aspect of the Ballets Russes, its distribution of praise had two monumental effects on the course of ballet history: It tempted Diaghilev to arrange future seasons for his ballet company in Europe, and it tempted Pavlova to strike out on her own. Having been offered other engagements outside Russia, she soon left both the Diaghilev company and the Maryinsky Theatre, eventually forming her own company. She became a kind of dance missionary, bringing ballet and her own unique artistry to practically every section of the globe. A whole generation of dancers, would-be dancers, and ballet fans emerged because they "had seen Pavlova." There were few masterpieces in her repertory other than Fokine's *Dying Swan,* but Pavlova, as dragonfly or snowflake or butterfly, infused even inferior choreography and insipid music with a special magic.

Many of the great traditions of nineteenth-century ballet technique and romantic artistry were carried into the twentieth century to nearly all corners of the world by the annual tours of Anna Pavlova, shown here in *The Dying Swan*, a two-minute solo choreographed for her by Fokine in 1905.

The years from 1909 to 1913 marked a period of notable success for all concerned. Diaghilev formed a permanent company, one completely independent from the Russian theaters. The prolific Fokine created *Schéhérazade, The Firebird, Carnaval, Spector of the Rose, Daphnis and Chloë, Petrouchka,* and eight other ballets of lesser fame. Igor Stravinsky, commissioned to compose music for *The Firebird,* became famous as a result and began his close collaboration with the Diaghilev Ballet. The costumes designed by Léon Bakst for *Schéhérazade* launched a wave of semioriental fashion for Parisian women.

The dancers were continually challenged by new and different roles. With the exit of Pavlova, Karsavina became the leading ballerina. Nijinsky revealed his unique gifts as a choreographer. His four ballets, notably *Afternoon of a Faun* and *The Rite of Spring,* seemed a denial of classical ballet; their angular, "primitive" movements and rhythmic motivation anticipated a vocabulary later developed by such modern dancers as Mary Wigman and Martha Graham.

Much to Diaghilev's pleasure, his troupe produced one novel ballet after another, although not all were successful with the public and the press. Then came 1914 and World War I. Despite the chaos of the times, Diaghilev was determined to continue his company. Around a newly discovered choreographic talent, Leonide Massine, a new repertory began to take shape. Promising young dancers were recruited. Cecchetti was engaged to guide these young talents in daily classes of strict technique.[33] Diaghilev had again assembled a group of extraordinary artists and the Ballets Russes continued, very like a tiny, independent kingdom of art in the midst of a world at war.

Massine produced several popular ballets. His most startling effort was the surrealist ballet *Parade,* with decor and costumes by Picasso. In later years, the choreographic skills of Bronislava Nijinska (sister of Vaslav) and George Balanchine (a 1924 defector from the Soviet Union) were encouraged.

Composers who worked with the company included Satie, Poulenc, Milhaud, de Falla, Prokofiev, Ravel, Debussy, and, of course, Stravinsky. In 1928, Stravinsky and Balanchine began a collaboration that extended to more than forty years. An early effort, *Apollon Musagète* (now known simply as *Apollo*), introduced a "neoclassical" style in which academic ballet training served as a base for stunning technical innovation.

Oakland Ballet, under the artistic leadership of director Ronn Guidi, revived a number of ballets originally created for Diaghilev's Ballets Russes. A 1989 addition to its repertory was Bronislava Nijinska's *Le Train Bleu* (1924), staged and directed by her daughter, Irina Nijinska, and dance historian Frank W. D. Ries. The original collaborators included Darius Milhaud (music), Jean Cocteau (libretto), and Gabrielle "Coco" Chanel, who designed the all-wool bathing suits. Pictured here are Oakland Ballet dancers Abra Rudisill and Michael Lowe as members of the young fashionable set frolicking on the Cote d'Azur.

The Diaghilev stage served as an inviting canvas for such painters as Braque, Picasso, Derain, and Rouault. The roster of dancers was ever-changing and ever-exciting. They lived a nomadic and precarious existence, these members of the first great ballet company, without backing from a state or royal treasury. Home became Monte Carlo for rehearsal periods and an annual season, but the company existed only from one season to the next, dependent on bookings in Europe, South America, and the United States; on alliances with influential impressarios of opera houses; and on the generosity of wealthy patrons. Somehow, necessary financing was always secured just in time. For twenty years, the Ballets Russes led the world to a new appreciation of ballet. But it was Diaghilev's company, and with his death in 1929 the organization collapsed, the dancers scattered, and an era ended.

## BALLET AFTER DIAGHILEV

The vision that Diaghilev had was too strong to die completely with him. During the 1930s, there emerged a series of companies whose names incorporated the magic box-office words "Ballet Russe" or "Monte Carlo" and whose repertories preserved many of the great ballets from the Diaghilev years. Massine continued to create remarkable ballets, some to symphonic scores, his lighter works including *Gaité Parisienne* and *Capriccio Espagnol*. The companies included many of the stars from the Diaghilev ballet plus an international list of new talents, such as Igor Youskevitch, Frederic Franklin,

Some of the innovative repertory from Diaghilev's Ballets Russes survived through revivals by subsequent companies. George Zoritch, soloist with Ballet Russe de Monte Carlo and Grand Ballet du Marquis de Cuevas, is pictured here in Fokine's *Le Spectre de la Rose* ("The Spirit of the Rose") created for Nijinsky in 1911.

George Zoritch, André Eglevsky, Mia Slavinska, and the "baby ballerinas" Toumanova, Riabouchinska, and Baronova.

The constant touring of these companies during the 1930s and 1940s produced a new generation of ballet fans. England and the United States were especially receptive, and serious efforts were made to encourage native talent and establish permanent companies in those countries. No state support for such projects existed in either England or the United States, but by the great determination and dedication of a few persons, companies were formed and, more important, ballet schools were established in both countries.

## BRITISH BALLET

In 1920, Marie Rambert founded a school and began the groundwork for what became Ballet Rambert, Britain's oldest dance company and now renamed the Rambert Dance Company. Always providing an atmosphere for experimentation, the company gave early choreographic opportunities to Frederick Ashton and Antony Tudor. Since 1966, it has been primarily a modern dance troupe, a reorganization fully endorsed by Rambert, who as a girl had studied eurhythmics, a system of translating musical rhythms into body movements. She had used these skills to coach Nijinsky, at Diaghilev's suggestion, in preparation for Stravinsky's challenging score for *Rite of Spring.*

Another grand dream was conceived and carried out by Ninette de Valois who, as a young London dancer named Edris Stannus, had studied with Edouard Espinosa and then with Cecchetti. In 1923, she joined the Diaghilev company in Paris. Her goal, however, was not the international touring example set by Diaghilev, but rather the establishment of a national ballet company in England.

From de Valois's London studio, founded in 1926, emerged a company known as the Vic-Wells, then as the Sadler's Wells Ballet when it moved to the theater by that name. The de Valois policy of carefully re-creating nineteenth-century classics was epitomized by the revival of the original Petipa version of *The Sleeping Beauty,* staged by former Maryinsky dancer Nicholas Sergeyev from the Stepanov notation. It became the company's signature piece, used in a gala performance after World War II for the reopening of the Royal Opera House at Covent Garden, the company's new home, and for its first triumphant New York season in 1949. The role of Princess Aurora in the ballet has been indelibly associated with Margot Fonteyn, a product of the de Valois school, who became one of the world's truly exquisite ballerinas.

The company was awarded a royal charter in 1956, thus becoming the Royal Ballet and fulfilling the de Valois dream. Principal choreographer Ashton, and later Kenneth MacMillan, built a balanced repertory of contemporary ballets and new productions of the classics.

Another British institution begun in the 1920s deserves mention in a ballet technique textbook: the Royal Academy of Dancing (RAD). Its initial purpose was to raise the artistic level of dancing and to improve teaching methods in Britain. Its first syllabus, written by Espinosa, reflected his French training but also the Italian, Danish, Russian, and English traditions of the other founding members. Annual examinations, now worldwide, and teachers' training courses continue the ideas of the Academy.

## THE AMERICAN SCENE

Across the Atlantic, performing outlets for American dancers in the early twentieth century included musical revues, vaudeville tours, and occasional concerts by small troupes from local studios—not unlike the dance opportunities in Britain at the time. Opera companies in New York, and later in San Francisco and Chicago, maintained a European repertory and performance model in which, at most, dance was an incidental divertissement.

However, a young Harvard graduate, Lincoln Kirstein, envisioned an American ballet company and fortunately had the financial means to implement his plans, for there was no government help, not even, as in most countries, a secretary or minister for the arts. Impressed with the neoclassical choreography of George Balanchine, Kirstein invited the young choreographer to the United States to found a company. Balanchine's famous reply, "But first, a school," resulted in the establishment of the School of American Ballet.

In that same year, 1934, Balanchine devised his first American ballet, *Serenade,* as a study in performance techniques for his students. The school and that particular ballet have flourished to this day, although the company had a rocky start. After periods of little activity and several reorganizations, the company finally in 1948 found a performing home, the New York City Center, and a new name, the New York City Ballet (NYCB).

The company repertory and style have always been dominated by Balanchine, even though Jerome Robbins, an American dancer–choreographer, was added as an associate director. Despite his Maryinsky background, Balanchine choreographed only a few full-length ballets—*Jewels, Don Quixote, A Midsummer Night's Dream,* and a perennially popular version of *The Nutcracker.* Instead, he usually followed the Diaghilev formula of three or four short ballets on each program. But unlike most ballets from the Diaghilev years, the Balanchine selections seldom have a story line or elaborate decor. Music, such as an intricate score from Stravinsky, was the catalyst for Balanchine's "pure dance" ballets, usually set on a bare stage and performed with incredible speed and stamina by dancers (most of whom trained in the company school) dressed in tights, leotards, or simple tunics.

Balanchine's 1957 ballet *Agon* packed an unprecedented amount of movement into only twenty minutes. Classical technique was stretched and explored as it never had been before. The complexities of Stravinsky's rhythms and twelve-tone style were matched by Balanchine's twelve disciplined dancers. It was a turning point for ballet, as the Balanchine–Stravinsky *Apollo* had been almost thirty years before.

A *pas de deux* from the Balanchine/Stravinsky collaboration *Agon* ("Contest," 1957) is pictured
as performed by its original New York City Ballet cast, Arthur Mitchell and Diana Adams.
This plotless ballet, with its revealing classroom dress and its exploration of the technical range
and complexity possible within the ballet medium, has had great impact on subsequent productions and perhaps even on ballet training.

The company seldom tours, enjoying lengthy seasons, a healthy endowment, and the stability of a home base, New York's Lincoln Center for the
Performing Arts. City Ballet, as it is familiarly known, has produced many
fine male dancers, such as Edward Villella, Jacques d'Amboise, and Arthur
Mitchell. But, to most minds, the "Balanchine dancer" was typified by such
streamlined ballerinas as Diana Adams, Tanaquil LeClerq, and Maria

Tallchief; later, Allegra Kent, Suzanne Farrell, and Patricia McBride; and more recently, Kyra Nichols and Darci Kistler, who at age eighteen became the youngest principal dancer in the company's history. Balanchine ballerinas perform with pistonlike pointe work and limber, over-the-head extensions, technical attributes now expected by most companies, many of whom have added Balanchine ballets to their repertories.

For a period after Balanchine's death in 1983, Danish-trained former principal NYCB dancer and superb partner Peter Martins and Robbins shared responsibility for running the company, but eventually Martins assumed full leadership. The company continues to nurture the legacy from Balanchine and, in 1998, celebrated its fiftieth-anniversary season in a gala all-Balanchine program—*Concerto Barocco, Symphony in C,* and *Orpheus*—that re-created the first NYCB performance in 1948. But its technique had changed, even since the 1980s. According to Martins, "The kids today [1996] are better. I remember when Helgi [Tomasson] and I danced together at New York City Ballet. We were the best dancers around. . . . That was 15 years ago. Now I have a *corps de ballet* of boys who can outdance what I did then."[34]

American Ballet Theatre (ABT) has followed quite a different path. Founded by Lucia Chase and Richard Pleasant, the company, until 1957 known simply as Ballet Theatre, has, from its opening season in 1940, been a kind of touring library of ballet. Its repertory tries to remain as strong in revived or revised classics as it is in works of established contemporary choreographers, both American and foreign, and in the experimental attempts of newcomers.

At the invitation of Ballet Theatre, Antony Tudor moved to America from England and brought a new dimension for ballet. It has been called a psychological element, for Tudor dealt with the motivations and emotions of ordinary people—their hopes, their struggles, their foibles—replacing the stylized poses of classical technique with natural gestures. Tudor required that his dancers be fine actors as well as strong technicians—a challenge met especially well by Nora Kaye, Hugh Laing, and Sallie Wilson. In 1942, Ballet Theatre produced Tudor's *Pillar of Fire,* which was an immediate success.

ABT has long attracted ballet superstars, from Alicia Alonso (Cuba) to Erik Bruhn (Denmark), and later Natalia Makarova (former Soviet Union). Another Soviet expatriate, Mikhail Baryshnikov, joined Makarova as a member of the company, becoming its artistic director in 1980. Baryshnikov's own high level of virtuosity has given a new boost to traditional ballet roles and to the technique itself. Dance critic Arlene Croce expressed it well:

> For Baryshnikov, a double *pirouette* or air turn is a linking step, and preparations barely exist. . . . He also performs invented steps. One is a turning *jeté* in which, at the last second, he changes the foot he's going to land on and his legs flash past each other in the air. . . . Baryshnikov's promise lies not in novel steps but in his power to push classical steps to a new extreme in logic, a new density of interest. He is a modern classical dancer.[35]

ABT continued to encourage choreographic innovation and technical expansion, as in, for example, its sponsorship of modern dance renegade Twyla Tharp's witty, unconventional compositions. Her 1976 ballet for ABT, *Push Comes to Shove,* both mocked and praised classical ballet and provided Baryshnikov with one of his most memorable and challenging roles. Under the current artistic director, former ABT star Kevin McKenzie, the company frequently presents full-length, narrative ballets. These costly endeavors sometimes are presented jointly with another company, such as the San Francisco Ballet (for *Othello* by modern dance and ballet choreographer Lar Lubovitch) or the Houston Ballet (for *The Snow Maiden* by Houston's artistic director, Ben Stevenson).

## BALLET ECLECTICISM AND TRADITIONALISM

Early in the twentieth century, some American dancers believed the codified technique and Russo-European traditions of ballet were an inappropriate and inadequate means of expression for their country and their time. Such persons became known as "modern" dancers because, following the inspiration of Isadora Duncan, they broke with all traditional forms in an effort to devise a more contemporary dance expression.

Their influence was felt in ballet circles, where choreographers began to look for subject matter from their native land and movements that would appropriately illustrate those themes. Among the first successful ballets of this type were *Filling Station* by Lew Christensen and *Billy the Kid* by Eugene Loring, both produced in 1938. The American West was the inspiration of another popular work, *Rodeo* (1942), by Agnes de Mille. Its success led de Mille to Broadway the next year for *Oklahoma!,* in which her western ballet-within-a-musical became an instant classic.

Jerome Robbins, like de Mille, brought to ballet choreography a varied background—ballet, modern, jazz, tap—that he brilliantly wove into a little masterpiece, *Fancy Free,* the saga of three sailors on leave in Manhattan, set to a new jazz score by Leonard Bernstein in 1944, and soon reworked into the Broadway musical *On the Town.* De Mille and Robbins began to successfully inhabit both worlds—ballet and Broadway. Among Robbins's many enduring shows are *The King and I, West Side Story* (another collaboration with Bernstein), *Fiddler on the Roof,* and *Gypsy.*

New York became the dance capital of the United States, but ballet activity already had spread from coast to coast. The San Francisco Ballet, established in 1933, is the oldest professional ballet company in the country. Emerging as a separate entity from the San Francisco Opera, the company, under the leadership of Willam Christensen, in 1940 offered the first full-length production of *Swan Lake* staged by an American. Four years later, the San Francisco Ballet presented *The Nutcracker* in the first full-length performance seen in the United States. Among the company's box office successes of the 1990s were its new productions of *Swan Lake* and *Giselle*

Nigel Courtney seems to fly across stage as Ariel in *The Tempest,* a full-length ballet based on Shakespeare's play. This ballet was created in 1980 for the San Francisco Ballet by then co-director Michael Smuin, who went on to establish his own company, Smuin Ballets/SF.

staged by the current company artistic director, Helgi Tomasson, former soloist with NYCB, and intriguing, unpredictable world premieres by modern dancer Mark Morris.

## U.S. BALLET TODAY

Although American ballet has decentralized, the leadership and repertories of many regional professional companies are highly influenced by the legacy of George Balanchine and the New York City Ballet. Former NYCB dancers who have founded companies include Arthur Mitchell (Dance Theatre of Harlem), Edward Villella (Miami City Ballet), and husband-and-wife team, Kent Stowell and Francia Russell (Pacific Northwest Ballet).

The costs of maintaining such companies are overwhelming to all but the most stouthearted and determined directors. Robert Joffrey was an outstanding example of success at great odds. Beginning in 1954 with six dancers, the Robert Joffrey Ballet toured in a station wagon, presenting a repertory of four Joffrey works that were performed in borrowed costumes to taped music. By the 1960s, the company had twenty dancers, a ten-piece orchestra, and funding from private foundations. Continuing to expand during the next twenty years, it came to share popular ranking with NYCB and ABT. Joffrey, who died in 1988, expected his dancers to perform as individuals in ballets of many diverse styles and periods, whether composed by his prolific assistant director, Gerald Arpino, now in charge of the Chicago-based company, or by visiting artists from the modern dance tradition. Revivals from the Diaghilev era and from Kurt Jooss's expressionistic European ballets of the 1930s added to the eclectic nature of the repertory.

Surviving financial crises is always on a company's agenda. Many a creative entrepreneur has had to be satisfied with establishing a small concert group whose members support themselves by means other than performing—all clearly professionals in every sense except that they do not receive a salary commensurate with the minimum required by the American Guild of Musical Artists (AGMA), the union for professional dancers. Other choreographers and dancers, finding the Broadway stage, films, and television more reliable for earning a decent wage, have helped to make the musical comedy perhaps America's greatest contribution to the theater and to create new audiences by introducing dance to the television screen.

Most companies—large or small, professional or semiprofessional—struggled according to the Diaghilev method: Tour a lot and try to make up deficits by soliciting gifts from wealthy patrons. Even this strategy usually failed to bring in enough money, and most director–choreographers saved themselves and their companies by teaching.

Gradually, large foundations were attracted to dance. In 1963, large grants were given by the Ford Foundation, principally to the NYCB and its

The Joffrey Ballet repertory includes several works created for the company by modern dance choreographers. In 1982 Laura Dean composed both the movement and the music for *Fire,* here performed by Patricia Brown and Luis Perez.

School of American Ballet, but with some support channeled to certain Balanchine-approved regional companies. Finally, aid began to come from government through the National Endowment for the Arts and from state arts councils, although always vulnerable to economic trends and priorities set by new administrations.

Fine professional (high standards/serious students) ballet schools are found in almost all large cities, and practically every telephone book in the country lists at least one ballet studio in its yellow pages. During the 1960s and 1970s, college and university dance-major programs, initially modern-dance oriented and supported in physical-education departments, eagerly added ballet courses to their curricula and began a gradual relocation into performing arts departments. Professional dancers were attracted to university faculties. The professional dance world and the academic dance world profited from the exchange, as ballet and modern dance benefited from mutual attractions and understandings. No longer can a modern dancer ignore ballet technique, nor can a ballet dancer remain "untainted" by other dance forms.

## BALLET INTERNATIONAL

The United States has produced many fine dancers who have achieved international renown. Among these are five Native American ballerinas, all born in Oklahoma in the 1920s: Yvonne Chouteau (Cherokee), Rosella Hightower (Choctaw), Moscelyne Larkin (Peoria/Shawnee), and the Tallchief sisters Maria and Marjorie (Osage).

For touring companies and guest artists, a New York review is as prized as a Paris review was once. Companies from far shores come for a New York season and often a tour of other cities. Moscow's Bolshoi Ballet was perhaps the most eagerly awaited visitor, making an enormously successful New York debut in 1959. Its prima ballerina, Galina Ulanova, had trained with Agrippina Vaganova in her method that now is the basis for ballet education in many countries as well as at the Vaganova Ballet Academy in St. Petersburg.[36]

In 1959, American audiences were stunned by Bolshoi virtuosity, especially the elevation and strength of its male dancers, who could carry their partners overhead in effortless lifts supported by only one hand. During the Cold War, dance exchanges between the two countries had interesting by-products, including the greater appreciation of male dancing in the West (spurred by the defection of Rudolf Nureyev) and a slimmer ballet silhouette for dancers in the East.

With the collapse of the Soviet Union, many Russian dancers now have opportunities elsewhere. One stunning example is ballerina Nina Anani-ashvili, who, under a special contract with the Bolshoi Ballet, has frequently worked abroad in addition to her yearly performances in Moscow. However, she emphasizes the importance of returning to the source of her training:

Whenever I am back in Moscow, I always take class with the company. I need regular check-ins with my two coaches, Raisa Struchkova and Marina Semyonova [former ballerinas with the Bolshoi Ballet]—I call it my spring cleaning! I learn so much from them, and they don't let me get sloppy in my work. You need a person to correct you even if you have danced the role a thousand times before![37]

Today continues to be the age of the guest artist, who can jet from capital to capital for one-night appearances and a hefty check. Good choreographers are always in demand, crisscrossing the globe from one assignment to another. Fortunately, more permanent residencies sometimes ensue, such as at the Nederlands Dans Theater, where Czech-born director Jiří Kylián developed his lyrical, wind-swept choreographic style. Another example is William Forsythe, an American whose innovative, startling choreography matured during his directorship of the Frankfurt Ballet in Germany.

An example of today's international dance scene is the career of Nicolaj Hübbe, who trained at the ballet school of the Royal Danish Ballet and at age twenty was appointed principal dancer with the company. He is shown here in the role of James in *La Sylphide,* a version of Filippo Taglioni's ballet created by August Bournonville that has remained in the repertory of the Royal Danish Ballet since 1836. In 1992 Hübbe left Copenhagen to join the New York City Ballet, where he is featured in quite a different repertory, one largely dominated by the neoclassical ballets of George Balanchine.

Although ballet developed from the culture of the Western world (as such, it meets the criteria for an ethnic dance form, according to anthropologist Joanne Kealiinohomoku),[38] it is now also a part of the rich dance offerings of Japan, China, Hong Kong, and many other Asian-Pacific cultures. Many companies, and most in the United States, have multinational dancers. Ballet has become a truly international art form, with annual competitions for aspiring artists (much like those for young pianists) held in ballet centers from Moscow to Jackson, Mississippi.

## TOMORROW'S BALLET

If ballet history has a message for the future it is this: Ballet companies will continue to enlarge the scope of their repertories and thus expand the technical possibilities of their dancers, whose training will then incorporate those desired technical changes.

For example, in 1992, the New York City Ballet began the Diamond Project (named for its benefactor, Irene Diamond), an ambitious choreographic showcase that presents new ballets by new choreographers, with the hope of expanding the NYCB repertory. One of the aspiring choreographers in the Project, NYCB dancer Christopher Wheeldon, later was appointed resident choreographer with the company.

In 1998, the Colorado Ballet performed Martha Graham's *Appalachian Spring,* the first American ballet company to present a Graham modern-dance work but doubtless not the last.

The boundaries of age are expanding also, for although ballet still is identified as a youthful occupation, the talents of mature dancers are gaining recognition. Baryshnikov, in his fifties, continued to amaze audiences as he channelled his skills into the contemporary repertory of his company, the White Oak Dance Project. Nederlands Dance Theater 3, a chamber company for ballet dancers over age forty, was established in 1991 by Kylián, and it has been successful in New York as well as in Europe.

Even as today's choreographers explore the possibilities of ballet's technical range and theatrical venue, other contemporary dancer–choreographers seek to reconstruct ballet's historical past. For example, several companies specialize in dances from the baroque era, which they have restored from the notation system (*chorégraphie*) of the time. The New York Baroque Dance Company, directed by Catherine Turocy, and Ris et Danceries, directed by Francine Lancelot in Paris, are two such historical dance ensembles. Using a variety of reconstruction techniques, Pierre Lacotte has mounted a number of ballets from the romantic era, in one case bringing back to the stage of the Paris Opéra much of the long-lost choreography of Filippo Taglioni's *La Sylphide.*

What unites all of these artists is the classical ballet tradition—most especially the transmission of ballet technique. It would seem that ballet has come a very long way from its early days as royal entertainment in the court of Louis XIV. But was it really so long ago? To trace one dancer's heritage, you can look, for example, at the ballet "genealogy" of the author of the book you are now reading. Foremost among my teachers were Margaret Craske and Dolores Mitrovich, each of whom studied with Enrico Cecchetti (Craske in England and Mitrovich in Italy). Cecchetti studied with Giovanni Lepri, a disciple of Blasis, who in turn had worked with Dauberval, a dancer with Noverre. Noverre trained with Dupré, who had worked with Pécour, the ballet master who succeeded Beauchamps at the Paris Opéra. Beauchamps gave dance lessons to Louis XIV.

That is a span of only ten ballet generations. The ballet family tree has many branches, but it is not so very tall after all, and every ballet dancer today can connect somewhere to one of those branches. Even though ballet roots go very deep (some like to say back to ritual dances of ancient cultures), its fascinating/exasperating, logical/unnatural, tender/provocative, balanced/venturesome dance technique has a relatively brief history.

And it is a highly personal history. One pair of feet has demonstrated for another pair, one hand has guided another body, one voice has encouraged another soul, one set of muscles has remembered what a mind may have forgotten. Ballet has not been, cannot be, transmitted alone from book or machine. It is an experience that must be lived. Ten generations have so lived it, studied it, performed it, taught it, redirected it. We can look forward to more.

## NOTES

1. The undated Domenico manuscript, *De arte saltandi e choreas ducendii* ("Of the art of leading *saltandi* and *choreas*"), is in the Bibliothèque Nationale, Paris. *Saltare* was a term implying pantomime or representative dance by professional performers; the term came to mean jumping or leaping. *Chorea* was a term later identified with *carole*, line or closed-circle dances with participants holding hands; these dances could be stately and stepped or lively with hops. These and other early dance terms are discussed by Ingrid Brainard in "Dance of the Middle Ages and Early Renaissance," in *The New Grove Dictionary of Music and Musicians,* vol. 5 (London: Macmillan, 1980), 180–85.

2. Ingrid Brainard, "Domenico da Piacenza," in *The New Grove Dictionary,* 532–33.

3. First established at the University of Wisconsin in Madison by Margaret H'Doubler in 1921.

4. Régine Kunzle, "In Search of L'Académie Royale de Danse," *York Dance Review* 7 (Spring 1978), 7.

5. Ibid., 8.

6. Ibid.

7. Quoted in "Fifteenth- and Early Sixteenth-Century Court Dances," in *Institute of Court Dances of the Renaissance and Baroque Periods,* ed. Juana de Laban (New York: Dance Notation Bureau, 1972), 4.

8. See Jennifer Neville, "Cavalieri's Theatrical Ballo 'O che nuovo miracolo': A Reconstruction," *Dance Chronicle* 21, no. 3 (1998): 353–88.

9. Texts by Fabritio Caroso are *Il ballarino* (Venice, 1581; facsimile reprint by Broude Brothers, 1967) and *Nobiltà de dame* (Venice, 1600; English translation by Julia Sutton, Oxford University Press, 1986). See also, *Le gratie d'amore* (Milan, 1602; facsimile reprint by Broude, 1969) by Cesare Negri.

10. *Pavana,* an adjective meaning "of Padua," implies that the dance took its name from that town. Some scholars believe the dance term (also *pavan, pavane*) derives from *pavón* (Spanish for peacock), indicating a relationship between the dignified, yet colorful dance and the elegant spread of a peacock's tail. *Gagliarda* (also *galliard, gaillarde*) means "vigorous, robust." *Saltarello,* or "little hop," is a dance form sometimes called *pas de brabant* or *alta danza. Canario* (also canary, *canarie*) is thought to be a dance form from the Canary Islands introduced to Spain in the sixteenth century and thence to the rest of the Continent.

11. Thoinot Arbeau was the pseudonym for Jehan Tabourot, a Catholic canon in Langres. His book, *Orchesography,* appeared in 1589. An English translation by Mary Stewart Evans is available, edited by Julia Sutton (Dover, 1967).

12. Arbeau, 81.

13. Quoted in *Le Balet Comique de la Royne,* 1581, trans. Carol and Lander MacClintock (American Institute of Musicology, 1971), 33.

14. *Le Balet Comique,* 90–91. Archimedes was a Greek mathematician and physicist, living 287?–212 B.C.

15. This first collection of country dances, entitled *The English Dancing Master,* was published by John Playford in London. Subsequent editions were titled *The Dancing Master* and, with additions of new dances, continued to appear into the next century.

16. According to Pierre Rameau, *The Dancing Master* (Paris, 1725), trans. Cyril W. Beaumont (New York: Dance Horizons, 1970), 5.

17. Joan Wildeblood, *The Polite World* (London: Davis-Poynter, 1973), 94.

18. Feuillet's notation was called *chorégraphie,* and the title of his book of notation is *Chorégraphie ou l'art de de'crire la danse* (". . . or the art of describing dance"). In addition to explanations of the notation symbols and tables of notated steps, the volume was bound with a collection of notated theatrical dances composed by Feuillet (including a ballet for nine dancers) and ballroom dances by Guillaume Louis Pécour, Beauchamps's successor at the Académie.

19. Quoted in Selma Jeanne Cohen, ed., *Dance as a Theatre Art* (New York: Harper & Row, 1974), 51.

20. Quoted in Lincoln Kirstein, *Dance: A Short History of Classic Theatrical Dancing* (New York: Dance Horizons, 1969), 209.

21. Jean Georges Noverre, *Letters on Dancing and Ballets,* trans. Cyril W. Beaumont (New York: Dance Horizons, 1968), 29, 99.

22. Ibid., 117.

23. Ibid., 99.

24. Translation by Mary Skeaping with Irmgard Berry (London: Dance Books, 1988), 128. Magri's original text, *Trattato teorico-prattico di ballo* ("Theoretical and practical treatise on dancing") was published in Naples.

25. Jack Anderson, *Ballet and Modern Dance: A Concise History,* 2d ed. (Princeton, N.J.: Princeton Book, 1992), 82.

26. Among the notable instructors were Jean-François Coulon (1787–1830) in Paris and one of his many students, Salvatore Taglioni (1789–1868), who established a school of ballet at the *teatro San Carlo* in Naples.

27. Blasis's text, *Traité élémentaire, théoretique et pratique de l'art de la danse* ("Elementary treatise, theoretical and practical on the art of dance"), was published in Milan when he was 25 years old. An English translation by Mary Stewart Evans is available (Dover, 1968). Blasis authored many dance texts, including *The Code of Terpsichore,* a greatly expanded version of the *Elementary treatise,* which he wrote while working in London in 1828.

28. *Théorie de la gymnastique de la dance théatrale* ("Theory of theatrical dance gymnastique"; Paris, 1859). Translated excerpts in Cohen, *Dance as a Theatre Art,* 71–77.

29. Théleur's book, *Letters on Dancing reducing This elegant and healthful Exercise to Easy Scientific Principles,* was published in London, with a second printing in 1832. The first edition has been republished in *Studies in Dance History* 2, no. 1 (Fall/Winter 1990). *Studies in Dance History* is a publication of the Society of Dance History Scholars.

30. Arthur Saint-Léon called his system of notation *sténochorégraphie.* An English translation by Raymond Lister of Saint-Léon's book, *La Sténochorégraphie ou Art d'écrire promptement la Danse ("Sténochorégraphie* or the art of quickly writing dance") was published by Lister (Cambridge, 1992).

31. Auguste Bournonville, *My Theatre Life* (Copenhagen, 1848–1878), trans. Patricia N. McAndrew (Middletown, Conn. Wesleyan University Press, 1979), 581 82.

32. André Eglevsky and John Gregory, *Heritage of a Ballet Master: Nicolas Legat* (Dance Horizons, 1977).

33. Cecchetti's method of instruction, including set *adagio* and *allegro* sequences for each day of the week, was compiled and published as *A Manual of the Theory and Practice of Classical Theatrical Dancing* by Cyril W. Beaumont and Stanislas Idzikowski in London in 1922 and later republished by Dover, 1975.

34. Quoted in Octavio Roca, "Peter Martins' 'Waltz Project' Pays Tribute to Balanchine," *San Francisco Chronicle Datebook,* 31 March 1996, 30.

35. Arlene Croce, "Mikhail Baryshnikov," in *The Dance Anthology,* ed. Cobbett Steinberg (New York: New American Library, 1980), 121–22.

36. Vaganova's book, *Fundamentals of the Classic Dance,* first published in Leningrad in 1934, appeared in translation by Anatole Chujoy as *Basic Principles of Classical Ballet/Russian Ballet Technique* (Dover, 1969).

37. Quoted in Margaret Willis, "Houston's Snow Maiden: Houston Ballet's Ben Stevenson Gives Nina Ananiashvili Her Opportunity to Dance a Classic Russian Heroine," *Dance Magazine,* March 1998, 72.

38. Joanne Kealiinohomoku, "An Anthropologist Looks at Ballet as a Form of Ethnic Dance," *Impulse* (1969–70), 24–33.

# Selected Reading and Viewing

## GENERAL REFERENCE

*Ballet 101: A Complete Guide to Learning and Loving the Ballet.* Robert Greskovic. New York: Hyperion.

*International Dictionary of Ballet,.* 2 vols. Martha Bremser, ed. Detroit/London/Washington, D.C.: St. James Press.

*International Encyclopedia of Dance,* 6 vols. Selma Jeanne Cohen, founding ed. New York: Oxford University Press.

*The Language of Ballet: A Dictionary.* Thalia Mara. Princeton, N.J.: Princeton Book.

*101 Stories of the Great Ballets.* George Balanchine and Francis Mason. Garden City, N.Y.: Doubleday.

*Oxford Dictionary of Dance.* Debra Craine and Judith Mackrell, eds. Oxford/New York: Oxford University Press.

*Technical Manual and Dictionary of Classical Ballet.* Gail Grant. New York: Dover.

## BALLET TECHNIQUE

*Alphabet of Classical Dance.* Nadezjhda Bazarova and Varvara Mey, eds. London: Dance Books.

*Ballet: Beyond the Basics.* Sandra Noll Hammond. New York: McGraw-Hill.

*Basic Principles of Classical Ballet: Russian Ballet Technique.* Agrippina Vaganova, trans. Anatole Chujoy. New York: Dover.

*Both Sides of the Mirror: The Science and Art of Ballet,* 2d ed. Anna Paskevska. Princeton, N.J.: Princeton Book.

*The Bournonville School: The Daily Classes.* Kirsten Ralov, ed. London: Dance Books.

*Classical Ballet: The Flow of Movement.* Tamara Karsavina. London: Adam & Charles Black.

*Classical Ballet Technique.* Gretchen Ward Warren. Gainesville: University Press of Florida.

*The Classic Ballet: Basic Technique and Terminology.* Lincoln Kirstein and Muriel Stuart. Gainesville: University Press of Florida.

*A Manual of the Theory and Practice of Classical Theatrical Dancing (Méthode Cecchetti),* rev. ed. Cyril Beaumont and Stanislas Idzikowski. New York: Dover.

*Physics and the Art of Dance: Understanding Movement.* Kenneth Laws. New York: Oxford University Press.

## BALLET HEALTH

*Advice for Dancers: Emotional Counsel and Practical Strategies.* Linda H. Hamilton. San Francisco: Jossey-Bass.

*Dance Injuries: Their Prevention and Cure,* 3d ed. Daniel D. Arnheim. Princeton, N.J.: Princeton Book.

*Dance Kinesiology,* 2d ed. Sally S. Fitt. New York: Schirmer Books.

*The Dancer's Foot Book: A Complete Guide to Footcare and Health for People Who Dance.* Terry L. Spilken. Princeton, N.J.: Princeton Book.

*Finding Balance: Fitness and Training for a Lifetime in Dance.* Gigi Berardi. Princeton, N.J.: Princeton Book.

*Fit and Well: Core Concepts and Labs in Physical Fitness and Wellness,* 3d ed. Thomas D. Fahey, Paul M. Insel, and Walton T. Roth. New York: McGraw-Hill.

*Inside Ballet Technique: Separating Anatomical Fact from Fiction in the Ballet Class.* Valerie Grieg. London: Dance Books.

*Stretch and Strengthen.* Judy Alter. Boston: Houghton Mifflin.

## BALLET PROFESSION

*Dance: The Art of Production: A Guide to Auditions, Music, Costuming, Lighting, Makeup, Programming, Management, Marketing, Fundraising,* 3d ed. Joan Schlaich and Betty DuPont. Princeton, N.J.: Princeton Book.

*Dancing: The All-in-One Guide for Dancers, Teachers, and Parents,* rev. ed. Ellen Jacob. Fairfield, Conn.: Variety Arts.

*How to Enjoy the Ballet.* Don McDonagh. Garden City, N.Y.: Doubleday, Dolphin Books.

*Off Balance: The Real World of Ballet.* Suzanne Gordon. New York: Pantheon Books.

## BALLET HISTORY

*Ballet and Modern Dance.* Susan Au. New York: Thames & Hudson.

*Ballet and Modern Dance: A Concise History,* 2d ed. Jack Anderson. Princeton, N.J.: Princeton Book.

*The Ballet of the Enlightenment.* Ivor Guest. London: Dance Books.

*Dance as a Theatre Art: Source Readings in Dance History from 1581 to the Present.* Selma Jeanne Cohen. Princeton, N.J.: Princeton Book.

*Dance: A Short History of Classic Theatrical Dancing.* Lincoln Kirstein. Princeton, N.J.: Princeton Book.

*Dancing Through History.* Joan Cass. Englewood, N.J.: Prentice Hall.

*Echoes of American Ballet.* Lillian Moore. Brooklyn, N.Y.: Dance Horizons.

*Era of the Russian Ballet.* Natalia Roslavleva. New York: Da Capo Press.

*The Pre-Romantic Ballet.* Marian Hannah Winter. New York: Pitman.

*Rethinking the Sylph: New Perspectives on the Romantic Ballet.* Lynn Garafola, ed. Hanover, Mass.: Wesleyan.

*The Romantic Ballet in England: Its Development, Fulfillment, and Decline.* Ivor Guest. Middletown, Conn.: Wesleyan University Press.

*The Romantic Ballet in Paris,* 2d ed. Ivor Guest. London: Dance Books,

*Time and the Dancing Image.* Deborah Jowitt. Berkeley: University of California Press.

## AMERICAN PERIODICALS

*Ballet Review: www.balletreview.com*

*Dance Chronicle: www.dekker.com*

*Dance Magazine: www.dancemagazine.com*

*Dance Teacher: www.dance-teacher.com*

*Journal of Dance Medicine and Science: www.iadms.org/jdms-ad.html*

*Pointe Magazine: www.pointemagazine.com*

## INTERNET SOURCES: BALLET VIDEO/DVD SELECTIONS

*www.dancehorizons.com* Among offerings listed:

> *The Balanchine Library* (selected choreographies and *The Balanchine Essays* on aspects of technique)
>
> *Footnotes Series* (examines the greatest ballets of all time)

*www.finisjhung.com* The Finis Jhung Ballet: Basic Ballet Series
*www.kultur.com* Among offerings listed:

> *Ballet Class for Beginners* David Howard
>
> *The New Ballet Workout for Wellness, Renewal, and Vitality* Melissa Lowe
>
> *Video Dictionary of Ballet* featuring Russian, French, and Cecchetti styles

## INTERNET SOURCES: BALLET COMPANIES

The following are just a few of the many ballet companies in the United States:

> American Ballet Theatre *www.abt.org*
>
> Boston Ballet *www.bostonballet.org*
>
> Houston Ballet *www.houstonballet.org*

Joffrey Ballet of Chicago *www.joffrey.com*
Miami City Ballet *www.miamicityballet.org*
New York City Ballet *www.nycballet.com*
Oakland Ballet *www.oaklandballet.org*
Pacific Northwest Ballet *www.pnb.org*
San Francisco Ballet *www.sfballet.org*

## INTERNET SOURCES: DANCE LIBRARIES AND ORGANIZATIONS

American Dance Therapy Association *www.adta.org*

CORPS de Ballet International, Inc. *www.corps-de-ballet.org* This professional organization is dedicated to the development, exploration, and advancement of ballet in higher education.

International Association for Dance Medicine *www.iadms.org*

Library of Congress *www.catalog.loc.gov*

New York Public Library *www.catnyp.nypl.org*

Preserve, Inc. *www.preserve-inc.org/library.html* The website of this organization—dedicated to "assuring dance life beyond performance"—includes listings of dance libraries, archives, and collections.

Save As: Dance *www.save-as-dance.org* Save As: Dance is a national partnership for advancing the ability of dance artists and dance communities to document and preserve their work and traditions. Its website lists arts funding resources; institutions of higher education with dance programs; dance companies, presenters, and publications; and other dance organizations with Internet sites.

Society of Dance History Scholars *www.sdhs.org* The website of the Society of Dance History Scholars—an organization dedicated to promoting study, research, discussion, performance, and publication in dance history and related fields—includes updated information on job opportunities, conference announcements, and awards for graduate students. Click on "Links Related to Dance" for other dance-related resources: organization, funding, publications, libraries, and research institutions.

# Photo Credits

**Chapter 2** p. 40, diagram by Peter Emmerich © 2002.

**Chapter 6** p. 134, Jan Hathaway; p. 138, Wendell Maruyama; p. 139, photograph by Walter Swarthout © 2002.

**Chapter 7** p. 148, from Cesare Negri, *Le Gratie d'Amore* (Milan, 1602), p. 80, reproduced from Monuments of Music and Music Literature in Facsimile (II/130), by permission of Broude Brothers Limited; pp. 150, 152, Jerome Robbins Dance Collection, The New York Public Library for the Performing Arts, Astor, Lenox and Tilden Foundations; p. 153, from Raoul-Auger Feuillet, *Recueil de Dances Composées par M. Pecour,* p. 43, La Bourgogne, in Feuillet, *Choregraphie* (Paris, 1700), reproduced from Monuments of Music and Music Literature (II/141), by permission of Broude Brothers Limited; p. 154 © Lois Greenfield, 1984; pp. 155, 156, 158, 159, 160, 163, Jerome Robbins Dance Collection, The New York Public Library for the Performing Arts, Astor, Lenox and Tilden Foundations; Foundations; p. 164, David Amzallag; p. 167, Judy Cameron; p. 170, Jerome Robbins Dance Collection, The New York Public Library for the Performing Arts, Astor, Lenox and Tilden Foundations; p. 171, Marty Sohl; p. 172, © Serge Lido/Sipa Press; p. 175, Martha Swope © Time, Inc., *Agon,* choreography by George Balanchine © The George Balanchine Trust; p. 178, Rudi Legname; p. 179, photo © Migdoll '99/Joffrey Ballet of Chicago; p. 181, David Amzallag.

# Technical Terms Index

Page numbers refer to major explanations of technical terms. Boldfaced numbers refer to illustrations. Additional entries for these terms are given in the General Index.

# General Index

Boldfaced page numbers refer to illustrations.

**195**